HEBRIDEAN FOLKSONGS

HEBRIDEAN FOLKSONGS

A Collection of Waulking Songs

BY

DONALD MACCORMICK

in Kilphedir in South Uist

in the year 1893

Some of them translated by the late
FR. ALLAN McDONALD

Completed and edited by
J. L. CAMPBELL

Tunes transcribed, from Recordings, by
FRANCIS COLLINSON

OXFORD
AT THE CLARENDON PRESS
1969

Oxford University Press, Ely House, London W. 1

GLASGOW NEW YORK TORONTO MELBOURNE WELLINGTON
CAPE TOWN SALISBURY IBADAN NAIROBI LUSAKA ADDIS ABABA
BOMBAY CALCUTTA MADRAS KARACHI LAHORE DACCA
KUALA LUMPUR SINGAPORE HONG KONG TOKYO

SEANN-ÒRAIN INNSE-GALL

Comh-Chruinneachadh do dh'Òrain Luadhaidh

LE

DÒMHNALL MAC CARMAIC
an Cille Pheadair an Ceann-a-deas Uibhist
anns a' bhliadhna
Ochd Ciad Diag Ceithir Fichead
's a trì diag

Feadhainn dhiu air an eadar-theangachadh le
MGR. AILEIN DÒMHNALLACH

Air an crìochnachadh 's air an deasachadh le
IAIN L. CAIMBEUL

Na fuinn air an sgrìobhadh le
FRANCIS COLLINSON

ATHA-NAN-DAMH
CLÒ-PHREAS CHLARENDON
1969

PRINTED IN GREAT BRITAIN

Ní math éadach gan úcadh.

Unwaulked cloth is not good.

FELIM MACDUGALL
Book of the Dean of Lismore (c. 1512)

'S cuimhnich thoir leat bannal ghruagach,
A luaighis an Cló ruagh go daingiunn.

And remember, bring with you a band of maidens
Who will waulk the Red Cloth firmly.

ALEXANDER MACDONALD
Ais-eiridh na Sean Chánoin Albannaich, p. 98 (1751)

Gasd' am farum aig a' bhannal
Th'air an teanal thall ud;
Luadhadh daingeann air na maidean
Chuireas plaid' an teanndachd;
Trom am buille, treun an ruighe,
Trang a' bhuidheann bhaindidh;
'N clò 'na shiubhal dol an tiughad,
Rann cur ruith gun taing air.

Splendid is the noise made by the company of
women gathered over yonder, firmly waulking cloth
on planks, tightening it; heavy are their blows,
strong their arms, busy is the modest band; the cloth
is kept moving, getting thicker, while a song sets
it in independent motion.

FR. ALLAN MCDONALD
Ceathramhnan a rinneadh do dh'Éirisgeidh (c. 1901)

FOREWORD

THE Gaelic-speaking Outer Hebrides are the richest storehouse of oral tradition, particularly of traditional folk-song, in Great Britain, if not in western Europe, today. An important type of traditional song surviving in these islands, including Skye, and apparently nowhere else, is the waulking song, called *òran luadhaidh* in Gaelic. Hitherto, no book has been entirely devoted to the subject of waulking songs, which are labour songs sung during the hand-fulling of home-made cloth. The nature of the songs themselves, and the manuscript that is the basis of the collection presented here, are described in detail in the opening sections of this book. Opportunity is taken to discuss the relationship of these songs to the art versions which have been made of some of them by Mrs. Kennedy-Fraser and others.

The musical transcriptions have been made, from disc, wire, and tape recordings which I and my collaborators made in South Uist, Barra, Eriskay, and Benbecula between 1937 and the present time, by my friend Francis Collinson, formerly musical research fellow of the School of Scottish Studies of Edinburgh University, at which copies of some of these recordings are deposited. It is a testimony to the vitality of the tradition that versions of the airs to which these songs are sung—in quite a number of cases, several versions—have been recovered for all but one of the forty songs printed here. Even today, some of the older singers can remember versions of the words which are as long as those taken down by earlier collectors such as Fr. Allan McDonald and Donald Mac-Cormick seventy years ago. But the majority of waulking songs cannot survive the cessation of the handloom production of tweed in the Hebrides by more than a generation, and it is as well that authoritative versions should be preserved in print.

In the course of nearly thirty years during which a great deal of the spare time of my wife and myself has been devoted to the recording of traditional Gaelic songs and stories, we have incurred indebtedness to innumerable friends, both in Scotland and in Nova

ix

FOREWORD

Scotia, for help and encouragement. Besides the singers, whose names are mentioned here in the Notes to the songs, and whose fidelity to the Gaelic tradition is worthy of the highest tribute, I must express my gratitude to the Leverhulme Foundation for an expense grant of £250 towards the cost of recording visits to the Outer Hebrides between 1949 and 1951—probably about a tenth of the sum spent by us on this work over all the years.

Mr. Collinson and I have also to express our gratitude to the McCaig Trust for a grant of £100 and to the Highland Development Board for one of £450 towards the expense of printing this book.

No collector of folklore or of folk-songs can work effectively in a Gaelic-speaking district without a knowledge of the language, or without local assistance. I wish particularly to express my gratitude for such help and encouragement to the late Major and Mrs. Finlay MacKenzie of the Lochboisdale Hotel in Uist; to the Rt. Revd. Mgr. Canon Ewen MacInnes, the late Neil Sinclair, the late Miss Annie Johnston, the late John MacPherson 'the Coddy', Neil Angus MacDonald, M.A., formerly headmaster of Castlebay School, and other members of the Barra Folklore Committee, for help while working in Barra; to the Revd. John Mac-Cormick and the Revd. Colin MacPherson for hospitality and help while working in Eriskay and Benbecula; to the late Revd. Alec MacKellaig, the late Revd. Donald MacDougall, the Revd. John MacLean, and Mr. and Mrs. Patrick MacPhee, while working in the Bornish district of South Uist; and in Benbecula, also to the Revd. Joseph Campbell, the late Dr. Calum MacLean, and to Mrs. A. J. MacLellan, Hacklett. I am also indebted to Mr. John MacInnes, clerk to the South Uist District Council, and to Dr. A. MacLean, Daliburgh, and the late Captain D. J. MacKinnon, Lochboisdale, himself a great folk-singer and the son of a great folk-singer, Roderick MacKinnon, of the Isle of Barra.

In Nova Scotia I have to thank many friends for help and encouragement, particularly the late Rt. Revd. Mgr. P. J. Nicholson, formerly President of St. Francis Xavier University, the Revd. Malcolm MacDonell, and the late J. G. MacKinnon, editor of *Mac Talla*.

I have to thank the Rt. Revd. Stephen McGill, Bishop of Argyll and the Isles, for the loan of the manuscript collection of waulking songs made by the late Donald MacLachlan, Oban; the Very Revd.

Canon Duncan MacLean, formerly parish priest of Bornish, and the late Donald MacIntyre, Paisley, for putting manuscript collections of the words of waulking songs that they had made in South Uist at my disposal; to the late Professor Angus Matheson for invaluable help with linguistic and historical problems; to the Revd. William Matheson for some very helpful suggestions in connexion with the glossarial index; to Miss S. J. Lockett for help in compiling this index and in typing part of the manuscript; to the authorities of the Linguistic Survey of Scotland at Edinburgh University for the loan of a Webster wire recorder but for which I would now be unable to play or copy my wire recordings, made between 1949 and 1955; to Mr. C. P. Finlayson, Keeper of Manuscripts at Edinburgh University, for much kind and courteous help in my searches in the Carmichael papers there; to Professor Derick Thomson, for reading this book in proof and making many valuable suggestions; and to the late Mr. Hector MacIver, M.A., who put the manuscript of Donald MacCormick's collection of waulking songs, for which I had long been searching, at my disposal. I am also indebted to my wife, Margaret Fay Shaw, for constant help and encouragement. My one regret is that this book appears after so many good friends who helped us to record these fine old songs have passed away.

My collaborator and I are indebted to Mr. Keith Henderson, O.B.E., for permission to reproduce the painting of a waulking which he made on the island of Barra around 1930.

J. L. CAMPBELL

Isle of Canna
9 December 1964

CORRIGENDA

p. 21, l. 29, *for* read *read* rear

p. 32, note 1, *for* this book *read* the book

p. 184, note to line 1010, for *dorics* read *dorus*

p. 197, l. 25, *for* Miss Effie Monk *read* Mrs. Effie Monk; also on pp. 306, 309, 328

p. 212, l. 2, *for* xiii *read* xii*d*; *for* xiv *read* xiv*b*

p. 214, l. 18, *for* xvii*c read* xvii

p. 221, l. 6, *for* xv*d read* xv*a*
    first diagram, sixth sign should be a crotchet rest

p. 232, l. 14, *for* long-short *read* short-long
    l. 16, *for* bar 6 *read* bar 7

p. 233, add dot to the second and third quavers in the last diagram

p. 234, *for* XXXIII*a read* XXXIII

p. 235, first diagram under Short-long, *for* III*b read* III

p. 252, last 3 lines, *for* time, *read* tune

p. 269, song X, Verse A, *read* (solo) *over 2nd bar*, (Chorus) *over 3rd*; *for* Mixolydean *read* Mixolydian

p. 273, *for* Eight (Ten) degrees *read* Nine (Eleven) degrees

CONTENTS

CONTENTS

LIST OF ILLUSTRATIONS

I

HEBRIDEAN
WAULKING SONGS

J. L. CAMPBELL

THE WAULKING DESCRIBED

UP to the beginning of the nineteenth century the normal way of fulling or waulking new-made cloth, that is, shrinking it and making it of even texture, was by means of fulling-mills, worked by water-power.[1] (Hence the expression 'milling songs', still used for 'waulking songs' in Nova Scotia.) The mill was constructed so that the water-wheel operated a series of pestles which pounded the cloth, which was impregnated with urine, soap, or fuller's earth, and placed in a vat or tank. But in the Highlands and Islands of Scotland, where water-mills were usually not available, the fulling of cloth, like the grinding of corn, continued to be done by manual labour, both being invariably performed to the accompaniment of singing. Today, curiously enough, water fulling-mills are entirely a thing of the past, but waulking by hand (though not by foot) still survives in the Outer Hebrides.[2]

[1] A description of fulling-mills and their method of operation can be found in the 1797 edition of *Encyclopædia Britannica*. Gaelic *ùcadh* or *fùcadh* derives from the English 'waulk', and the *O.E.D.* references to Old English *wealcan* 'to roll, toss' and Old High German *walchan* 'to full, to cudgel', suggest strongly that 'walk' ('to go about') derives from 'waulk' ('to full') and not vice versa. The usual Gaelic term, *luadhadh*, means to roll or toss. The *O.E.D.* statement that the term 'walk-mill' derives from the walking of a horse seems very unlikely to be correct, as there is abundant evidence that the normal driving power of waulking-mills was running water.

There is an account of waulking-mills in a manuscript of 1581 quoted in a published history of the well-known tweed manufacturers, Henry Ballantyne and Sons, of Walkerburn in Peeblesshire. The ruins of a waulk-mill exist on the estate of Kersewell, in Lanarkshire; the former owner of this estate, Miss Grizel Bertram, has told Francis Collinson that she remembers as a child her nurse telling her that the young women of the neighbourhood used to come to help waulk the cloth in this mill. Her nurse described how a number of women used to sit around a table or bench, presumably to feed the cloth into the mill, extract and fold it, and so on. Miss Bertram thinks her nurse told her that these women used to sing songs at the table as they worked, but cannot say what kind of songs were sung.

Other waulk-mills are well known to have existed at Walkerburn, near Peebles, at Nine Mile Burn, Midlothian, and at Dufftown in Banffshire.

[2] The *Encyclopædia Britannica* of 1797 says that the fulling of stockings, caps, etc., should be done with the feet or the hands, as the fulling-mills were liable to damage such articles.

The earliest extensive description of a waulking is that by Thomas Pennant, who gives an account of one he witnessed on the Isle of Skye in 1772. This is quoted in full here, and the woodcut by Moses Grifiths illustrating it is reproduced in this book.

LUAGH. On my return am entertained with a rehearsal, I may call it, of the *Luagh*, or, *walking of cloth*, a substitute for the fulling-mill: twelve or fourteen women, divided into two equal numbers, sit down on each side of a long board, ribbed lengthways, placing the cloth on it: first they begin to work it backwards and forwards with their hands, singing at the same time, as at the *Quern*: when they have tired their hands, every female uses her feet for the same purpose, and six or seven pair of naked feet are in the most violent agitation, working one against the other: as by this time they grow very earnest in their labors, the fury of the song rises; at length it arrives to such a pitch, that without breach of charity you would imagine a troop of female demoniacs to have been assembled.

They sing in the same manner when they are cutting down the corn, when thirty or forty join in chorus, keeping time to the sound of a bagpipe, as the *Grecian* lasses were wont to do to that of a lyre during vintage in the days of *Homer*. The subject of the songs at the *Luaghadh*, the *Quern*, and on this occasion, are sometimes love, sometimes panegyric, and often a rehearsal of the deeds of the antient heroes, but commonly all the tunes slow and melancholy.

Singing at the *Quern* is now almost out of date since the introduction of water-mills. The laird can oblige his tenants, as in *England*, to make use of this more expeditious kind of grinding; and empowers his miller to search out and break any *Querns* he can find, as machines that defraud him of the toll.[1]

Pennant's account is illustrated with a woodcut of ten women waulking with their feet, and two working a quern. Considerably earlier Martin Martin tells us how an English visitor to North Uist

happen'd to come into a House where he found only ten Women, and they were employ'd (as he suppos'd) in a strange manner, *viz.* their Arms and Legs were bare, being five on a side; and between them lay a Board, upon which they had laid a piece of Cloth, and were thickning of it with their Hands and Feet, and singing all the while. The *English*-man presently concluded it to be a little *Bedlam*, which he did not expect in so remote a Corner: and this he told to Mr. *John Macklean*, who possesses the Island. Mr. *Macklean* answer'd, he never saw any mad People in those Islands: but this would not satisfy him, till they both

[1] *Tour in Scotland*, ii, p. 328.

Women at the quern and at foot waulking at Talisker, Isle of Skye, in the eighteenth century. Reproduction of original woodcut by Moses Grifith. (See Thomas Pennant, *A Tour in Scotland*, II. 329)

went to the place where the Women were at work; and then Mr. *Macklean* having told him, that it was their common way of thickning Cloth, he was convinc'd, tho surpriz'd at the manner of it.[1]

Most of the early travellers in the Highlands and Islands mention the singing of the people while at work harvesting with the sickle, grinding with the quern, or rowing. Waulkings, which men were not then allowed to attend, are less frequently referred to. But today it is the waulking songs alone which survive to any extent; the other forms of labour, at which the singing of the people was so noticeable, have disappeared, and most of the songs associated with them have been lost, except in so far as they have been sung at waulkings.

An interesting description of waulking is rather surprisingly to be found on p. 136 of William Shaw's *An Analysis of the Gaelic Language* (1778):

There is a species of poetry peculiar to the Gael called *Iurram* and *Orain luathaidh*. The music of the *Iurram* has always that mixture of grandeur and melancholy that never fails to gain its end. They are sung on board of ships and buirlings[2] by the sailors, when they row or work, to deceive the time. The subject is generally the life and actions of some chief or relation. The language is such as to express the sentiments and actions described; the music, expression, and strokes of the oars, coinciding in such exact time, both the sailor and passenger forget their hardships and fatigue, even in the most inclement seasons.

The *Oran luathaidh*, with the same view, is sung when they work on shore, and derives its name from *lu[a]thadh*, milling or fulling. Till very lately, fulling of cloth by mills was not known in the Highlands, and in some parts is not yet introduced. They fulled their cloth by laying it wet on an extended frame of rods wattled together, around which were placed as many women as could conveniently be employed, who, by an alternate motion of their feet, kept the cloth in perpetual rotation. One of them, in the mean time, sung the verse, and all the rest at once joined in the chorus. And even to this day, when these songs are sung in genteel company, a lady's handkerchief or a gentleman's bonnet supplies the place of a piece of cloth, every one taking hold of a corner. The time of this species of singing is not so quick as that of the *Reel*, not so slow as the *Iurram*. It is exceedingly lively, however, and justifies what a French gentleman observed of the Scots music: *La musique Eccoissoise sur tout pour le divertissement & toucher le coeur.*

[1] *A Description of the Western Islands of Scotland*, second edition, p. 57. The incident took place in the late seventeenth century.   [2] i.e. galleys.

5

Shaw gives the chorus and four couplets of Duncan Ban Mac-
Intyre's *Togamaid fonn air luadhadh a' chlòlain*.[1]

Necker de Saussure describes the *iorram* and the *òran luadhaidh*
in the second volume of his *Voyage en Écosse et aux Iles Hébrides*,
pp. 272 and 348. After telling how appropriate the wild airs of the
iorrams sounded against the background of stormy seas and rocky
coasts, he gives an account of waulking songs he heard at a dance
on Iona on 17 August 1807:

Dans l'intervalle d'un *reel* à l'autre, ils chantoient en chœur des airs
gäelics. Quoique ces chants, comme ceux que nous avions entendus sur
mer, fussent composés de deux parties distinctes, l'une chantée par un
homme seul, l'autre entonnée en chœur par toute la compagnie, ils en
différoient un peu par le rythme, et les sujets des paroles, nous dit-on,
n'étoient pas du même genre; les airs faits pour être chantés sur l'eau et
accompagnés par le bruit des rames se nomment *Jorrams*; les autres
portent le nom de *Oran luathaidh*, et ne se chantent que sur terre, pour
délasser les ouvriers dans leurs travaux; ce sont des espèces de ballades
ou de récits d'avantures, quelquefois héroïques ou tragiques, quelquefois aussi burlesques et divertissantes.

Les hommes et les femmes s'asseyoient en rond autour de la chambre,
et se donnoient la main, ou tenoient deux à deux le bout d'un mouchoir
qu'ils agitoient en cadence pendant les chœurs. On dit qu'un pareil
mouvement imite l'opération de fouler le drap, et que ces chants, comme
leur nom l'indique, accompagnoient jadis ce genre de travail.

Between one reel and another, they sang Gaelic songs in chorus.
Although these songs, like those which we had heard at sea, were
composed of two distinct parts, one sung by a soloist, and the other
chanted in chorus by the whole company, they differed from them a
little in tempo, and the subjects of the words, we were told, were not
of the same kind; the songs made to be sung on the water, accompanied
by the sound of oars, are called *Iorrams*; the others are called *Òrain
Luadhaidh*, and are only sung on land, to lighten workers at their work;
these are kinds of ballads or of recitations of adventures, sometimes
heroic or tragic, sometimes, too, funny or amusing.

Men and women sat in a circle around the room, and held each other's
hands, or held two by two the corners of a handkerchief which they
moved in time with the music during the choruses. We were told that
such a movement imitates the operation of waulking the cloth, and that
these songs, as their name indicates, formerly used to accompany this
kind of work.

[1] See M. F. Shaw, *Folksongs and Folklore of South Uist*, p. 204.

By the time Necker de Saussure visited the Highlands and Islands, fulling-mills, driven by water, had become widespread on the mainland.

Records of Argyll (p. 297) refers to Campbell of Ormidale having dammed a river in 1755 to provide power for one—an action which provoked a pitched battle with his neighbour Campbell of Glendaruel, which was only stopped by the parish minister. There was a fulling-mill in existence in the parish of Kilninian, in the Isle of Mull, at the time of the Old Statistical Account (1794). Hand waulking of cloth only survived in the Outer Hebrides and a few other remote places. It is interesting to note that 'milling songs' are still sung in the Gaelic-speaking parts of Cape Breton, Nova Scotia, in the style which Necker de Saussure describes.

Another early nineteenth-century allusion to waulking occurs in Lockhart's *Life of Sir Walter Scott*.[1] This observation was written at Dunvegan Castle on 24 August 1814, when Scott and Lockhart were the guests of MacLeod of Dunvegan, whose ancestors are so often mentioned in waulking songs. 'The day being delightfully fair and warm, we walk up to the church of Kilmore. In a cottage, at no great distance, we heard the women singing as they *waulked* the cloth by rubbing it with their hands and feet and screaming all the while in a sort of chorus. At a distance, the sound was wild and sweet enough, but rather discordant when you approached too near the performers.' The fact that waulking was done with the feet as well as with the hands in Skye is confirmed by Pennant's illustration of a waulking at Talisker, already referred to, and by Mary MacKellar's description of a waulking, see p. 13.

Two more recent descriptions of waulking are worth quoting. One was published by Miss Goodrich Freer in an article on 'Prince Charlie in Eriskay' in *Blackwood's Magazine* in February 1901, and reproduced in her book *Outer Isles* (p. 254) the next year. As it was Fr. Allan McDonald himself who introduced Miss Freer to this waulking, and as his influence can clearly be seen in this article, her account is peculiarly suitable for quotation in this book. Miss Freer, who did not know Gaelic herself, describes a waulking held in one of the old Hebridean 'black houses', which themselves have all but disappeared.

'There are red cheeks', says a proverb of the Outer Hebrides, 'before

[1] Vol. iii, p. 230.

the tailor and the fulling women',[1] their visits being the two occasions when the public is admitted into the intimate domestic life of the family. The tailor is peripatetic, and as he visits from house to house he carries with him the gossip of the neighbourhood. He knows when the meal tub is getting low, and when the whisky bottle is withheld from the guest. So, too, when the cloth is being dressed after it is taken out of the loom. It needs eight or ten women to do the work, and as many as the house will hold to look on. None may refuse an invitation to a fulling, and as it requires skilled labour, and the work is voluntary, it is an opportunity for the exercise of all possible hospitality: to give less than the best would be, indeed, an occasion for scandal and 'red cheeks'.

The 'fulling' is a scene of the utmost friendliness: the talk is intimate, and yet a certain ceremony and dignity are observed, and the customs, probably many centuries old, are adhered to rigidly. The songs which accompany the work are preserved orally, and are of the deepest interest; some are love ditties; some are religious, some political, all have a quaint picturesqueness of language, which, like many things in these Islands, is almost oriental. One sees, on such occasions as these, something of the under-current of the life of the people; in the song, one hears, as it were, the keynotes of the views and the faith which they have inherited. They are an emotional people, but so reticent that one who would know what traditions they still cherish has need of some such opportunity as this.

The scene is almost weird. It is an evening in the early autumn. The house is long and low, it has neither floor nor ceiling; but the walls are thick, and the thatch, of divots, or sods of grass, fastened on with heather ropes, is an excellent protection from cold and draught. A peat fire burns in a hollow in the clay floor, and the smoke seeks escape through an opening in the roof. A kettle, singing gaily, is suspended from an iron chain, and round flat cakes, supported by stones, are arranged in a circle about the fire.

The scant furniture of the house has been cleared to one side, and three long planks, supported table-wise at either end, so as to slope towards the door, occupy the open space. Chairs are scarce, but forms and boxes are placed so as to seat the women who are to do the work of the evening. Ten big muscular young women they are, with bare arms, and long coarse aprons over their gowns. They take much heed to the right height and firmness of their seats, as indeed the violent exercise they are about to enter upon requires. The house is already well filled with humanity, and but ill-ventilated, while two or three smoking

---

[1] This proverb was taken down by Fr. Allan McDonald in the winter of 1897–8. 'Eibheal air gruaidh mnathan-luadhaidh is tàilleirean.' He adds 'one would be much ashamed if he had not proper food for them'.

Fr. Allan McDonald at a waulking on the island of Eriskay in the summer of 1898. (Photograph by Walter Blaikie)

paraffin-lamps further subtract from the available oxygen. Later we learn to be thankful for the additional reek of peat and tobacco, for the climax of ill savour is not reached till the hostess brings in the web of cloth freshly dipped in some nauseous compound[1] which contends with its original smell of fish and hot sheep,—fish oil and tallow being the most fragrant of the various dressings applied to the wool, from which the process of fulling is to cleanse it.

Five to each side they sit, and the dripping cloth is passed from hand to hand, while the moisture runs down the sloping boards to the floor. The movements of the women, at first slow, are in perfect rhythm, and, like all co-ordinated movement in these islands, their direction is *deiseil* —sunwards. It is only at first that we can observe the details of their operations, for soon the process becomes so rapid that we can distinguish nothing but the swaying of their figures, and the rapid thud of the cloth, keeping time to the rhythm of their song.

And what strange singing it is! Deep-toned and monotonous, the rhythm very marked, the thud of the wet cloth regular as the beat of a drum, the melody seldom extending beyond five notes, each syllable having its separate note, and no pause made from beginning to end of the song, which is necessarily in four time. The verses are couplets,[2] and each is sung first by one woman alone, and then taken up by all.

The course of the web along the board describes a series of zigzags, each woman's movement forming the letter V, of which she herself is the base, and each point being marked by the loud thud of the cloth upon the board, always in four time. At *one* she receives the cloth from her neighbour on the right, leaning forward and throwing it down at arm's length; at *two* she draws herself upright and brings it down again immediately in front of her, twisting it as she does so; at *three* she passes it, again at arm's length, to her neighbour on the left; and at *four*, once more upright, she brings her hands again in front of her, still beating time, and is thus ready for *one*, *da capo*, for the rhythm is ceaseless.

Each song averages about eight minutes, and is about fifty couplets[3] in length. As each one is finished, the women throw down the web and their arms drop. They are exhausted and breathless, as well they may be, for to sing and work as they do, throwing themselves violently forward so that the cloth they are handling becomes absolutely hot in the process, is no light work.

In a minute or two they begin again. A 'song-less' web (*clò bodaich*) is unlucky, and, without any pre-arrangement, another strikes up an air.

---

[1] Urine. The urea acts as a mordant and fixes the dye.

[2] Miss Freer's remarks on the time of the tunes and the versification are over-simplifications. See p. 198.

[3] This would be an unusual length. Probably Miss Goodrich Freer did not realize that each couplet or line is sung twice.

Like the last, it is a love song, its sentiment of the most florid description. After this we have another in which the rival merits of two adjacent islands are discussed,[1] and then the women, having worked more than half-an-hour, examine the cloth. It is carefully measured: a piece of cloth must always be finished at a sitting, and in course of fulling it should shrink an inch to every foot of length.[2] The women measure on the back of the hand, occasionally verifying their estimate on a half-yard wand—eight feet to the yard being the Highland measurement.

'It will take three or four songs more', they say, and the picturesque phrase seems in keeping with the scene about us.

While the work has gone on, more visitors have strolled in. The hostess is moving about, now that the cessation of work makes movement possible in the cramped space. The dogs have clustered about the fire, relieved at the stopping of the singing. The hens are complaining on the beams overhead; the cat, who had climbed to the top of one of the cupboard beds, is expressing disgust as only a cat can. With every hair of her fur she protests against the crowd, the smell—above all, the noise; but it is better to bear the ills she has than to run the gauntlet of the dogs.

Now they begin again: the women are rested, and the singing becomes more vigorous, the melody is marked and rapid, the aspirates of the Gaelic breathe an audible excitement. Four long and short syllables go to a line, and the accent this time is very definite, and the thud of the cloth takes on a sharper sound as the web dries. . . .

The song is finished, and the women, exhausted, lean forward on the table. The sudden cessation of sound and movement is almost painful. The discontented cat shakes a disgusted paw, the dogs look hopefully towards the door. The fulling is over, the cloth lies reeking on the table. . . .

The ceremonial is not yet ended. Two of the women stand up and roll the cloth from opposite ends till they meet in the middle, and then, still keeping time, four of them fall upon the roll and proceed to pat it violently, straightening out the creases, and those unemployed strike up another song, this time of different metre. This finished, one standing up calls out, 'The rhymes, the rhymes!' And those who have been working reply: 'Three rhymes, four rhymes, five and a half rhymes.' This is very mysterious—probably the last remains of some forgotten ceremony.

Then the cloth is unwound, and again very carefully rolled up, this time into one firm bale, and then all rise and stand in reverent silence while the leader of the fulling-women pronounces the quaint, old-world

---

[1] Cf. No. xxiii here.

[2] On 4 May 1898 Fr. Allan McDonald recorded that he attended a waulking and that the cloth originally 50 feet long shrunk 4 feet 3 inches in the waulking.

grace with which their work concludes. Laying one hand on the cloth, she says:

> Let not the Evil Eye afflict, let not be mangled
> The man about whom thou goest, for ever.
> When he goes into battle or combat
> The protection of the Lord be with him.

And then some man of the party—it would not be etiquette for a woman —turns to the owner and says with emphasis:—

> 'May you possess it and wear it.'

And the cloth is fulled.

Miss Goodrich Freer writes as a visitor, though with Fr. Allan McDonald at her elbow. A vivid account of a waulking by a lady who must have taken part in them is given in a paper by Mary MacKellar, the Skye Gaelic poetess, read for her by Mr. John Whyte to the Gaelic Society of Inverness on 9 March 1887:

The Waulking Day may now be called one of the institutions of the past. It belonged to the time when the Highland women manufactured their own clothing, and also that of their households. . . . The making of fine material, and the designing of beautiful patterns, and the dyeing of the wool into the different shades, was a delight to the Highland women; and to see their husbands and sons arrayed in becoming garments of their own handiwork gave a dignity to many lives that were otherwise commonplace and uninteresting, and gave rise to a healthy emulation among them as to who should make the finest plaid or the prettiest web. . . .

It was a great labour to produce a good web. The wool had to be carefully washed, and then finely teased. Then the carding and the spinning and the dyeing had to be gone through, and when the right number of cuts for the number of yards wanted were wound into balls, the proud and victorious owner of them took them to the weaver to have the pattern set. She never went on that mission empty handed. She always took to the webster a cogful of meal, some butter, a kebbuck of cheese, a braxy ham, or whatever in the way of food happened to be most plentiful at the time. This offering was supposed to make him work cheerfully at his loom, so that he would leave a blessing on the cloth.

Every matron and maiden in the township knew when the web was expected home from the weaver's, and they could be heard humming some of the waulking songs that they would be expected to sing. The day came at last on which they were invited to help. . . and shortly after breakfast they gathered at what might be termed the festive house. A table was covered and sumptuously laid with whisky, divers kinds of bread, butter, cheese, and cold mutton, and any other delicacy at hand. The matrons examined the web, and discussed the colours, the pattern, and the texture, while the maidens carried stoups of water, or pails, from neighbouring houses, of a liquid called by them *màighstir* or *mac a' mhàighstir*.[1]

The web was put into a large tub of water and soap, and well tramped. A strong door was taken off its hinges, and laid on rests, so as to enable them to sit comfortably around it, and the web, saturated with the soapy water, was laid loosely upon it, and forthwith the work began. All seemed full of light-hearted gladness, and of bustle and latent excitement, and as each laid hold of the cloth, with their sleeves tucked up to the shoulders, one could see the amount of force they represented. . . . These good women, with strong, willing hands, take hold of the web, and the work proceeds, slowly at first, but bye and bye, when the songs commence, the latent excitement bursts into a blaze.

The greater number of these songs are tragic, and, in ballad style, have a story in them equal in interest to any three volume novel. . . . These Gaelic songs were never sung to a listless, uninterested audience. Every face was beaming with interest in every word of it that expressed feeling or suggested sentiment. One [woman] sings the song, while all take up the chorus, weird and plaintive, and as they toss and tumble the cloth, passing the folds from hand to hand, a stranger, who saw them at the work for the first time, might be pardoned for thinking them mad.[2] Alexander MacDonald, the poet (1700–1770) could not have used a better expression to tell the rough treatment he wished given to the 'Redcoats' than when he wished for a band of maidens to waulk the red web with firm hands. . . .

All the songs are called into requisition that have a chorus appropriate for the rhythm necessary for the hands in working the cloth to advantage. . . . The rhythm of hands and cloth together at this work may have been the origin of the Highland habit of holding a handkerchief by the corners, and keeping time with it during the singing of a Gaelic song. . . .[3]

After this part of the work was over, a table full of luxuries was spread —tea in abundance, and oatcakes, scones, butter, cheese, crowdie, cold beef, fresh eggs, or whatever was in season. The married women were expected all to take a full glass of whisky, whilst the maidens merely put the glass to their lips. There were no men at the table, and the hostess either said grace herself, or asked some pious matron to do so, and then came the extraordinary coaxing of them all to eat, making pieces for them, loading their plates with whatever was best, and all politely

[1] Urine, as before. Nineteenth-century writers are most reticent about identifying the liquid!

[2] See p. 4.　　　　　　　　　　　　　　　　[3] See p. 5.

saying 'they were not hungry'; all in high spirits, with radiant faces, interchanging witty remarks [in Gaelic], quoting proverbs, repeating snatches of songs to illustrate or give force to their remarks; and this closed the first part of the day's work.

After what is called the *luadhadh-làmh* or hand-waulking is done, the cloth is carefully rolled up in web form. The matrons then generally return home, leaving the maidens to the *luadhadh-chas* or foot-waulking. This is their best time. Shoes and stockings are stripped off, and with petticoats kilted to the knees, they sit on two rows of stools with the cloth on the floor between them, and there they kick it with heart and good will, singing merrily the while, and keeping time with their feet to the rhythm of the song. Soapy suds are kept on the cloth, and the web is continually turned round to let the waulking benefit each part alike. The maidens are in high glee, and the special choruses sung at this work are fitted for giving any amount of improvisation. . . .[1]

Before the waulking had commenced in the forenoon, each of the girls present had cut a knotted end of thrums off the corners of the web, and placed it above the door. The first one that placed it there was to get a husband of the same name as the first male, man or child, that entered the house; the second was to get a husband of the name of the second male that entered, and so on. This gave rise to great fun, and if a young man of the name of Donald came in under the thrums of a girl whose sweetheart in the meantime was named Duncan, it gave rise to a good deal of chaff. When a young man dropped into a house where the waulking was going on, he generally got a rough handling. He was summarily taken hold of by them and muffled up in the web, and thoroughly soaked with the luke-warm soapy water with which the web had been kept wet all the time. . . .[2]

During the foot-waulking, the web was rolled different ways three times, so that all parts would get the benefit, and after it was done they beat it with the open hands for some time. Then some old woman shook it out of the roll, and with a charm put all the witches from having any power over it, saying *Roinn a h-aon, roinn a dhà, roinn a trì, roinn a ceithir, roinn a còig, roinn a sia, roinn a seachd, cha n-aodach seo a shagart no chlèir*, 'Division one, division two, division three, division four, division five, division six, division seven, this is not cloth for priest or cleric'[3] and so on. Then the girls took it to the river or burn, where they tramped

---

[1] These songs were of a 'pairing-off' nature, such as *Cò bheir mi leam air an luing Éireannaich*, see *Folksongs and Folklore of South Uist*, p. 268.

[2] John MacFadyen tells the same thing of waulkings in the Isle of Mull, see *Sgeulaiche nan Caol*, p. 43.

[3] Cf. Alexander Carmichael, *Carmina Gadelica*, i. 307. The complete formula was 'this is not cloth for priest or cleric, but for so-and-so my beloved'. *Roinn* seems to be the word Miss Goodrich Freer rendered as 'rhyme', see p. 10.

all the soapy suds out of it, and all the part of the dye that might be loosened in the course of the day's work. They afterwards spread it out, carefully stretched, to dry, and having tidied themselves up, and got on their shoes and stockings, they return home. . . . They used to return to their homes singing some marching song.

In conclusion, I may mention here that the next thing done with the cloth was for two or three strong men to stretch and roll it as firmly and tightly as possible on a narrow board, or strong stick, whilst it was damp. This was called *coinnleachadh*, and it was left for several days in that condition, so that it might become smooth and stiff. When it came off the stick with a sound that seemed like a declaration of its strength, it was called *fìor-aodach* ['true cloth']. It was then unrolled to get dried in the sun, and after that it was rolled up again ready for the tailor, who had already been spoken to for coming to the house as soon as he could to make the required suits for young and old.

Though Mary MacKellar writes of the waulking day in 1887 as already an institution of the past in the Highlands, it is significant that out of ten songs which she quotes as then being sung at waulkings, at least seven have been recorded from the living Gaelic tradition of South Uist and Barra since 1930, demonstrating again the importance of these islands in the conservation of traditions that have disappeared elsewhere.

It is interesting that Mary MacKellar's account agrees with Pennant's in telling how the waulking was begun with the hands and finished with the feet. Alexander Carmichael mentions that 'occasionally the waulking-board is laid on the ground instead of on trestles, and the women work the cloth with their feet instead of with their hands'.[1] But use of the feet for waulking seems to have ceased entirely in the Hebrides, though according to Professor Otto Andersson it is the usual method in Sweden and Finland, but without the accompaniment of the kind of songs that are sung in Gaelic Scotland.[2]

A waulking on the Isle of Barra is described by the late Miss Annie Johnston, a gifted Barra lady who had an intimate knowledge of the Gaelic oral tradition of her native island, and did much to help preserve it; several airs recorded from her are printed in this book. Her account, which was written in Gaelic, is translated;

[1] *Carmina Gadelica*, i. 306.
[2] *On Gaelic Folksongs from the Isle of Lewis*, Budkavlen, 1952, pp. 15–19. In French Canada it was done with paddles, see paper by Professor Marius Barbeau in vol. viii of the *Journal of the International Folkmusic Council*, p. 40.

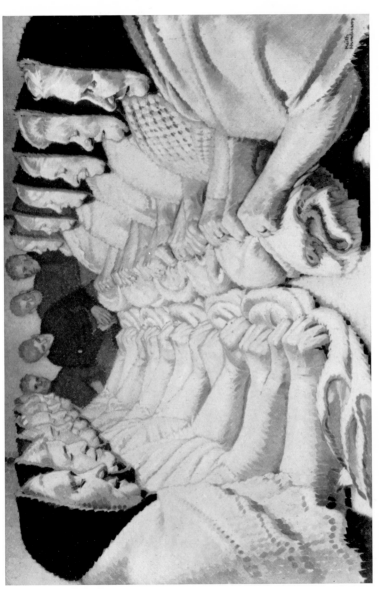

A waulking on the island of Barra, c. 1930. Reproduction of the painting by Keith Henderson, O.B.E.

it was originally printed in the introduction to *Gaelic Folksongs from the Isle of Barra.*

When the web of cloth came home from the loom, they used to decide which night they would have the waulking. There was the food to be prepared, fresh butter, oatcakes and barley cakes to be made, whisky to be brought home, crowdie and *gruthim* [a mixture of butter and crowdie] to be made, a hen or two to be killed and prepared, and then word would be sent to the waulking women. There would be a host, and the waulking-board would be in his care. This was usually made of wooden planks put together, or else, if they had one, a door would do.

The number of waulking women was according to the size of the cloth, and if it was blue cloth, there had to be two teams, working in turn, to make it really tight. Usually five or six was the number that could sit on each side of the waulking-board. The women used to come, wearing calico petticoats, drugget coats and tibbet aprons. Then the hostess used to baptize the cloth, that is, she shook holy water on it in the name of the Trinity, and put it in a tub of urine. They used to say that nothing was so good for taking the oil out [of the cloth] as urine. They used to take the cloth out of the tub and put it on the board, as you saw, and doubled it on the board thus. Then the woman who was best at singing began with a slow song, and then a 'warming-up song', and after that a short light song to encourage them because they were getting tired.[1]

After this the hostess would measure the cloth with her middle finger, and usually there was not much shrinking in it at the first three songs. Then another one would begin; she would sing three songs too, and as the cloth had been warmed by the first three songs, it would shrink more at the second attempt, and at the third attempt it ought to be ready, if it were blanket or white cloth.

At first it was eight finger lengths (ells) broad. When the cloth was ready, it would be three inches narrower in breadth anyway.

If it were blue cloth, that is, the cloth the men wore on board the boats, it would be made much thicker, and another band of waulkers would need to go to the board when the first band was tired.

When the cloth was as thick as was desired, the women then used to put it on the *coinneal*, that is, rolling it up in a roll, and singing an *òran basaidh*, 'clapping song'. Clapping songs were usually light and funny, such as:

'Who will I take with me on the Irish ship?' or, 'Ho my sweetheart, hé my sweetheart' and so on.

---

[1] It was considered unlucky for the same song to be sung twice at a waulking, as Alexander Carmichael records (*Carmina Gadelica*, iv. 89).

I never heard them have a blessing in Barra, though I asked many people about it; but one of the waulking women would say to the host, if the cloth were for him, 'Enjoy and use it, pay the dance, and throw across the next web.' If it were for a young man, 'Enjoy and use it, tear and rend it, and marry before it wears out.'

Then the waulking women used to wash themselves, and come in for food and a dram, and the young men used to put the waulking-board out into the barn, and the young folk would collect for a dance.

Such was the operation of waulking hand-made cloth, which was performed with minor variations in different islands of the Hebrides, as can be seen from other descriptions, such as those by Alexander Carmichael, Frances Tolmie, John MacFadyen, F. G. Rea, and others mentioned in the bibliography of this book. Nothing shows better than these accounts how work in the Gaelic-speaking Highlands and Islands was performed as a joyful social creative activity, integrated into the lives of the people and expressing their personalities, and how their great store of traditional folksong enriched their lives and lightened their labours—a very different, and a happier state of affairs than the rootlessness and monotony of modern urban factory existence enlivened only by mass media of entertainment.

THE SUBJECTS OF THE SONGS

THE texts of many of these songs take us back into the Highlands and Islands of the sixteenth and seventeenth centuries, as described by writers such as John Major (1521), Hector Boece (1527), Bishop Leslie (1578), and George Buchanan (1582).[1] They show us vividly a proud and independent pastoral people, deeply attached to their hereditary chiefs, delighting in the hunt and in the arts of love and war, and of Jacobite tradition (in so far as they had any politics at all). It was a world of which the traditions went back to Cù Chulainn and the Cattle Raid of Cooley, which came to an end in Ireland with the Battle of Kinsale and the Flight of the Earls at the beginning of the seventeenth century, but which in the Highlands and Islands of Scotland survived, at least in part, until 1746. In the older waulking songs, the clothing and arms and social habits described are those of the sixteenth and seventeenth centuries, or perhaps rather one can say, are immemorial habits that were still persisting in the sixteenth and seventeenth centuries. Amongst men, long hair and a fair complexion were esteemed. Clothing mentioned includes the steel helmet (*clogada cruadhach*), doublet, shirt (*léine*), plaid (*breacan*), belt (*crios*), hose, garters, and shoes. In the belt were carried the dirk (*sgian*) and pistol; at the side was carried the sword (*claidheamh chinnghil*, a silver-hilted sword). Bows and arrows were also used, well into the seventeenth century; guns (*gunna chaol*) were beginning to come into use. Professor W. J. Watson has pointed out that guns were late in coming into use in the Highlands, and that no Gaelic song in which they are mentioned is likely to have been composed before 1600, if as early.

The favourite diet of the Highlanders was venison, beef, oat and barley cakes, and preparations of milk. Potatoes were unknown at the time these songs were made. Fish, except salmon, were not much esteemed. Drink included wine from France, whisky and brandy from the Lowlands, gin (*sineubhar*), and beer. Another

[1] See Hume Brown, *Scotland before 1700*.

luxury was silk from Spain (*sioda reamhar ruadh na Spàine*) and linen from Galway. Galway in Ireland must have had a considerable trade with the Hebrides at one time.

The animals hunted were the seal, red deer, roe deer, otter, swan, goose, grouse, salmon, and trout; the livestock owned was, above all, cattle, but also sheep (kept primarily for wool), and horses. The ships were galleys using both sails and oars. There are many allusions to these galleys in the early seventeenth-century minutes of the Privy Council of Scotland, which was concerned to procure their destruction and so limit the independence of the Hebridean chiefs. The recreations of the Highlanders were backgammon (*tàileasg*), dicing, dancing, poetry and song, and the music of bagpipe, fiddle, and harp.

The subjects of the songs are usually the praise of great men, of the chiefs and their magnificence and hospitality; the hunt; love (if the lover is of noble origin, there is no shame in an illegitimate pregnancy); and laments for the dead.

Similes are drawn directly from nature, and the language is pure, simple, and concrete, and often highly poetical, as might be expected from a people whose everyday life was permeated with an oral literature of poetry, song, and story, and with whom the professional poet-historians were held in high honour. Chevilles and conceptions borrowed from the court poetry of these frequently appear in popular Gaelic songs of the seventeenth century.[1]

The question has been raised whether the words of waulking songs were originally composed for the purpose of the waulking, or were songs or ballads, originally made to be sung to quite different airs, later forced to submit to the melodic structure of waulking airs; and whether waulking songs owe their frequently disjointed form to stanzas or sections having been forgotten in the course of oral transmission.[2] The answer to the first question seems to be that though pre-existing ballads were—and still are—sometimes used for waulking by being sung to waulking airs, the great majority of these songs were extemporized at the waulking-board,

[1] See J. C. Watson, *The Poems of Mary MacLeod*, p. xxi.

[2] See *Éigse*, viii, parts 1, 2, and 4, and ix, part 2, where this question was debated at length by James Ross and the writer. These changes in subject usually coincide with a change in end-rhyme (involving a slight variation in the air if a long rhyming vowel is substituted for a short one). Donald MacCormick marks such changes with the word *atharraich* 'change' or *tionndaidh* 'turn'. For a description of the metres of waulking songs, see p. 198 here.

and that different parts of the same song may well have been extemporized by different persons present, in order to make the songs long enough for the waulking of the cloth. This process of extemporization and not the omission of passages is sufficient to account for the abrupt changes of subject[1] that occur in the songs as we find them. As they have been taken down, they are remarkably consistent in these 'breaks' over the past seventy years: no amount of collation of versions taken down at different times and places seems to produce anything to fill the gaps. Moreover in Cape Breton, which has been separated from Gaelic-speaking Scotland completely since around 1835, exactly the same kind of 'breaks' occur in the same places in the same kind of songs.

On the other hand, it is indisputable that ballads have been adapted for use as waulking songs. The best instance of this is the Arthurian ballad known as *Am Bròn Binn*, 'The Sweet Sorrow'. A version of this was printed by the late Dr. George Henderson in the *Miscellany presented to Kuno Meyer* in 1912. In this Dr. Henderson says: 'In 1892 the ballad *The Melodious Sorrow* (Am Bròn Binn) was sung to me at Dalibrog, S. Uist, by Mòr Nic Fhionghain, in a semi-recitative air such as is associated with the Ossianic Lays and with one or two hymns like *Laoidh Mhic Cealair*' (p. 20). On p. 27 he remarks that 'the ballad (i.e. *Am Bròn Binn*) must at one time have been popular although it does not seem old in its present form, for there is still another variant sung as a waulking song!' I myself have recorded it as a ballad, sung to a recitative type of air, from Mrs. Patrick MacCormick at Hacklett in Benbecula on 21 November 1949, and as a waulking song from Mrs. MacDougall (Anna Raghnaill Eachainn) in Barra in March 1938.

There is an interesting reference to the singing of Ossianic ballads as labour songs in the Isle of Man in the eighteenth century, in British Museum Additional MS. 11215, fol. 6: in a letter from John Buchanan to Professor Thorkelin, which tells how, when the Bishop of Man's old gardener overheard a discussion about James MacPherson's Ossian, he

stept in on hearing frequent mention of Fingal and Oshian and Cuchullan, &c., and told them he knew who could sing a good song about those men and Ochullin, and that was his Brother's Wife, a very

---

[1] Marked by double repetition of the refrain when sung, see p. 214.

antient Woman. On which they sent for the old Dame who very readily
sung them eight or ten verses which my friend immediately took down
in writing, and next day on recollection she brought them the rest, and
of which he obliged me with a Copy. I must own I was much surprized
and delighted with the discovery & similarity of the subject to some of
Oshian's Poems, vizt Love, & Warriors, & Hunting & Jealousys, & the
barbarous Vengeance of those heroick Ages, of all wch we meet with so
many passages in the poem of Fingal. My friend asked her, where she
learned this old Song, she said from her Mother & Grandmother & many
more—that they used to sing them at their work & Wheels [i.e. spinning
wheels].

The date of the letter is 25 October 1789; it was printed in the
Catalogue of the Manuscripts relating to Wales in the British Museum,
p. 953 (Cymmrodorion Record Series, 4, iv).

A song which only exists as a waulking song but which may well
have originated as a ballad is *A Mhic a' Mhaoir* 'O, son of the
Steward'.[1] Another is *A' Bhean Iadach* 'The Jealous Woman',[2]
of which versions have been recovered in various places in the
Gaelic-speaking districts of Scotland and Ireland. On the other
hand, waulking songs in the form of flytings, such as No. XXIII
here, or No. 73 in the Tolmie Collection,[3] both of which are dis-
putes between the bardesses of MacDonald of Clanranald and
MacNeil of Barra, and songs which, like No. XIV here, are in the
form of a dialogue between a man and a woman, give a particularly
strong impression of having been extemporized. In some songs it
happens that musical stress coincides with metrically unstressed
syllables. This in itself is no proof that the words of such songs
were originally composed to another tune: it is something just as
likely to happen when lines are extemporized in labour songs sung
to melodies of very marked rhythm. It is interesting that where
such musical stress falls on an obscure vowel (e.g. forms of the
definite article such as *a'*, *na*, *nan*) the pronunciation of this is
often changed by traditional songs when so stressed from ə to
open *o*.

There is also strong evidence that many of the songs, in the form
in which we now have them, were extemporized, from the extent

[1] *Gaelic Folksongs from the Isle of Barra*, p. 30.
[2] *F.F.S.U.*, p. 254. Another probable example is No. XVII here, see Notes.
[3] The version of this song in the Tolmie Collection is not complete. Much
fuller versions have been recorded in Barra, Vatersay, and Cape Breton. (*Cha
déid Mór a Bharraidh bhrònaich.*)

to which identical, or very similar, lines and passages describing stock situations or personalities occur over and over again, so that it is really quite impossible to say that they belong originally to one song more than to another. Such lines and passages must have existed in large numbers in the unconscious minds of the women who extemporized at the waulking-boards, and who had been immersed in the Gaelic oral tradition from their childhood. It is therefore quite possible for the words of a waulking song to have been 'composed' in the seventeenth century from the point of view of the personal allusions made in it, and yet to contain passages of verse which must have been made much earlier.

Some instances that occur here may be mentioned. In many of these songs there occurs a stock passage in which the poetess compares the luxury in which she was reared with the poverty of her present circumstances. Such passages occur here in VII, lines 236–41, XXIX. 1045–51, and XXXII. 1131–4. Then there are very similar passages on the magnificence of the household of a great chief (V. 147–54, VIII. 287–90, XXXII. 1136–9). Identical passages describing what the author or authoress would do if he or she possessed the strength of Cù Chulainn occur in VI. 217–22 and VIII. 308–13.

Amongst a people who were devoted to the chase, the successful hunter has always been a subject for praise, and many similar passages occur on this theme, see here V. 175–80, XI. 397–408, XII. 416–22, XIII. 470–5, XIV. 490–4, XV. 542–8, XXVIII. 1004–8, XXX. 1083–5, XXXIII. 1168–71, XXXIV. 1190–4, XXXVII. 1326–30, and XXXIX. 1363–6. Note, for instance, such a line as (*sealgair*) *na circeige duinne bheireadh gur as an fhuarniod*, 'the hunter of the grouse that would read a brood in the cold nest', occurring in two completely different songs (XII. 421–2 and XXXVII. 1329). Were the whole corpus of waulking songs to be taken into consideration, the list of passages that occur repeatedly in different songs could be considerably extended; for example, the passage XXV. 893–900, where a girl complains that her lover is kept from her by her lack of a dowry, occurs in several different songs. The passage XXXIII. 1164–71 where the girl says she will go with no one but her own love, a hunter, is identical with the opening passage of a different song, printed by K. C. Craig on p. 19 of his collection. The glossarial index to this book has been compiled partly to facilitate the study of such stock passages and expressions; the whole subject of their occurrence in Scottish Gaelic waulking songs and of their origin awaits further investigation.[1]

In these traditional waulking songs we have a large body of verse, several thousand lines in fact, never printed to any extent until the MacDonald Collection of Gaelic Poetry appeared in 1911, and never made the entire subject of any book until the publication of K. C. Craig's *Orain Luaidh Màiri Nighean Alasdair*, which consists of texts alone, without translation, music, or explanatory notes, in 1949. Some of this verse consists of pre-existing ballads adapted for the purpose of waulking the cloth, but the bulk of it was extemporized by women at the waulking-board, using freely passages and conceptions from an older literature. The authors of this verse are, from internal evidence, nearly all women, as might be expected. The words of most of the surviving songs were composed in the seventeenth century in a style so similar that most of them might well have been made by the same person, which of course is not the case. The only persons I have heard named as the authoresses of waulking songs are Mary MacLeod (Màiri nighean Alasdair Ruaidh, the seventeenth-century Skye poetess), who is said to have composed the words of No. XVII here; Nic Iain Fhinn, who is said to have been born on the island of Mingulay and to have composed No. XXXVII here; Nic a' Mhanaich, a South Uist woman who had a flyting with Nic Iain Fhinn; and Nighean Aonghuis 'ic Dhòmhnaill Bhàin, who is said by the late Revd. A. MacDonald, minister of Killearnan, to have composed No. XX here.[2]

It can be safely said that apart from Ossianic or Arthurian ballads such as *Am Bròn Binn* that have been adapted for waulking, the subject of no waulking song known to us is older than the downfall of the Lords of the Isles (i.e. the end of the fifteenth century), indeed it is doubtful if any are older than the middle of the sixteenth century. But cloth must have been waulked in the Highlands before 1550, and many of the tunes of waulking songs

---

[1] See Stith Thompson, 'The Challenge of Folklore', *P.M.L.A.*, September 1964. 'A study of the unlettered singers in Yugoslavia has shown that it is not the actual text of a ballad or epic song which they hold in their memory and which permits rapid improvisation, but rather a vast store of formulas and of formulistic statements which can be applied to almost any situation.' This was the situation in the Highlands and Islands when these waulking songs were extemporized in the seventeenth and eighteenth centuries. The same kind of thing applies in the telling of Gaelic folktales.

[2] Killearnan MS. collection of Gaelic Songs, p. 16.

give the impression of being very archaic. It is therefore probable that fresh words were extemporized to the old waulking-song airs, particularly during the period of 1550 to 1650 when great disorder existed in the Highlands and Islands, when clan warfare, following the failure of the last attempt to restore the Lordship of the Isles, became frequent and bitter and was complicated by the politics of the Reformation in Scotland, culminating in the Civil War, in which Highlanders under Montrose played a distinguished part. Later on, the eighteenth-century poets Alexander MacDonald and Duncan Bàn MacIntyre composed songs to waulking airs: this was the first literary use of the waulking-song form. A recent instance was the song in praise of the Vatersay raiders of 1908 by Malcolm MacFarlane.[1]

[1] See *The Old and the New Highlands and Hebrides*, p. 154.

THE WAULKING SONG IN
EIGHTEENTH-CENTURY
PRINTED GAELIC LITERATURE

THE first original work printed in Scottish Gaelic is the first edition of Alexander MacDonald's Poems, *Ais-Eiridh na Sean Chánoin Albannaich*, published in 1751. This contains a well-known poem in waulking-song form, which MacDonald called *Oran-luaigh no fúcaidh, a rinn duin'-uasal d'a leannan, air dhi dol thar fairrge. Air fonn, Agus ho Mhórag, no hó-rou no hó-rou ghealladh*, i.e. 'A waulking or milling song, which a gentleman made to his sweetheart, after she had gone over the sea. To the tune, *Agus ho Mhórag* (etc.).'

MacDonald's first edition is said to have been suppressed by the Hanoverian government, though no reference to the order for its destruction has yet been found in contemporary records. This song, however, has passed into oral tradition, possibly from his own recitation of it in the first instance, and a version is printed, with tune and translation, in Donald Campbell's *Treatise on the Language, Poetry, and Music of the Highland Clans*, published in 1862 (pp. 176–81 of text and p. 3 of music). This is the first instance known to me of the publication of text, translation, and tune of a Scottish Gaelic waulking song. *Agus hó Mhórag* is still popular. I recorded another traditional version of it from Roderick Mac-Kinnon (Ruairi Iain Bhàin), Northbay, Isle of Barra, in March 1938.

Alexander MacDonald also wrote another poem on the same subject in the form of a waulking song, *Òganaich ùir a' chùil teudaich*, of which a fragment is found in Gaelic MS. LXIII of the National Library of Scotland: this too survived in oral tradition; after the last war I found a version of the full text in the papers of Alexander Carmichael, and later recorded the tune from Captain D. J. MacKinnon, a son of Roderick MacKinnon above-mentioned.

The first edition of the poems of Duncan MacIntyre (1768) also contains a poem in the form of an 'Oran Luaidh', *Togamaid fonn air luadh' a' chlóthlain*, 'Let us raise a tune at the waulking of the cloth'. This song, too, has become popular and is part of the oral tradition of Uist and Barra: see Margaret Fay Shaw, *Folksongs and Folklore of South Uist*, p. 204.

Waulking songs, and the closely related *iorrams*, have appeared in small numbers in the anthologies beginning with Ranald Mac-Donald's Eigg collection in 1776 (I recorded the song *'S e mo rùn do chùl bòidheach*, printed on p. 351 of the Eigg Collection, sung as a waulking song in Cape Breton, in 1937). There are two or three waulking songs in the Gillies collection (1786), including *'S fhad tha mi 'm ònaran* (p. 124), with a reference to the publication of the tune as No. 91 in Patrick MacDonald's collection of Highland music (published *c.* 1780): this song survives in the oral tradition of South Uist, and a version was published by Margaret Fay Shaw in *Folksongs and Folklore of South Uist* in 1955. The Gillies collection also contains a version of *Chunnaic mise mo leannan/ 'S cha d'aithnich e 'n dé mi* (p. 245); this also survives in the oral tradition of South Uist and Barra, and I have recorded a spirited version of it from Roderick MacKinnon in 1938, and two versions can be found in *Folksongs and Folklore of South Uist*, p. 228. These instances illustrate how songs originating on the mainland but probably now forgotten there have survived in the oral tradition of the Outer Hebrides, an important aspect of that tradition.

But generally waulking songs, not being felt suitable for literary treatment or for solo singing at concerts, have been neglected by the compilers of Gaelic anthologies and Gaelic song-books. In particular, the objective presentation of texts, with translations and authentic airs, has been delayed, and did not take place to any extent until the publication of Frances Tolmie's collection of Gaelic folk-music by the English Folksong Society in 1911. This contains 105 songs of which 38 are waulking songs, but the Gaelic texts are not always given in full. Some of the airs had been put at the disposal of Keith Norman MacDonald for inclusion in the Gesto collection of Highland music, which was published in 1895.

In 1949 the late K. C. Craig published the Gaelic texts of 155 waulking songs taken down from a single reciter, Màiri nighean Alasdair 'ac Dhòmhnaill at Snaoiseabhal in South Uist, a valuable piece of work that brought home to students of Gaelic the wealth of the oral tradition of South Uist. This was followed by the publication in 1950 of *Gaelic Folksongs from the Isle of Barra* with five twelve-inch discs selected from the recordings made by the writer in 1938, with book of words and translations. Nine of the ten songs so presented are connected with the waulking of the cloth.

In 1954 the fifth volume of Alexander Carmichael's *Carmina Gadelica* appeared, containing a section devoted to the texts of fourteen waulking songs, with translations, and in 1955 Margaret Fay Shaw's *Folksongs and Folklore of South Uist*, which includes the tunes and texts, with translations, of thirty-two waulking songs (of which versions of ten are found in the MacCormick MS.), was published. In 1960 the School of Scottish Studies put out a long-playing disc of Scots and Gaelic songs chosen from a large number of recordings, with a booklet of words and translations; this includes one or two waulking songs, and is an excellent introduction to the whole subject of Scottish folk-music.

ART VERSIONS OF WAULKING SONGS

USE of the airs and textual motifs of waulking songs as a basis for the construction of art songs is almost entirely associated with the names of Mrs. Kennedy-Fraser and the Revd. Dr. Kenneth MacLeod; until the publication of *Songs of the Hebrides*, it was seldom attempted. The earliest instance we have discovered is the arrangement of the waulking song *Mas tu mo mhàthair 's gura fiadh thu* 'If you are my mother and you are a deer', 'Oisein's Warning to his Mother', that is to be found in the first volume of Alexander Campbell's and Walter Scott's *Albyn's Anthology*, pp. 48 and 49. This was published in 1816. Campbell says in a footnote that 'This is one of the ancient Melodies to which many of the Poems ascribed to OSSIAN are chanted. This air, together with the Vocal Poetry and four other ancient melodies, the EDITOR took down, (with the assistance of the Revd. RODERICK MACLEAN) from the recitation of RODERICK MACQUEEN, Grass-keeper[1] at Carnish, North Uist, in August 1815.'

From Campbell's description it might be thought that the melody represented one of the chants to which the old Ossianic ballads were (and still sometimes are) recited, of which an example can be seen in Amy Murray's *Father Allan's Island*, p. 100. But it is clear from the syllables of the chorus, which begins *Bheir mi hoirin o ha*, and from the air itself, that the transcriber is attempting to represent a waulking song. This is confirmed in a striking way by J. F. Campbell's *Leabhar na Féinne*, published in 1872, where no fewer than six versions of the same song are given, the choruses being similar to that printed in *Albyn's Anthology* (*Bheir mi hoireann o a haw*, etc.). Three of the six versions J. F. Campbell gives were taken down in North Uist, one by Miss Frances Tolmie in 1871, of which Campbell says that it was 'written this year in North Uist, by

---

[1] A grass-keeper, *coimheadaidh* in Gaelic, was the person who was responsible for keeping cattle and sheep out of the unfenced crops in the summertime in the days when arable ground was worked in runrig. 'Carnish' is usually written 'Carinish'.

Miss Tolmie, from the repetition of women who used to sing this song at their work, but who have been forbidden to sing any more secular music, and given up the practice as wicked'. The air taken down by Miss Tolmie is printed in her collection, No. 89; the resemblance to that printed in *Albyn's Anthology* is distinct. Miss Tolmie refers to the song as being almost forgotten in Skye in her time: I have not been able to find anyone in South Uist or Barra who could sing it, though old people had heard of it.

Adaptations of three waulking songs ('*S fhad' tha mi m'ònaran, Dh'éirich mi moch madainn Chéitein*, and *A Mhic a' Mhaoir*) were attempted by Finlay Dun in *Orain na'h-Albain*, which was published around 1860.[1] The success of Mrs. Kennedy-Fraser's *Songs of the Hebrides* has inspired some imitators, notably the two volumes of *Gaelic Songs of the Isles of the West* by Fr. John MacMillan, Barra, with the collaboration of Patrick McGlynn and F. M. Lewis; but *Songs of the Hebrides* remains much the most important and most striking effort to adapt Gaelic folk-songs, including waulking songs, as art versions for concert-platform purposes.

As most waulking songs consist of different sections, probably originally extemporized, on unrelated subjects, and all are naturally sung unaccompanied, with the choruses in unison and the soloist having the folk-singer's liberty of introducing slight variations into the airs, which are in gapped scales (modes), adaptation of waulking songs for concert performance is a matter of considerable difficulty and involves radical interference with their natural structure.[2] Mrs. Kennedy-Fraser in *Songs of the Hebrides* (three volumes, 1909, 1917, and 1921), *From the Hebrides* (1925), and *More Songs of the Hebrides* (1929) attempted this, originally with the help of Kenneth MacLeod, on a considerable scale, and with varying success: the critic's attitude to her versions will depend to a considerable degree on his knowledge of what constitutes genuine folk-music and even more upon his knowledge of the original traditional versions of the Hebridean songs themselves. It can be said here that the Gaelic texts printed in the first volume of *Songs of the Hebrides*, where Kenneth MacLeod's hand is most evident, are fuller and more authentic than in any of the succeeding

[1] Pp. 22, 12, and 74. See the Gillies Collection, p. 124, for a version of the first, and *Gaelic Folksongs from the Isle of Barra*, p. 30, for a version of the last.

[2] During the last generation, a native style of unaccompanied solo singing of these songs has been developed, mostly by singers from Barra, using a slower tempo and not repeating verses. This style is not unpleasing.

volumes. Now that so much recording work has been done in the Outer Hebrides since 1937, sufficient material exists for a critical inquiry into the origins of *Songs of the Hebrides*. Indeed the publication of this present work is a contribution to such an inquiry. Versions of fourteen of the forty songs printed here are to be found in *Songs of the Hebrides*, and comparison will not only show how Mrs. Kennedy-Fraser treated her material, but prove that her collection by no means exhausted the field, as her uncritical admirers have claimed, greatly to the detriment of any effort systematically to preserve and establish the authentic versions of the songs. Thus we have George Malcolm Thomson writing in 1929 of

the discovery by Mrs. Kennedy-Fraser of an exquisite folk-poetry and folk-music among the Gaelic-speaking fisherfolk of Eriskay and other Hebridean islands. It is one of the most romantic and fortunate accidents in modern history that this small and lovely world yielded up its treasure before it passed away.[1]

while in 1934 Sir Robert Rait and Dr. George Pryde wrote that:

In our own day Mrs. Marjorie [*sic*] Kennedy-Fraser tapped an almost untried source in Gaelic folk-poetry (though Burns did use a few Gaelic airs) and made the nation her debtor with her edition of songs of the Hebrides. To deride work of this kind as a tampering with the genuine product of the folk-spirit is inept and ungracious, yet it is still occasionally done. Not only is it clear that the essentials of the originals are generally preserved and that the alterations and additions are improvements; it is even doubtful if, in many cases, anything would have survived without the interested labours of these collectors.[2]

while fourteen pages later these writers express the surprising opinion that 'the chief approach to Gaelic letters for Scotland as a whole remains the admirable translations of Mrs. Kennedy Fraser'.[3]

Dr. Agnes Mure MacKenzie, too, refers to Mrs. Kennedy-Fraser, her sister, and her daughter, doing 'extensive work in collecting, no more than barely in time, the remnants of Gaelic song', but she at least can see that 'the English translations she attached to them were unluckily of a dreadful soulfulness, and the

---

[1] *A Short History of Scotland*, p. 299.
[2] *Scotland* (in the Modern World series), p. 302.
[3] Ibid., p. 316. (No hyphen here!)

settings of some were unduly elaborate'[1]—not one of these writers was aware of the fact that Mrs. Kennedy-Fraser herself was incapable of translating a Gaelic song!

Fully aware of the risk we run of incurring the charges of ineptitude and ungraciousness made by the authors of *Scotland* in the Modern World series, quoted above, the writer and his musical collaborator, Mr. Francis Collinson, publish this collection both in order to honour the memories of Donald MacCormick and Fr. Allan McDonald, collectors who preceded Mrs. Kennedy-Fraser, and the traditional singers who have kept the authentic versions of the songs alive in our own time, and to help to establish and make known to the world the traditional forms of some of the real 'songs of the Hebrides'.

[1] *Scotland in Modern Times* (1941), pp. 208, 209. Readers interested in Mrs. Kennedy-Fraser, her treatment of her originals, and her indebtedness to other collectors, should read 'The Debt of Marjory Kennedy Fraser to Frances Tolmie', by Ethel Bassin (*T.G.S. I.* xxxix–xl. 334); the articles on 'Songs of the Hebrides' in the *Scotsman* of 6, 7, and 8 January 1958 by Francis Collinson; and that on the same subject by J. L. Campbell in the *Scots Magazine* of the same month.

THE DONALD MacCORMICK
COLLECTION

T H E existence of this manuscript was first revealed by the discovery
of an entry made by the late Fr. Allan McDonald of Eriskay (1859–
1905)[1] written in January or February 1897 in the fifth volume of
his folklore notebooks, which is as follows:

I transcribe a stanza or two of 'Orain Luaghaidh' [waulking songs]
with 'Fonn' [chorus] from Donald MacCormack [sic] Kilphedir's[2]
collection so that I may have a cue for the different airs to be collated.
I will number them according as they come in his collection. My impression is that the same assonant rhyme should run thro' each line
from the beginning to the end of each piece and that where this is not
the case, that different songs have been mixed together.[3]

This entry is followed by the opening lines and choruses of
thirty waulking songs.

There is a very interesting description of Donald MacCormick
himself by the late F. G. Rea, who was headmaster of Garry-
namonie School in Fr. Allan McDonald's parish in South Uist
from 1890 to 1894 and again from 1904 to 1913, in his reminiscences
recently published under the title of *A School in South Uist*. Rea,
an Englishman, began his duties as headmaster on 2 January 1890,
and the school log-book records the first visit of the Compulsory
Officer to him on 20 January. In those days the Compulsory Officer
was a busy man: children were frequently absent from school, in
the winter-time from bad weather and epidemics, in the spring
herding cattle, keeping them out of the growing crops[4] (much of the
crofters' arable ground being unfenced), and in the autumn being
wanted for the harvest work. Donald MacCormick's visits both to

---

[1] For accounts of Fr. Allan McDonald, see Amy Murray, *Fr. Allan's Island*;
Mrs. Kennedy-Fraser, *A Life of Song*; J. L. Campbell, *Fr. Allan McDonald,
Priest, Poet, and Folklorist*, and *Gaelic Words from South Uist, collected by Fr.
Allan McDonald*; F. Rea, *A School in South Uist*.

[2] Kilphedir was the village where MacCormick lived.

[3] It is rather evidence of extemporization, see p. 19.

[4] Cf. line 276 here!

the schools of the parish, and to the houses of defaulters, were frequent. His salary is said to have been only a few pounds a year. This is how Rea describes him:

The attendance officer visited the school at intervals for reports of the attendance. He was a type of man I had never met before. A fairly educated man who spoke, read and wrote Gaelic and English quite fluently, he had a thoroughly independent outlook on men and matters, and his logical critical view on life in general tinged with a little philosophy quite interested me. He was a native of the island, between forty and fifty years of age, of medium height and build, hair turning gray, and had clean-cut good features in which were set a pair of lean gray eyes. I judged that he had travelled a lot in his earlier days but he had evidently settled down, for he then had a fair farm and quite a number of cows and horses.

If he came to the school in the afternoon I generally invited him to the house when lessons were over, for I enjoyed conversing with him. His knowledge of the then current politics and prominent men, and his keen judgment of them; his power of discussing the merits and demerits of standard authors and their works really astounded me; for here was, perhaps, the last place I should have looked for such a character.

Had the worthy Mr. Rea been better acquainted with Gaelic-speaking Scotland or Ireland he would not have been so surprised at finding such a personality as MacCormick in a place like South Uist, which had been the home of the poet-historians of the Clanranald family up to the middle of the eighteenth century. Donald MacCormick belonged to the type of the old hedge schoolmasters that were a feature of life in the Scottish and Irish Gàidhealtachds in the seventeenth and eighteenth centuries.

Besides being a collector of oral tradition—Fr. Allan McDonald's early folklore notebooks contain anecdotes and a collection of Gaelic proverbs contributed by MacCormick—he was also a poet. Three hymns written by him were included in the Catholic Gaelic hymnal which Fr. Allan McDonald published at Oban in 1893[1]— a hymn in praise of the Blessed Virgin, a hymn to St. Michael, and the 'Farmer's Hymn' (*Bho nach diamhanas nì cùis duinn*). Donald MacCormick also wrote an elegy on Father George Rigg, referred to on p. 34 here.[2]

---

[1] See J. L. Campbell, 'The Sources of the Gaelic Hymnal', *Innes Review*, vii. 101. MacCormick's hymns are on pp. 124, 127, and 130 of this book.

[2] Printed in the *Stornoway Gazette* of 5 July 1960. Two letters written in

As far as this collection of waulking songs was concerned, inquiries in South Uist yielded the information that MacCormick had probably taken down the words from the singing of his mother and sister. He had left no heirs in Uist who might possess any of his manuscripts now, and it was believed that his manuscript collection of waulking songs had probably been taken away by Alexander Carmichael the well-known folklore collector on one of his visits to South Uist.

The papers of Alexander Carmichael had passed to his son-in-law, the late Professor W. J. Watson, who in turn had bequeathed them to Edinburgh University Library on his decease shortly after the last war. They comprise a very large amount of material— Gaelic stories, songs, ballads, incantations, place-names, folklore, local tradition, lexicographical material, and so on, much of it collected in the Hebrides by Carmichael himself, some of it contributed by other collectors. Carmichael's papers were uncatalogued. A search through them revealed no trace of Donald Mac-Cormick's manuscript: but the very last bundle of papers examined was found to contain verse translations of fifteen of the songs in it in Fr. Allan McDonald's handwriting in pencil, with references to the pages of the original manuscript. A translation of another was found in a notebook of Fr. Allan McDonald's devoted to waulking songs, which also contained translations of different versions of three other songs in the MacCormick collection. Attempts at musical transcriptions of most of the songs in the MacCormick collection by Miss Evelyn Benedict, an American lady who visited Eriskay in 1905, were also found; these, however, cannot be regarded as successful.

A fresh search was begun in the Carmichael papers in case Donald MacCormick's manuscript had been overlooked, when quite unexpectedly I received word from the late Mr. Hector MacIver that, knowing that I was engaged in research on Fr. Allan McDonald and his folklore collections, he was sending me a document connected with him which he had been given some time ago by Fr. Allan McDonald's niece, the late Miss Margaret MacInnes. When this arrived, it turned out to be the long-sought MacCormick manuscript collection of waulking songs.

Gaelic by MacCormick also survive. One was printed in *Gairm*, No. 28, p. 369, the other in *An Gàidheal*, xlvii, p. 11. MacCormick also left a manuscript *Urnuigh roimh n'Aifrinn* [*sic*], 'A Prayer before Mass'.

The manuscript is an octavo notebook bearing the title

Cochruinneachadh
Do
Dhorain Lùaidh
Le Domhnull M'Càrmaic
N, Cillpheadair N,
Ceann a Deas,
Uist.
Anns, a Bhliadhna
Ochd Ciad diag Ceithirfichead
S, a Tridiag.

i.e. 'A Collection of Waulking Songs made by Donald MacCormick in Kilphedir in South Uist, in the Year 1893'. 'Age 56' is added in pencil, apparently in Fr. Allan McDonald's handwriting. The notebook itself contains the texts of thirty-six waulking songs (two of which are almost identical versions of the same song[1]) and a love song, *Mo ghaol òigeir a' chùil duinn*, which is not printed here (see Killearnan MS., p. 144, and the *MacDonald Collection of Gaelic Poetry*, p. 365). On a loose leaf there are two more waulking songs, and on another there is an original elegy by MacCormick on the late Fr. George Rigg who succeeded Fr. Allan McDonald as parish priest of Daliburgh in 1894 and died a heroic death in the fever epidemic of 1897, having caught the sickness through ministering to poor people who would otherwise have been left unattended.

The songs in the notebook occupy ninety-six numbered pages, but the opening lines transcribed by Fr. Allan McDonald early in 1897 only go as far as page 80,[2] though he had made translations of two and a half of the six songs that are written after that page. The loose-leaf sheet with two waulking songs is paginated 45 to 48, but it was not torn out of this notebook, and was probably extracted from another of the same size. MacCormick went to some trouble to indicate how the songs should be sung, as regards the repetition of lines or couplets and the division of choruses, but says nothing of the persons from whom he took down the words.

---

[1] pp. 45, 78 (No. XXIX here). This proves the collection must have been made over an extended period of time.

[2] As do the entries in MacCormick's 'Clarr Innse' or List of Contents. This must have been the extent of the manuscript in early 1897.

The project of publishing a book devoted to Hebridean waulking songs, to be edited by Fr. Allan McDonald, had been considered as long ago as 1902. On 2 September of that year, Ella Carmichael, the daughter of Alexander Carmichael, who with her brother had paid a visit to Eriskay a few days previously, wrote to Fr. Allan McDonald regarding a Gaelic Texts society which it was proposed should be founded in Edinburgh, with the backing of Walter Blaikie, a personal friend of Fr. Allan's and one of the directors of the firm of T. & A. Constable that had published Alexander Carmichael's *Carmina Gadelica*. The object of this society was to be the publication of collections of Gaelic oral literature such as Fr. Allan McDonald's. Ella Carmichael wrote:

I am very pleased to be able to tell Mr. Blaikie that you will go over and roughly shape your MSS this coming winter, and though we would all have liked the first volume to be entirely yours, I think perhaps what you said on Sunday is the best—to prepare a collection of waulking songs. You have some and I have a few and my father has a few and Miss Fanny Tolmie has some and a Mr. Kenneth MacLeod—who is a missionary at Lochboisdale (perhaps you know him?) has some. Miss Tolmie has the music of a good many and can get more, and with your very kind offer to 'block in' the translations of some we might be able to get something ready for spring if things get sufficiently into form otherwise.

On 23 March 1903 Ella Carmichael, returning to Fr. Allan McDonald six volumes of his folklore manuscript collection, remarked that Blaikie would like to have Fr. Allan's material fairly soon, either tales or waulking songs, preferably the latter: 'If you agree that they are best you could have those written down by Miss Tolmie, Kenneth MacLeod, myself etc. for translation and editing.'

There follows a long gap in the correspondence, lasting nearly a year. Then a letter from Ella Carmichael, dated 29 February 1904, in which she says: 'You will be thinking with regard to our Gaelic Texts Society we have gone to sleep. We have not quite done that however but we have decided to have a magazine instead of a Texts Society.'

The magazine was to be the *Celtic Review*, which started publication in the summer of the same year: it was to be financed by Walter Blaikie, and edited by Ella Carmichael, with the Professor of Celtic at Edinburgh University, Donald MacKinnon, acting as consulting editor. Fr. Allan McDonald was pressed to contribute some folklore, preferably oral tradition about St. Columba, to the first issue. He did not do so; in fact the first articles of this kind that he published were sent to *Guth na Bliadhna*, a Catholic Highland Gaelic and English quarterly which was founded and edited by Ruairi Erskine of Marr at about the same time that the *Celtic Review* was founded.

The project of publishing a book devoted to waulking songs was dropped; later, Kenneth MacLeod and Frances Tolmie achieved reputation in the respective spheres of the romantic and the objective presentation of Hebridean folksong. Fr. Allan McDonald laid aside the work he had begun in translating waulking songs from his own and Donald MacCormick's collections in anticipation of the projected Gaelic Texts Society. 'How I regret I can't take down the airs' he had written in his diary on 4 May 1898 after attending a waulking on Eriskay. Not until the visits of Evelyn Benedict and Amy Murray who came separately to Eriskay in the summer of 1905, the last of Fr. Allan McDonald's life, did anyone come who would try to help him by making objective transcriptions of the airs of the many songs of which he had collected the words. Amy Murray, who was by far the better folk-musician of the two, says she took down over a hundred airs on Eriskay;[1] only forty of her transcriptions survive, twenty-six in print, and fourteen in one of Fr. Allan McDonald's notebooks. In the case of Mrs. Kennedy-Fraser, who visited Eriskay the same summer, it was a matter of Fr. Allan McDonald's helping her rather than of her helping him:[2] had he lived, he and Amy Murray might well have developed a collaboration that would have much surpassed in interest that of Mrs. Kennedy-Fraser and Kenneth MacLeod.

It seemed to us well worth-while completing the work which Donald MacCormick began in 1893 and which Fr. Allan McDonald started to prepare for publication ten years later, for by the time that Donald MacCormick's manuscript was recovered, the recordings my wife and I had already made in South Uist, Benbecula, Barra, and Eriskay included versions of thirty-four of the thirty-seven waulking songs in the MacCormick collection. Three waulking songs from Fr. Allan McDonald's collection, which he had himself translated, were added to make the number up to a

[1] *Fr. Allan's Island*, p. 86.
[2] 'A Life of Song', pp. 107–18; *Scots Magazine*, January 1958, p. 307.

round forty: the airs of these too had already been recorded. Many of the songs in MacCormick's collection are still quite well known in South Uist, Benbecula, and Barra, but MacCormick's versions of the words are very good ones and were written down two generations ago, when such things were more in conscious memory than they are today. The translation was completed in Fr. Allan McDonald's style, notes were added, and an extensive glossarial index was made to illustrate the language of the songs, and, as is described in the Foreword, the transcription of the airs from the recordings was undertaken by Mr. Francis Collinson. With the publication of the present volume, the project suggested in 1902 by the late Walter Blaikie of a book devoted to the waulking song is at last realized.

II

THE MacCORMICK
COLLECTION OF
WAULKING SONGS

INDEX OF FIRST LINES

INDEX OF FIRST LINES

TEXT WITH
TRANSLATIONS

DONALD MacCORMICK'S
TEXT AND NOTES

I

Ailein Duinn, o hó hì, shiùbhlainn leat

Ailein Duinn, o hó hì, shiùbhlainn leat,
Hi ri ri, ri u ó, hi o hùg hòireann ó,
Ailein Duinn, o hó hì, shiùbhlainn leat.

'S bochd an nochd na bheil air m'aire,
Miad na sìne, fuachd na gaillinn
Ailein Duinn, *etc.*

Miad na sìne, fuachd na gaillinn
Dh'fhuadaicheadh na fir o'n charraig,
Ailein Duinn, *etc.*

Dh'fhuadaicheadh na fir o'n charraig,
Chuireadh iad a' bhòid dha'n aindeoin
Ailein Duinn, *etc.*

Far an trom an laigh a' ghailleann,   5
Cha b'e siod leam ar dìol caladh,
Ach Caolas Diadhair anns na Hearadh,
Far am bi na féidh air bhearradh,
Dóbhran donn is laogh breac ballach.

[*Atharraich*]

Gura mise th'air mo léireadh   10
Cha n-e bàs a' chruidh 'sa Chéitein,
No tainead mo bhuaile spréidhe,
Ach a fhlichead 's tha do léine,
'S tu bhith 'm bàrr nan tonn ag éirigh
Mucan mara bhith 'gad reubadh,   15
Bhith 'gad ghearradh as a chéile;

44

TRANSLATION

I

Brown-haired Allan, I'd go with thee

(*For tune, see pp. 241–4*)

Brown-haired Allan, o hó hì, I'd go with thee
Hi ri ri, *etc.*
Ailean Donn, o hó hì, I'd go with thee.

Tonight sad thoughts my mind are filling,
The strength of the storm, the cold of th' tempest

The strength of th' storm, the cold of th' tempest
That drove the men from the shore's shelter,

That drove the men from the shore's shelter,
Sent them on a voyage unwilling

Where the gale blows so heavy;   5
'Twas not, I think, your choice of harbour,
Rather Diadhair Sound in Harris,
Where the deer are on the hilltops,
Otter brown and fawn all spotted.

[*Change*]

Truly I am sore tormented,   10
Not by death of stock in springtime,
Nor by th' fewness of my cattle,
But by thy clothing's dampness,
And that thou art on wavetop floating
While sea monsters rend thy body,   15
And are tearing thee asunder;

45

Ailein Duinn, a laoigh mo chéilleadh,
Gura h-òg a thug mi spéis dhut,
Nuair a bha thu 'n sgoil na Beurla
Nuair a bha sinn ann le chéile;　　　　　　　20
[*Atharraich*]
　　Gum pàigheadh Dia siod ri t'anam
　　Mhiad 's a fhuair mi d' chuid gun cheannach,
　　Pìosan caola geal' an anart,
　　Nèapagain do 'n t-sìoda bhallach,
　　Thug thu fhéin, a ghaoil, a Manainn.　　　25
　　Ailein Duinn, a mhiann nan leannan,
　　Chuala mi gun deach thu fairis
　　Air a' bhàta làidir dharaich;
　　Ma 's fhìor siod, cha bhi mi fallain,
　　Gu là bràch cha dian mi bainis.　　　　　30
　　M'iarrtas air Rìgh na Cathrach
　　Gun mo chur an ùir no 'n gaineamh,
　　An talamh toll no 'n àite falaich,
　　'N seòmbar cùil no 'n àite daingeann,
　　Ach 'sa bhall am bheil thu, Ailein!　　　35
[*Atharraich*]
　　'S truagh, a Rìgh! nach mi bha 'n làimh riut,
　　Ge bè bàgh no sgeir an tràigh thu,
　　Ge bè tiùrr am fàg an làn thu,
　　'S cùl do chinn air bhac mo làimhe,
　　Do chùl dualach, cuachach, fàinneach.　　40
　　Dh'òlainn deoch, ge b'oil le càch e,
　　Cha b'ann do bhùrn no do shàile,
　　No do dh'fhìon dearg na Spàinte,
　　Ach fuil do chuim 's tu 'n déidh do bhàthadh;
　　Gura buidhe nochd dha d' mhàthair,　　　45
　　Bho nach 'eil thu beò 's tu bàite.

　　Ailein Duinn, o hó hì, shiùbhlainn leat,
　　Hi ri ri, ri u ó, hi o hùg hòireann ó,
　　Ailein Duinn, o hó hì, shiùbhlainn leat.

Tha e ri ràdh, an am dol a thiolagadh a' bhoireannaich seo, gura h-ann thairis air Caolas Diadair a bha i ri h-adhlacadh. Gun dàinig muir-bàite air an sgiobadh, air chor 's gum b' éiginn daibh a' chiste-laighe a chur a mach air a' mhuir. Gun d'fhalbh i calg-dhìreach an aghaidh an

Ailean Donn, king of my senses
Young I was when first I lov'd thee,
When you were getting English schooling
When we were in school together; 20

[*Change*]

May God repay thy soul, I'm praying
What of thy own store thou gav'st me,
Silver shining, wrapped in linen,
Speckled tablecloths, all silken,
Which you brought from Manann's Island. 25
Ailean Donn, my chosen sweetheart,
I did hear that you went over
On the vessel, strong and oaken;
If 'tis true, I'll not recover,
Till Doomsday I'll have no wedding. 30
I pray unto the King of Heaven
In earth or sand I'll not be buried,
Nor in quagmire or place of hiding
Nor in back-room, nor in stronghold,
But the spot where thou art, Ailean! 35

[*Change*]

Alas, O God, I was not beside thee
Whatever bay or rock thou'lt come on
Whatever tide-mark the flood will leave thee
Thy head in my hand-palm cradled
With curling, flowing hair in ringlets 40
I'd drink a drink, though all abhor it
Not of the sea, nor of fresh water,
Nor of the red Spanish claret
But thy heart's blood, after thy drowning;
Thanks tonight unto thy mother 45
Since thou art drowned and liv'st no longer.

It is told that when this woman was going to be buried, she was to be
buried on the far side of Diadair Sound; that a tempest came upon the
crew, so that they had to put the coffin overboard; that the coffin went
right against the tide and the wind, and that it sank at the very spot

t-sruth agus na gaoithe. Gun deach i fodha 'san dearbh-bhad 'na bhàthadh a leannan 's gun dàinig fiath agus sìth air a' mhuir 's gun shàbhail na daoine a bh'ann am mór-chunnart am beatha a chall.

II

'S mise bhean bhochd, chianail, thùrsach

Hì il ìnn, ò hò,
Hù il ò, ro bha hò,
Hì li rinn e hò,
Ho ro hù il ò ho hì.

'S mise bhean bhochd, chianail, thùrsach,
Cha chadal dhomh 's cha n-e 'n dùsgadh,
Hì il ìnn, *etc.*

Cha chadal dhomh, 's cha n-e 'n dùsgadh
Chunnaic mi do choill' 'ga rùsgadh
Hì il ìnn, *etc.*

Marcraich' 'n eich dhuibh air thùs innt'   50
Marcraich' na fàlaire crùidhich,
Nan strian sleamhain 's nan each sunndach.

Atharraich

Mhic Iain Mhùideartaich na féile,
Chunnaic mi latha bha feum ort,
Latha Cnoc nan Dos bha gleus ort,   55
Latha Chill' Saoide bu mhór t'fheum ann
Toirt an iarainn fhuair a féithean,
Fuil 'ga dòrtadh 's feòil 'ga reubadh,
Fir gun cheangal air an ceudfath,
'S mnathan a' fàgail an céilleadh.   60

Atharraich

Gura h-iad mo rùn mo bhràithrean
Raghnall 's Niall, Lachlann 's Teàrlach,
Alasdair na gruaige fàinnich,

48

where her sweetheart had been drowned, whereupon peace and calm came upon the sea, and the men, who were in great danger of losing their lives, were saved.

II

I am a poor, sad, sorrowful woman

(*For tune, see p. 245*)

I am a poor, sad, sorrowful woman
Sleep's not mine nor yet a-waking,

Sleep's not mine nor yet a-waking,
I have seen thy wood stripped naked

The black steed's rider foremost rode her   50
The well shod palfrey's rider came then
With slippery reins and horses playful.

Change

Son of Moydart's John free-spending
I saw the day that you were needed,
At Cnoc nan Dos you proved your manhood,   55
At Kilsythe great was your value
With cold iron cutting sinews
While blood was spilt and flesh was rended
Men their reason burst the bonds of
Wives grow witless mid the shambles.   60

Change

Dearly do I love my brothers
Ranald, Neil, Lachlan, Charlie,
Alasdair of curling tresses,

Cha b'i 'n Aoine rinn ur n-àireamh,
Ach a' bhean a chaill a nàire.   65

Atharraich

'S truagh, a Rìgh! nach fhaicinn-s' ise,
A taobh leòinte 's a glùn briste,
'S gun aon léigh fo'n ghréin ach mise!
Chuirinn creuchd am beul gach niosgaid,
Air mo làimh gun dearbhainn misneach!   70
Bhristinn cnàimh 's gun tàirninn silteach,
Chuirinn ùir air bruaich do lice,
Gus an càirinn thu 'san islig,
'S gus an dùininn thu 'sa chiste.

Atharraich

'S mise bhean bhochd, dhubhach, dheurach,   75
'S cha n-ann mu lughad mo spréidhe,—
Mu Iain Mùideartach na féile
Cha deach an làmh dheas gu feum dhut.

Atharraich

'S muladach, muladach, thà mi
Dìreadh na beinne 's 'ga teàrnadh,   80
Thuit mo chridhe, 's fad' o'n là sin,
Cha tog fiodhall e, no clàrsach,
No pìob mhór nam feadan àrda.

Tha fonn an òrain mhaisich seo ri ghabhail no ri chantuinn as déidh
a h-uile dà shreath, agus ri chantuinn dùbailte, air neo tionndadh air,
gach uair a thigear gu atharrachadh fuaim.

III

Nighean ud thall, bheil thu 't'fhaireachadh?

Hi ri a bhò
Ho rò ghealladh i,
Ho ì o hó.

Nighean ud thall, Hi ri *etc.*   bheil thu 't'fhaireachadh? Hi ri *etc.*
Nach seall thu mach   bheil a' ghealach ann?   85

Aoine's numbering[1] you were safe from
But the shameless quean betrayed you.   65

Change

Alas, o God! I cannot see her,
Her body wounded, her knee shattered,
Myself the only leech to heal her!
Each sore's mouth a gash I'll pierce in,
By my hand, I swear I'll flinch not,   70
I'd break her bones and make her blood flow,
I'd heap the earth upon your gravestone,
Till the death-planks hold you stiffened,
Till I close you in your coffin.

Change

I am a poor, sad, tearful woman   75
Not because few are my cattle
But for Moidart's John free spending
Right hand was ineffective for you

Change

I am sorrow, sorrow laden,
Climbing mountain or descending,   80
Long ago my heart has fallen
Harp cannot raise it, nor fiddle,
Nor the tall-droned great bagpipe.

The refrain of this fine song is to be sung or said after every two lines, and to be sung twice, or returned to, every time one comes to a change of rhyme.

III

Woman would you, if you're waking yet

(*For tune, see pp. 246–50*)

Woman would you   if you're waking yet,
Look if the moon   shows her face to us?   85

---

[1] i.e. drowning was not your fate. See note.

No bheil a’ ghaoth   ’n iar gun charachadh?
’M faod am bàta   bàn dol thairis (a)?
H-aghaidh air cuan,   a cùl ri fearann (a)
Air muir dubhghorm,   ’s air chuan cambhileach.

Atharraich

Raghnaill, a rùin,   cum do ghealladh rium   90
Cum an dùchas   bh’aig do sheanaire
Dian do thaigh mór   an ceann an rathaide
Far an dian na   h-uaislean tathaich (a).

Atharraich

Taghlaidh Mac Leòid,   ’s Mac ’ic Alasdair,
’S taghlaidh m’eudail   Mac ’ic Ailein ann,   95

Atharraich

Ceannard air sluagh   an uair fearachais,
Cha b’e ’m buideal   beag bu mhath leat, (a)
Cha b’iad na stòip,   ach na galain (a)
Togsaidean fìon’   air an ceannaibh riut,
Mar dh’òladh càch,   phàigheadh Ailein (a).   100

Atharraich

A bhean a chuir   orm an ailis, (a)
Gun robh mi ri   call nan leanabh, (a)
Mo chìochan làn   ’s mo ghlùn falamh—(a)
Cha n-iarr mise   pian ad anam-sa
Ach a bhith agad   fios mo ghalair-sa   105
Chuir mi cóigear   anns an talamh dhiu,
Ùna ’s Sìne,   Mór is Anna,
Ailein a’chùil   rinn mo sgaradh dhiu
Chuir e mo cheum   ann an aineamhachd
Chuir e mo chuailein   donn an tainead (a).   110

Atharraich

’S fada ’s is cian   chì mi sealladh uam,
Chì mi Rùm is   Eige ’s Canaidh uam,
Ge tà, cha n-fhaic   mi na Hearadh uam
Far an robh mi   òg ’nam leanabh (a)
Mùirneach meadhrach,   gu ciùin arralach.   115

Tha gach rann de’n òran seo ri ghabhail no ri chantuinn dà uair no dùbailte, a h-aon ’ga sheinn, mar anns gach òran, ’s càch a’ seinn an fhuinn.

Or if west wind   blows unchangingly,
If the boat can   cross the waves tonight,
Prow to ocean,   stern to safe land here,
On sea dark blue   where surge lips gape away.

Change

Your word you gave me,   Ronald, stand to it,   90
Keep the custom   grandsire taught to you,
Build your house where   high road draws to end,
Where the nobles   oft may gather in.

Change

Of these McLeod   and Mac ic Alister,
And whom I love   the great McAllan's son.   95

Change

Chieftain of hosts   in hour of manliness,
No (mean) bottle   would his asking be,
Stoups and gallons   all too paltry were;
Hogsheads of wine   endlong and taps a-flow,
Whate'er they drank   the score was Allan's sure.   100

Change

Ill wife who cast   it up in scorn to me
That I lost the   children born to me—
I wish her soul   no other torment than
That she have   my ill a knowledge of,
Her breast be full,   her knee hold no fosterling: 105
Five laid I down   with earth to cover them,
Anna and Mór,   Jean and Winifred
Long haired Allan   rent me most of all,
My step e'er since   on earth has trodden slow
My thick brown hair   is thin and glossless now.   110

Change

Far and wide the   sea I'm scanning now,
Rum I see and   Eigg and Canna too,
I see not the   hills of Harris land
Where in childhood's   days I ran about
Gladly, gaily,   cares then cankered not.   115

Every verse of this song should be sung or recited twice, or double,
one person singing it, as in every song, and the rest singing the refrain.

Nach fhreagair thu, Chairistiana?

    É hó hì ura bhì,
    Ho ro ho ì, ó ho ro ho,
    É hó hì ura bhì.

Nach fhreagair thu, Chairistiana?
        É hó, *etc.*

Nam freagradh, gun cluinninn fhìn thu,
        É hó, *etc.*

Bha mi bliadhna 'n cùirt an rìgh leat,
'S ged chanainn e, bha mi a trì ann—
Fuaigheal anairt, 'g gearradh shìoda,   120
'S a' cur gràinne air léintean rìomhach.

Atharraich

    Thug mi turus do Ghleann Comhann,
    'S bha 'm muir àrd 's an caolas domhain
    Gheàrr mi leum 's cha d'rinn mi thomhas,
    Gun leum na h-uiseagan romham,   125
    'S thuirt iad rium nach dianainn gnothach,
    Nach fhaighinn mo mhuime romham,
    Ceann na céille, beul na comhairl',
    Sgrìobhadh 's a leughadh an leobhar;
    Bhiodh na h-uaislean ort a' tadhal   130
    Cha b'ann gu mealladh an gnothaich.

Atharraich

    'S iomadh long is bàrc is biaoirlinn
    Is luingeas a tha 'm bial Chaol Ìle
    Tighinn a dh'iarraidh Cairistiana;
    Cha n-ann gu pùsadh mhic rìgh leat,   135
    Gus do chur 'san talamh ìseal,
    Fo leaca troma na dìleann.

Atharraich

    Fhleasgaich òig na gruaige duibhe,

54

IV

Why not answer, Cairistiana?

(*For tune, see pp. 251–4*)

Why not answer, Cairistiana?

If you did 'tis I would hear you;

Spent we both a year in king's court,
Truth to tell we spent full three there,
Sewing linen, silk a-scruding,   120
Snow white sheets embroidering neatly.

Change

Journeyed I the way Glencoe lies,
Deep the kyle while tide it flowed high,
For I leapt the span I know not,
Larks sprang startled up before me,   125
Luckless errand mine they told me,
Weema I'd not find before me,
Head of wisdom, lips to solace,
You could write and read the volume;
Nobles often came a-calling,   130
But they got not what they sought for.

Change

Many a ship and bark and galley,
Islay's Kyle with shipping teemeth,
Come to fetch thee, Cairistiana;
But 'tis not to wed a king's son,   135
To put you in the earth beneath us,
Heavy leaking flags to keep thee.

Change

Gentle youth whose hair is blackest,

55

'S ann an nochd as mór do mhulad;
Do leannan a staigh fo dhubhar   140
An ciste nam bòrd air a cumadh,
An déidh na saoir a bhith 'ga dubhadh.

Tha fonn an òrain ghrinn seo ri chantuinn leis an luchd freagraidh an
déidh a h-uile sreith, no ceathramh, no rann, ma's e 's freagarraich, a'
bhean-òrain a' cantuinn nan rann, càch 'ga freagairt leis an fhonn.

V

Cha n-eil mi gun nì air m'aire

Hó ró, na hu linn ó ro,
Cha n-eil mi gun nì air m'aire,
Och ó rinn ó, falbh orra seinn.

Cha n-eil mi gun nì air m'aire,
Hó ró, na hu linn ó ro
Ge b'e ris an dian mi ghearain,
Och ó rinn ó, falbh orra seinn.

Ge b'e ris an dian mi ghearain,
Hó ró, *etc.*
'S e m'eudail mhór Mac 'ic Ailein,   145
Och ó rinn, *etc.*

'S e m'eudail mhór Mac 'ic Ailein,
Cha n-e Mac Leòid 's mi 'na fhearann;
Dhomhsa b'aithne beus do thalla
'San fheasgar chiùin fhiathail earraich—
Muc 'ga ròsladh, bó 'ga feannadh,
Lòmhnaichean òir air coin sheanga,   150
Fiamh an duin' òig air an t-seannduin',
Fiamh na maighdin air a' chaillich,
Gruagaichean 'gan toirt do dh'fhearaibh,
Fir òga danns' air am bainis.

[*Atharraich*]
Mhoire! 's e m'eudail 's mo luaidh thu,   155
Mhic an fhir bho thùr na stuaidhe,
Dhomhsa b'aithne 'm beus bu dual dut—

56

Great this night thy weight of sadness,
She you love within in darkness,   140
In chest of boards the wright has fashioned,
E'en now they coated it with blackness.

The refrain of this fine song is to be sung by the persons singing in
chorus, after every line or verse, if it is most suitable, the soloist singing
the verses, and the rest answering her with the refrain.

V

I'm not free from thoughts that harass

(*For tune, see p. 255*)

I'm not free from thoughts that harass,

Yet to none I'll bare my anguish,

Yet to none I'll bare my anguish,

My one darling is Clanranald,   145

My one darling is Clanranald
Not McLeod I live his land in—
I know well thy great hall's fastness
On the spring eve full of calmness
Swine a-roasting, kine a-slaughtering,
Golden leashes on the staghounds,   150
Hue of youth on brow of grandson,
Maiden blush on cheek of grandam,
Virgins o'er to lovers handed,
Marriage feasts keep young a-dancing.
[*Change*]
Thou my darling art my heart's one,   155
Son of him from gabled castle,
Well I know the style you're heir to—

57

Taigh mór farsuinn, ùrlar sguabte,
Teine mór air bheagan luatha,
Ruitheadh ùbhla sìos is suas ann,   160
Deagh-bhean-taighe bhith 'na uachdar,
Seòmbraichean glaiste 'n taobh shuas di,
Seòmbraichean am biodh daoin'-uaisle
'G òl a cupannan 's a cuachan,
Nìonagan glana ri fuaigheal,   165
Cur an t-sìoda dhuinn 'na dhualaibh.

[*Atharraich*]

'N cuala sibh ormsa cor Dhòmhnaill?
Mo chur anns a' cheap 'nam ònar
Ceangal nan taod air mo dhòrnaibh;
Dhia, gu dé ur n-adhbhar dhòmhsa?   170
'S nach do ghoid mi molt a mòintich,
Cha mhó ghoid mi gobhar chròcach,
'S cha do chuir mi caor' air ròpa,
'S cha do ghoid mi sguab na dòrlach.

[*Atharraich*]

Cha do rinn mi siod, no urad;   175
B'fheàrr leam a bhith falbh le m' ghunna,
'G ialadh air mo ghlùin 's air m'uilinn,
Fiadhach air fiadh ruadh a' mhunaidh,
'N eala bhàn as bòidhche guileag,
'S an ròin mhaoil o thaobh na tuinne.   180
Falbhaidh mi 's cha dian mi fuireach,
Nàile! creicidh mi mo ghunna!
Nì mi dha'n stoc clàran cumain,
Nì mi dha'n ghleus iarann-muilinn,
'S nì mi car mu shiar a Muile.   185

[*Atharraich*]

Tha Alasdair air a' mhórthir,
Mac an fhir a chumadh còir ruinn,
Thug e dusan crùn a dh'òr dhomh,
Thug e siod, is buaile bhò dhomh,
Chuir e long fo chrainn 's fo sheòl dhomh.   190

[*Atharraich*]

Nam bithinn a' falbh na mara

58

Large wide mansions, floor swept barely,
Mighty fire, of ashes sparing,
Apple rolls from end to end of,   160
Right good wife in further chamber,
And beyond more rooms a-fastened,
Rooms where duine wassals gather,
Drinking cups and bowls a-quaffing,
Girls a-hemming fair and happy,   165
Brown silk thread all deftly platting.

[*Change*]

Heard ye how I fared from Donald?
In the stocks he thrust me lonely,
Bound my wrists with cutting cording;
O my God he had no cause for't,   170
Wether none from moorland stole I,
Nor yet stole I goat long hornèd,
Nor a sheep bound I with cording,
Nor a sheaf nor wisp from cornfield.

[*Change*]

None did I nor aught so wrong am,   175
Rather roam with gun the borders,
Bend my knee and elbow stalking,
Hunt the red deer of the mountain,
Swan so fair the sweetest songster,
Thick-head seal from round the coast line.   180
I will go—stay here no longer,
I will sell my gun to some one,
Stock I'll rend to staves for cogie,
Lock a mill-pin I will form it,
West of Mull I'll take a voyage.   185

[*Change*]

Alastair is on the mainland,
He whose sire true justice showed me,
Once he gave me twelve crowns golden
And with that a cattle fold full
Ship with masts and sails well ordered.   190

[*Change*]

If I were o'er ocean roving

59

Air a' bhiaoirlinn chaoil-duibh dharaich,
Agam a bhiodh car 'ga mealladh,
Chuirinn a siùil air a h-aineoil,
'S chuirinn sàbhailt i gu cala,   195
Gu acarsaid nan seòl geala.

Tha gach rann de'n òran seo ri ghabhail no ri chantuinn dà uair le
fhonn, 's tha 'm fonn ri ghabhail dùbailte, gach uair a tha 'n fhuaim ag
atharrachadh. Dh'fhiach mi ri ligeil fhaicinn 'san toiseach cia mar a tha
e ri sheinn.

VI

Tha 'n latha 'n diu gu fliuch fuaraidh

Ó, hi ù o, ì ò
Tha 'n latha 'n diu, ì ò
Ó, hi ù o, ì ò
Gu fliuch fuaraidh, ì ò,
Ó, *etc.*
Tha sneachd le, ì ò,
Ó, *etc.*
Gaoith a tuath ann, ì ò,
Ó, *etc.*

Mo chasan, na,	gabhail fuachda;
Tha mi togairt	do'n bhail' uachdrach, 200
Gu taigh mór, na,	Nìll mhic Ruairidh,
Taigh mór farsuinn	am biodh na h-uaislean.

[*Atharraich*]

'S mise chunnaic	'n diu an t-iaonadh
Air nighean duinn	[a' chuailein chraobhaich;]
Chaidh i do'n tràigh	bhuain a' mhaoraich, 205
Sheas i air lic	's rinn i sraonadh,
Chaidh i 'n riochd	na béiste maoile,
Thug i mach ri	snàmh nan caolas,
Sgoilteadh i 'n cuan	gacha taobh dhi;
Cha chreidear mi,	's mi 'nam aonar, 210

60

In the dark slim barge of oak tree,
And could steer her at my own will,
Course I'd set her now she knows not,
And I'd put her into port in   195
Th' anchorage with white sails gleaming.

Every verse of this song should be sung or recited twice, with its
refrain, and the refrain should be sung twice, every time the rhyme is
changed. I tried to show at the beginning how it is sung.

VI

The day today is wet and chilling

(*For tune, see pp. 256–8*)

The day today   is wet and chilling;

With the north wind   it is snowing,

In my feet   the cold I'm feeling;
I am taking to   the upper township,   200
To the big house   of Niall mac Ruairi,
Capacious dwelling   where nobles gather.

[*Change*]
'Tis I today   who saw the exploit
A brown haired girl   [of flowing tresses]
She went to the shore   to gather shellfish   205
She sat on a flagstone   and made a movement,
She changed her form   into an otter,
She made away   to swim the narrows,
She clave the sea   on each side of her;
I'm not believed   without another   210

61

| Gus am faigh mi | tuilleadh dhaoine, |
| Fear no dithis | gacha taobh dhiom. |

[*Atharraich*]

Nam bithinn-se	làidir eòlach,
Neart Chù Chulainn	a bhith am dhòrnaibh,
Chuirinn am blàr	le Cloinn Dòmhnaill,
Le sìol Ailein	nan long leòmhainn.

215

[*Atharraich*]

Nam bithinn-se	làidir fearail,
Neart Chù Chulainn	a bhith am bhallaibh,
B'aithne dhomh fhìn	chùirt a leanainn,
Cha b'i cùirt Mhic	'Ille Chaluim,
Cùirt a' Ghruamaich	cùirt a' Ghallaich,
Cùirt an Dòmhnaill	Ghuirm nach maireann.

220

Tha gach rann do'n òran sgiobalta seo ri 'n seinn dà uair, mar iomadh
de na h-òrain luadhaidh, am fonn leis gach turus 's a' crìochnachadh le
ì ò.

VII

Di-Sathuirne ghabh mi mulad

Hi ri ù o, hi ri ù o,
Di-Sathuirne ghabh mi mulad
Hì rì a bhó ho libh ó,
Ì o challa, hi ri u bhi ù o hù o.

Di-Sathuirne ghabh mi mulad
Hi ri ù o, hi ri ù o,
Di-Dòmhnaich a ghabh mi uil' e
Hì rì a bhó *etc.*

Di-Dòmhnaich a ghabh mi uil' e
Hi ri ù o, hi ri ù o,
'S ann Di-Luain a rinn mi 'n tuiream;
Hì rì a bhó *etc.*

225

Chunnaic mi bhith gabhail umad,
Gabhail mu'n bheul a bha lurach,

| Until I find | further people, |
| A man or two | on each side of me. |

[*Change*]

Would that I were	strong and knowing
Cu Chulainn's strength	in my handfists
I would side	with brave Clan Donald,	215
Ship and lion	rule Clanranald.

[*Change*]

Would that I were	strong and manly,
Cu Chulainn's strength	in all my members,
I know well	the court I'd stand by,
Not the court of	Gille Chaluim,	220
But the Gruamach's	court and Gallach's
Donald Gorm's	whose course is ended.

Every verse of this neat song is to be sung twice, as with many of the waulking songs, the refrain every time, and ending with ì ò.

VII

Saturday I felt the gloom come

(*For tune, see pp. 259–62*)

Saturday I felt the gloom come

Sunday it came on in fulness,

Sunday it came on in fulness,

Monday dirge I was a-crooning,   225

Busy hands I saw around you,
Closing lips I loved to look on,

63

Gabhail mu'n t-sùil a bha cuimir,
Togail nan seòl ris a' churach,
Seòladh gu tìr àrd a' mhurain,   230
Far nach cluinntear fuaim na tuinne,
Ach fuaim an t-sìobain ris a' mhuran,
Fuaim a' challtainn ris a' chuileann,
Fuaim na craoibhe ris an duilleig,
Fuaim na sìne ris an uinneig.   235

[*Atharraich*]

Ochóin, a chiall, mo thriall dhachaigh
Gu baile bòidheach a' chlachain,
Far an d'fhuair mi gu h-òg m'altrum,
Cha b'ann air sàile nam partan,
Air fìon, air beòir, 's air leann daithte,   240
Air bainne-cìoch nam ban basgheal.

[*Atharraich*]

Chuir Seumas duine g'am ghlacadh
Ma chuir, cha ligeadh e leas siod,
Cha b'i mèirle fhuaradh agam,
Cha d'fhuair iad feòil aig mo chasan,   245
Ma fhuair, cha b'fheòil chruidh no chapull,
B'ionnraic e na fhuaradh agam—
Gruagach dhonn an lùib mo bhreacain,
Iseabail òg an fhuilt chleachdaich,
'S gile a bian na cliabh na h-eala,   250
'S deirge a gruaidh na cuach air chrannaibh,
'S guirme a sùil na driùchd na mainneadh,
'S mìlse a pòg na òl na meala.

[*Atharraich*]

Ach nam faighinn siod air m'fhacal
Dà fhear dhiag do dh'fhearaibh tapaidh,
Ceathrar air fhichead is caiftinn,   255
Le'n cuid chlaidhmhnean geura sgaiteach,
Cha n-iarrainn bàta dha'n aiseag—
Gur math gum fóghnadh mo chasan—
Bhithinn an Dun-Tuilm mun caidlinn,   260
Dh'innsinn sgeul daibh nach 'eil aca,
Dh'fhàgainn Seumas Bàn gun astar,

64

Closing eye that shone in beauty,
Hoisting canvas to the currach,
Sailing whither bent-grass groweth,   230
Where unheard is roar of ocean
Or the sand-drift whistling onward,
Of hazel swishing to the holly,
Trees a-moaning to the foliage,
Tempest roaring at the doorway.   235

[*Change*]

Alas! O dear! my turning homeward
To the Clachan's pretty homestead,
Where they reared me in my young days
Not on partan salt sea water,
Ale and beer, red wine my draught was,   240
Milk from breast of matrons snow-palmed.

[*Change*]

James sent men to take me captive,
He need not have done that action,
What they found it was not rapine,
Flesh they found not by my hearthstone,   245
Yet they did—not horse or mart flesh,
What I had I had it faultless—·
Brown haired maid wrapped in my tartan,
Locks of gold in graceful platting,
Whiter her skin than the swan's breast,   250
Redder her cheek than rowan bunches,
Bluer her eyes than morning's dew drops,
Sweeter her kiss than draught of honey.

[*Change*]

Would I had it for the asking,
Twelve young fellows stout and active,   255
Twenty-four and one as Captain
Served with sword keen edged for hacking,
I would ask no boat for transport
Well our feet would serve and faster
Duntuilm I'd reach e'er sleep could,   260
Tale I'd tell them that they lack now,·
Hamish Ban would ne'er stir after,

Dh'fhàgainn a phiuthar gun bhràthair,
'S dh'fhàgainn a mhàthair gun mhac aic',
Dh'fhàgainn a mhuime gun dalta,   265
'S a bhean òg gun chéile leapadh.

[*Atharraich*]

Tha 'n latha 'n diu gu fliuch frasach
Dh'fhalbh mo ghràdh air bàta 'n aisig
Cha n-ann gus do chàirdean fhaicinn
No gu sgoil thoirt dhaibh an asgaidh—   270
Gus do chur 'san ùir am pasgadh,
An ciste chaoil 's na saoir 'ga ghlasadh,
An léine chaoil an anart ascaoin.

Dh'fhiach mi ann an toiseach an òrain seo mar bu chòir a leantuinn
gu chrìch; tha e glé mhaiseach, 's air leith math, agus sunndach, air son
luadhaidh. Bheireadh còmhlan nighean òga ann am dhùthaich air clò,
dha thainead, leis an òran ud, 's le trì no ceithir do na h-òrain a tha
roimhe, gun seasadh e air oir.

VIII

Rinn mi mocheirigh gu éirigh

Hó hó, ho la ill ó,
Ho ì ó ho nàilibh i,
Hó hó, ho la ill ó.

Rinn mi mocheirigh gu éirigh,
    Hó hó, etc.

Cha b'ann a shobhadh na spréidhe,   275
No ghleidheadh an fhochainn Chéitein,
Ach chumail coinneamh ri m'fheudail—
Nighean mhic Ailein, na bi 'n eud rium,
Tha mi 'n troma-ghaol orra cheudghaol,
Tha mi sin, ma 's oil leat fhéin e;   280
Rachainn leat ro' chuan na h-Éireann,
Far am bi muir àrd ag éirigh,
Loingeas a' losgadh ri chéile,

Sister his I'd leave no brother,
Son I would not leave to mother,
'Weema' I'd leave her none to foster,   265
Bride of bed mate I would rob her.

[*Change*]

Wet the day with rain a splashing,
Gone my love is by the transport,
Not to see her friends in passing,
Not to teach them unpaid lesson,   270
But to lay there neath the flagstone,
In the spare chest wright has fastened
In the unkind shrouding wrapt up.

I showed at the beginning of this song how it should be sung through
to its end; it is very attractive, and especially good, and suitable for a
waulking. A company of young women in my district would, with this
song and three or four of the songs before it, make any cloth, however
thin, so that it would stand on its edge.

VIII

Haste made I to rise all early

(*For tune, see pp. 263–7*)

Haste made I to rise all early,

Not indeed for cattle herding,   275
Nor to keep the braird of Mayday,
But to tryst with him I favoured—
Clanranald's daughter be not envious,
For thy first love I'm a-phrenzied,
I am so howe'er ye mind it.   280
I'd cross with him the sea of Erin
Where the billows raise their heads up,
Fleets a-firing wild and vengeful,

Mucan mara móra séitill.

[*Atharraich*]

Rachainn leat ro' chùl-taigh dùinte,   285
Far am faighinn modh is mùirne,
Daoin' uaisle mu bhòrdaibh dùmhail,
Ruidhleadh mu seach air an ùrlar,
Le pìob mhór nam feadan dùmhail,
Le pìob bheag nam feadan siùbhlach.   290

[*Atharraich*]

Rachainn leat ro' chuidh' na spréidhe,
Far am bi laoigh òg' a' leumnaich
Mnathan a' caoi, crodh a' geumraich,
Gaoir nan creach 'gan toirt o chéile,
'S nach aithnich mi mo chuid fhéin diu.   295
Mhnathan, nach tog sibh fo m'éighe?
Togaidh mise, leagaibh péin e,
'S ann dhomh fhìn bu chòir a h-éigheach.

[*Atharraich*]

Ochan, 's och mar a tha mise,
An dùthaich a bhith gun cheann-cinnidh,   300
Freasdal làn an dùirn a ghiollan;
Nan éireadh gach ian le fhine,
Dh'éireadh na Dòmhnallaich linne.
Camshronaich o'n gharbh-bheinn bhioraich,
'S Leathainich nach leubh an giorag,   305
Chuireadh Sìol Leòid air an uilinn—
'S tìom dhuinn, a ghaoil, a bhith tilleadh.

[*Atharraich*]

Nam bithinn-se làidir fearail,
'S neart Chù Chulainn a bhith 'm bhallaibh,
B'aithne dhomh co chùirt a leanainn   310
Cha b'i cùirt Mhic 'Ille Chaluim
Cùirt a' Ghruamaich, cùirt a' Ghallaich,
Cùirt an Dòmhnaill Ghuirm nach maireann.

[*Atharraich*]

Nam bithinn-se làidir eòlach,
'S gum b'aithne dhomh mo bhogha sheòladh,   315

68

Mighty whales spouting spray up.

[*Change*]

I'd go with thee to fastened chamber,   285
Right attention would be paid me,
Duine wassals round your tables,
Reels around in endless mazes,
With the great reed pipe a-straining,
And the pipe of sweetest cadence.   290

[*Change*]

Cattle pen with thee I'd go thro',
Where young calves are even sporting,
Matrons wailing, kine a lowing,
For my tears the bonds that hold them,
'Mong them all my own I know not,   295
Matrons join me in th' hullo'ing
I will start you with the chorus,
Who but I should cry the same song?

[*Change*]

Och nan och but how I'm feeling
That the land should know no chieftain,   300
Trusting to a fist-full stripling;
Birds should flock each to its kindred,
Then Clan Donald would be with us,
Cam'rons from the hills well timbered
And MacLeans who read not trembling,   305
We'd fell MacLeod upon his elbow—
'Tis time, love, for us to be returning.

[*Change*]

Would that I were strong and manly,
Cu Chulainn's strength in all my members,
I well know the court I'd stand by,   310
Not the court of Gille Chaluim
But the Gruamach's court and Gallach's,
Donald Gorm's whose course is ended.

[*Change*]

Would that I were strong and knowing,
Knew to set the arrow winging,   315

Chuirinn am blàr le Cloinn Dòmhnaill,
Le Sìol Ailein nan long leòmhann.

[*Atharraich*]

Chuirinn fhìn mo gheall 's mo theannagheall
Dh'fhaodainn siod, ge bè mo cheann e,
Gun cuireadh sibh creach 'na deannruith,   320
Steach le leathad corrach gainntir,
O mhullach beinne gu bial fainge.

Tha fonn an òrain shnasail seo ri chantuinn dà uair an déidh a chéile
gach uair a tha 'n fhuaim ag atharrachadh, agus aon uair an déidh gach
ceathramh no rainn, mar a lig mi fhaicinn 'san toiseach.

IX

Dh'éirich mise moch Di-Dòmhnaich

Ì hoireann ò hi ri o ho,
Ù hoireann ò hi ri rì u,
Ì hoireann ò hi ri o ho.

Dh'éirich mise moch Di-Dòmhnaich,
Chaidh mi sgiobalta 'nam chòmhdach.
Ì hoireann ò *etc.*

Chaidh mi sgiobalta 'nam chòmhdach,
Ann am stocainnean 's am' bhrògan,   325
Ì hoireann ò *etc.*

Ann am stocainnean 's am' bhrògan,
Cha robh uisge mór no ceò ann,
Ì hoireann ò *etc.*

Grian gheal air aghaidh nam mórbheann;
Thug mi gu siubhal na mòintich,
Thànaig mo leannan am chòmhdhail,
'S shuidh sinn air taobh cnocain còmhla,   330
'S theann sinn ri mire 's ri gòraich'
Mar as minic a rinn ar seòrsa;

I would side with brave Clan Donald,
Ship and Lion rule Clanranald.

[*Change*]

    I would swear and swear it doubly,
    Though my head should be the forfeit,
    That you'd make the foray scurry   320
    Down the steeps thro' passes rugged
    From the hills to pen a running.

The refrain of this attractive song is to be sung twice over every
time the rhyme changes, and once after every verse or line, as I showed
at the beginning.

IX

I rose early Sunday morning

(*For tune, see p. 268*)

I rose early Sunday morning,
And all neatly donned my clothing.

And all neatly donned my clothing.
I fit on my hose and shoes too.   325

I fit on my hose and shoes too.
There was then no rain or fog on,

Sun on mountain faces shone white;
I set out to roam the moorland:
And my sweetheart came across me,
Then we rested on a knoweside,   330
Whiled an hour in playful sporting,
As the foolish young are wont to;

'S e thànaig as a sin dòibheirt,
Bhagair e mo léine shròiceadh,
Rinn e liadan beag' am chòta,   335
Chuir e stìom mo chinn 'na h-òrdan—
Chunnaic thu, Rìgh! nach b'i chòir i!

Atharraich

Fhir ud a shiùbhlas a' mhòinteach,
Fois orr 'o cheum, biomaid còmhla—
Thoir mo shoiridh-sa gu m'eòlas,   340
Bhuam do Sgorabreac an eòrna,
'S thoir fios gu m' phiuthair a Chnòideart,
'S innis dhi mar dh'éirich dhòmhsa,
Rinn mi 'n dìolanas ro'n phòsadh,
Laigh mi le glas-ghiollan gòrach,   345
Nach dug cìr no stìom no bròg dhomh,
Nach dug fàinne far a mheòir dhomh,
Cha dug, no 'm bréid, 's e bu chòir dha.

Atharraich

Ach nam bithinn-sa 's taigh-òsda
Dh'aithnghinn fear mhealladh na h-òinsich,   350
Làmh air a cìochan 's 'ga pògadh,
Paidirean is preasain bhòidheach,
'S muladach caileag 'na h-ònar
Am bothan beag an iomall mòintich,
Chleachd bhith 'n cuideachd nam fear òga.   355

Atharraich

Iain Mhic Chaluim 'ic Dhòmhnaill,
Cha digeadh tu nuair bu chòir dhut,
Tacan beag mun rinn mi 'n còrdadh,
Gun laighinn leat an déidh còrdaidh,
Dhianainn bainis is mór-phòsadh   360
An taigh mór an ùrlair chòmhnard,
Far am bi daoin' uaisle mu bhòrdaibh.

72

Thence arose a deed of sorrow,
To lay bare my bosom strove he
Into shreds he tore my clothing 335
My head ribbon he disordered
Thou, O God, didst see he wronged me.

Change

Thou who on the moorland wandrest,
Stay thy step so that I join thee—
Take my blessing to the homeland, 340
Sgorabreac where barley grows well,
Tell my sister, she in Knoydart,
Tell what evil has befallen—
Babe unborn ere groom betrothed me,
To a foolish lad ungrown yet, 345
Shoe nor ribbon nor a comb e'en,
Gave he me, nor ring bestowed he,
Nor the kertch which sure he owed me.

Change

Had I been to inns accustomed,
I'd have known gay deceivers, 350
Leading girls astray with kisses,
Tempting them with pretty presents;
Sad's the girl who lives in loneness
In a cot on mossland border
Whom the young men once all thronged to. 355

Change

John McCallum son of Donald
Wherefore stayed you when you ought not
Ere the contract first was ordered
Ever after I'd have sought you,
Feast and wedding we'd have holden 360
In the hall of level flooring,
Boards surrounded all with nobles.

X

'S fliuch an oidhche 'n nochd 's gur fuar i

Éileadh na ùrabh o ho,
'S fliuch an oidhche, o hù o ho,
Éileadh na ùrabh o ho,
'N nochd 's gur fuar i, o hù o ho,
Éileadh na ùrabh o ho,

Thug am bàta, o hù *etc.*
'S beag mo chùram
'S mo leannan air
Òganach deas
Làmh air an stiùir
Cha b'fhear cearraig
No fear làimhe deis'
Guma slàn do'n
Dh'fhàg e luchdmhor
Fulangach gu
'N saoil sibh péin (na)
Do m' leithid fhìn
Bhith 'm bothaig bhig
Fo dhìolanas
Gun òl cupa, o hù o ho,
Éileadh na hùrabh o ho,
Gun òl cuaiche, o hù o ho.

bàn an cuan oirr', o hù *etc.*
as a fuadach,   365
bhòrd a fuaraidh,
do dhuin' uasal,
nuair bu chruaidhe,
bheireadh uat i,
is fuachd air.   370
làimh a dh'fhuaigh i,
làidir luath i,
siubhal chuantan,
nach mór an truaighe,
do gheala-ghruagaich   375
an iomall tuatha,
mhic duin' uasail,

Tha roinn do'n fhonn aig an òran seo ri bhith air a chantuinn an déidh gach rainn no sreith leis an luchd-freagairt.

74

X

Wet the night is, full of coldness

(*For tune, see p. 269*)

Wet the night is, full of coldness,

The white boat sped	far out to ocean,
No fear that now	her course she'll go from 365
My lover sits	the windward board on
A handsome youth	of family noble,
Holding the helm	when weather worst is,
No left hand man	would take her over,
No right hand man,	when the cold comes. 370
Health to the hand	that bound her moulding
He left her loaded	strong, swift to go in,
Enduring well	to leap o'er ocean.
Think ye not	my plight is woeful,
That a girl	like me all doleful 375
In a cot	in glen all lonely
Be in shame	from sin of noble
That I drink	not cup nor bowl from.

Part of the refrain of this song is to be sung after each verse or line by the women singing in chorus.

Thug mi gaol do'n nighinn duinn

Hó hì ri rì ù,
Hi hoireann ò hó,
Hó hì ri rì ù,

[ESAN:]

Thug mi gaol do'n nighinn duinn,
Hó hì ri rì ù, *etc.*

Beul a ghabhail an fhuinn,   380
Gu h-aotrom neo-throm,
'S tu mar chuthaig an coill',
'S tu mar smeòraich an craoibh.

Atharraich

Nighean bhuidhe, nighean bhàn,
Dhut a thug mi mo ghràdh,   385
Nì nach ceil mi air càch,
Gus an déid mi 'san làr,
Anns an anart chaol bhàn,
An ciste chumhaig nan clàr.

Atharraich

[ISE:]

Gura mise tha fo ghruaim,   390
A h-uile là is Di-luain,
Thug am bàt' oirre 'n cuan,
Ged a shéideadh i cruaidh,
Bhiodh mo ghràdh 'ga cur suas,
Làmh stiùradh nan stuadh,   395
I bhith deas no bhith tuath.

[*Atharraich*]

Gura mise tha gun aighear,
Tha mo shealgair 'na laighe—
Mo cheist sealgair nan aighean,
Cas 'gan iarraidh 's 'gam faighinn,   400

XI

A brown maiden I wooed

(*For tune, see p. 270*)

[HE:]
    A brown maiden I wooed,

      She could sing me so true,   380
      Light, sprightly all through
      Like the wildwood cuckoo,
      Like the thrush on the bough.

Change
      Maiden golden and fair
      For thee only I care,   385
      I will hide it nowhere
      Till I lie in the lair,
      In the linen so bare,
      In the deal chest so spare.

Change
[SHE:]
      'Tis I am in woe   390
      Every day as it goes,
      For to sea he has flown,
      Tho' the wildest wind roars
      To the windward she'll go,
      He will steer the seas o'er   395
      Whate'er airt the wind blows.

[*Change*]
      All my joy is a-dying,
      For my lover's a-lying,
      The swift hunter of wild hind
      Foot to track and to find them,   400

'S 'gan teàrnadh le leathad.
Choilich dhuibh am bàrr meangain
'S e t'fhùdar caol a nì 'n spreadhadh,
'S i do luaidhe nì snaidheadh
Gacha taobh na Beinn' Cheathaich;   405
Miann mo shùl bhith 'gad amharc
Le do mhìolchoin air lomhain—
Thug mi gaol do'n nighinn duinn.

Tha an t-òran seo air a roinn eadar dithis a bha leannanachd, a' chiad
earrann a' tòiseachadh leis an fhear, 's tha e crìochnachadh le freagradh
a leannain.

XII

Gura mise tha fo mhulad, 's mi air tulaich na buaile

O ho ao ri rì o ho,
Hi rì ò ho rò hu o,
O ho ao ri rì o ho.

Gura mise tha fo mhulad
O ho ao, *etc.*

'S mi air tulaich na buaile;   410
Cha d'fhuair mi 'n raoir cadal
Air an leabaidh, 's mi 'm ònar,
'S mi 'g ionndrainn mo leannain
Fleasgach fearail, ciùin, eòlach,
Fear a chinne Mhic Cailein   415
Thig o thalla nan ròiseal.

[*Atharraich*]

Bu tu sealgair a' chathain
Théid do'n athar a' ruaiseadh,
Agus nàmhaid ròin theilich
Thig o sgeirean a' chuain ghlais,   420
'S na circeige duinne
Bheireadh gur as an fhuarniod.

78

Down the slopes you could drive them.
Of the black cock a-swaying
Your powder bursts wide out,
And your lead does the slaying
Ben Ceathaich—each side of;   405
'Tis my longing to see thee
With thy greyhounds on leashes—
A dear maiden I wooed.

This song is divided between two who were in love, the first part
beginning with the man, and ending with the answer of his sweetheart.

XII

I am full of sorrow

(*For tune, see p. 271*)

I am full of sorrow

On the mound of the cow fold;   410
Last night on my bed
I was sleepless and lonely,
For my lover I was longing
A youth wise, calm and manly,
Of the race of Mac Cailein   415
From the hall of the banners.

[*Change*]
Hunter of wild geese
That take to flight quickly,
Foeman of the fat selchie
From the grey ocean's skerries,   420
And of the brown moor-hen
Who raised her brood from the cold nest.

79

Guma slàn do na gillean
   Thug a mhireag a' chuain orr',
Ge bè rachadh dha'n tilleadh   425
   Bhiodh an iomairt ud cruaidh dha,
Gum biodh leòis air am basan,
   Agus laise 'nan gruaidhean.

    .   .   .   .   .

   Ach a Ruairi, 's a Ruairi!   430
Na creid gun duirt mise
   Gun gibhtinn mo ghruagach;
Cha ghibhtinn 's cha gheallainn,
   'S cha mhalairtinn uam i,
Cha dugainn air òr i   435
   No air chòrn an t-sròil uaine,
'S mi air thì bhith 'ga faire
   Mum mealladh fear uam i.
Cha n-e eagal an ùmhlaidh
   No mùiseag dhaoin' uailse,   440
Ach air eagal thu seasamh
   Anns an t-seisein trì uairean.

Tha fonn an òrain a tha gu àrd ri sheinn an déidh a h-uile sreith no
ceathramh, mar as bicheanta chanar ris, 's an ceathramh fhéin ri
chantainn dà uair no dùbailte.

XIII

Gura mise tha làn airteil

   Hi liù, hi leò, hò ro éileadh,
   Hi liù, hi leò, ro hù, a hò,
   Hi liù, hi leò, hò ro éileadh.

Gura mise tha làn airteil,
Dìreadh 's a' teàrnadh na leacaich.
   Hi liù, *etc.*

Dìreadh 's a' teàrnadh na leacaich,
Buachailleachd nan gamhna breaca.   445

Here's a health to the stalwarts
　　Who took to the ocean;
He who'd go to repel them　　　　　　　　425
　　Would find the contest a hard one,
On their palms would be blisters
　　And their cheeks would be blazing.

　　　.　　.　　.　　.　　.　　.

But Rory, o Rory!　　　　　　　　　　430
　　Don't believe that I told them
That I'd give up my maiden
　　I'd not give her, nor promise,
Nor would I exchange her;
　　For gold I'd not give her　　　　　　435
Nor for roll of green satin,
　　Intently I watch her,
Lest anyone lure her from me.
　　'Tis not a fine I'm afraid of
Nor threats of the gentry,　　　　　　　440
　　But that they may make thee
Stand thrice at the Session.

The refrain of the above song is to be sung after every line or verse,
as it is often called, and the verse itself is to be sung twice, or doubled.

XIII

Truly I am full of sorrow

(*For tune, see pp. 272–8*)

Truly I am full of sorrow,
Climbing and descending the hillside,

Climbing and descending th' hillside,
While I'm speckled stirks a-herding,　　445

Buachailleachd nan gamhna breaca,
'S gun am buachaille 'nam faisge.

'S gun, *etc.*

[*Atharraich*]

Dhìrich mi mach a Bheinn Ghruamach,
'S chaidh mi timchioll air a bruachan,
Rànaig mi lag an fhraoich uaine.
Chìr mi mo cheann, dh'fhàg mi ghruag ann,   450
Dh'fhàg, is falt mo chinn 'na dhualan,
'S cha n-fhacas fear a' chùil dualaich,
Cha n-fhaca, 's gum b'fhada bhuam e,
Ged a sheall mi far mo ghuaille.
Gura diumbach mi do'n té tuathaich,   455
No thé eile bheireadh uam thu,
'S gur mi fhìn bu mhutha luaidh ort,
A chunnaic, no chì, no chuala,
No chuir an saoghal air uachdar,
No chuir an domhan mu chuairt da;   460
Dh'fhairlich orm a chur air fuadach,
Chur a deas no chur a tuath uam,
Thug e 'n latha 'n diu fo ghruaim dhiom,
Gun òl cupa, gun òl cuaiche.
Gura h-e mo cheist an t-uasal,   465
Chunnaic mi 'n dé seachad suas thu,
'S éileadh ort am pleatadh cuaiche,
Osan geàrr mu d' chalpa luathgheal,
Boineid chùil-bhig air deagh-ghruaig ort,
'S do ghunna-snaip orr 'o ghualainn,   470
Dol a shealg na h-eilde ruaidhe,
An eala cha dig slàn o d' luaidhe,
No 'n giadh glas as moiche ghluaiseas,
Lacha bheag a' charra-chinn ghuanaich—
No ròin léith o bheul na stuaidhe.   475

While I'm speckled stirks a-herding,
In the absence of the herdsman.

[*Change*]

I climbed out to the Gloomy Mountain
And went round about its braesides,
I reached the valley of green heather.
I combed my head, I left its hair there,   450
I left my head's hair there in ringlets,
I saw not him whose hair is curling,
I saw him not, far was he from me,
Though I looked across my shoulder.
With the northerner I am angry,   455
Or other lass who'd take thee from me,
Since 'twas myself who greatest loved thee,
Who ever saw, or sees, or heard of,
Or who set the world above him,
Or who put the world around him;   460
I failed to banish melancholy,
To send it south or send it northwards,
It made me spend today in sorrow,
Without cup or quaich a-drinking.
The young noble is my darling,   465
I saw you yesterday go past me
With your dress in folds all pleated,
On thy fair swift calf, short stocking,
On your fine hair, a neat bonnet,
With your gun upon your shoulder   470
Going to hunt the tawny roedeer,
The swan will not escape your gunfire,
Or the grey goose that wakes earliest,
Or the mallard, giddy headed,
Or the grey seal at sea's edges.   475

XIV

Gura mise tha fo ghruaman

É ho libh ò, ro hoireann ò,
É ho libh ò, hò ri ghealladh.

[ISE:]

Gura mise tha fo ghruaman,
　'S luath leam a thàinig an t-earrach.
　　É ho libh ò, *etc.*

Nist o rinn mo chriosan éirigh
　Cha n-urrainn mi fhéin 'ga theannadh.

Air feabhas gun dian mi m'éileadh　　　　　　480
　Tha 'n crios ag éirigh dha m'aindeoin.

Toiseach bainne a' tighinn am chìochan
　O'n òg as glan sìoladh fala.

Mo cheist air péidse Fir Ròthag,
　B'e sin an t-òganach smearail.　　　　　　485

Calpa cruinn an t-siubhail eutrom,
　Cha lùbadh tu feur no gaineamh.

Traigh chuimir an stocainn bhàinghil
　Dhìreadh a' bheinn àrd gun anail.

Giamanach gunna nach diùltadh　　　　　　490
　Nuair chaogadh tu 'n t-sùil 's a' mhala.

Giamanach gunna bheòil bhòidhich,
　Leagadh tu na h-eòin far chrannaibh.

Dé mar nì mi dhut an t-òran,
　'S gun mi eòlach mu d' dhà sheanair?　　　　　　495

Dé mar nì mi dhut an t-aodach,
　'S gun mo chaoirich anns na gleannan?

Ogha nan seanairean còire,
　Dha'm bi 'n crodh mu'n chrò as t-earrach.

84

XIV

'Tis I who am melancholy

(*For tune, see pp. 279–80*)

[SHE:]

'Tis I who am melancholy,
  Quickly, I feel, has come the springtime.

Now, since my belt is stretching,
  To tighten it I am unable.

However well my plaid is put on   480
  In spite of me the belt is stretching.

In my breasts first milk is coming—
  Nobly born is my young lover.

Roag's page is my darling,
  A young fellow strong and active,   485

Neat calf of light footstep,
  Sand nor grass would bend beneath you.

Neat foot in whitest stocking
  Would climb the high hill without breathing.

Hunter whose gun would never falter   490
  When you cocked your eye and eyebrow.

Hunter whose gun is unfailing,
  You would knock the birds off branches.

How shall I make for you the ballad,
  Without knowledge of your grandsires?   495

How shall I make for you the clothing
  Without my sheep in the valleys?

Grandson of kindly grandsires
  Who have kine in fold at springtime.

Ogha nan seanairean uasal, 500
  Dha'm biodh na cruachan 's na teanail.

Rinn mi 'n cadal beag an raoir leat,
  'S b'e siod 'n caoimhneas bu mhath leam.

Fhuair mi 'n cadal beag le brìodal
  Le òigeir nam mìogshùil meallach. 505

Ghabh thu seachad orm Di-Dòmhnaich,
  'S chuir siod dòltramachd air m'aire.

ESAN 'GA FREAGAIRT:
  Shaoil mi nach robh thu cho gòrach
  'S gun creideadh tu còmhradh balaich.

'S nach robh thu idir cho suarach 510
  'S gun creideadh tu tuaileas caile.

'S nach dug 's nach dobhair mi fuath dhut,
  Gus am fuaighear mi 'san anart.

Gu'n càirear 'sa chiste chaoil mi
  An déidh na saoir a bhith 'ga ceangal. 515

Gus an déid mi null air sàile—
  Bidh siùil bhàna ri crainn gheala,

Gus am bi na fir 'gam ghiùlain
  Gu eaglais nan tùran geala.

Mo cheist nighean donn na spréidhe 520
  Muineal glé-gheal is gruaidh thana.

Mo cheist nighean donn na buaile,
  'S ann leam fhìn nach b'fhuathach t'fhaicinn.

Mo cheist nighean donn nam mìogshùil
  Cha n-eil mi air thì do mheallaidh. 525

Gur tric a bha mi 's tu bànran
  Muigh am bàthaich a' chruidh-bhainne.

Gur tric a bha mi 's tu brìodal
  'S mo làmh air do chìochan geala.

Brollach geal mun dig an sìoda, 530
  Gruaidh mhìn-dearg fo'n glan sealladh.

86

Grandson of noble grandsires 500
Who had wealth accumulated.

Last night I slept a while beside you
—That was a kindness, well I liked it.

Tenderly I slept a little
Beside the youth whose smile beguiled me. 505

You went past me on the Sunday
Which cast gloom upon my spirit.

HE ANSWERING HER:

I thought that you were not so silly
That you'd believe a stripling's tattle.

I thought that you were not so foolish 510
That you'd believe a hussy's malice.

I never did, nor shall I hate you,
Until in linen I am shrouded.

Until I'm placed in narrow coffin
After the carpenters have bound it, 515

Until I go across the water—
White sails on bright masts will be hoisted.

Until the men do take my body
To the church with its white steeple.

I love the brown girl of the cattle 520
Of whitest neck and cheek most slender.

I love the brown girl of the cowfold
For me, to see thee's no displeasure.

I love the brown girl with eyes smiling
I'm not meaning thy deception. 525

Often you and I were talking
Softly outside in the cowbyre.

Often you and I did murmur
While I gently did caress you.

White thy bosom, silk becomes it, 530
Soft red cheek beneath pure glances.

87

'S i nochd a' chiad oidhche 'n fhoghair

E ho ì ri ò,
'S i nochd a' chiad oidhche 'n fhoghair,
    E ho hì ri ri o hó gu,
    E ho hì ri rì o,
    Hì a bhó hi ù rù.
'S i nochd a' chiad oidhche 'n fhoghair,
    E ho ì ri ò,
'S an raoir a chuala mi an fhaghaid,
    E ho hì ri ri o hó gu,
    E ho hì ri rì o,
    Hì a bhó hi ù rù.

'S an raoir a chuala mi an fhaghaid,
    E ho ì ri ó,

Eadar ceann a' bhàigh 's an fhadhail,
    E ho hì ri ri o hó gu, *etc.*

Cha ghuth gallain 's cha ghuth gadhair—   535
Guth na mnà 's i 'm bàrr a meadhail,
'S còmhlan fhear òga 'na deaghaidh,
O, 's i fhéin a bha 'gan taghadh,
Dh'fhàg i 'n diùbhaidh 's ghabh i a raghainn,
Ghabh i 'n t-òigeir seòlta, seadhach,   540
Òganach gun tòir 'na dheaghaidh,
Théid e 'na bheinn am bi 'n fhaghaid,
Le ghille 's le chù 'na dheaghaidh,
Le gunna caol a' bheòil laghaich,
'S le do mhìolchoin ghearrachoin ghadhair,   545
'S leat am fiadh air thùs na graighe,
Nì thu fùdar gorm a thaghadh,
Nì thu 'n luaidhe ghlas a leaghadh.

Atharraich

M'iarrtas air Rìgh na gréine,
Nach millear thu an còir no 'n eugcoir,   550
No mu òl a' bhuideil bhréige.

XV

Tonight's the first night of the autumn

(*For tune, see pp. 231–3*)

Tonight's the first night of the autumn,
   E ho ì ri ò,
Last night I heard the hunters calling,
   E ho hi ri, *etc.*

Last night I heard the hunters calling,

'Twixt the bayhead and the fording,

'Twas no lad nor hound that voiced it—   535
Voice of woman 'twas all haughty,
Whom a band of gallants followed,
Whom she loved she could make choice of,
Him she chose was best among them
Youth she chose full skilled and knowing,   540
With no feud to fear from foemen;
He'll go to hunt upon the mountain,
With fowling piece of well-shaped muzzle,
With his lad and dog behind him,
With your greyhounds and your lurchers   545
Yours will be the deer herd's leader,
Gunpowder you'll be choosing,
Grey lead you'll be melting.

Change
My prayer to the King of Heaven
That you're not lost in right or wrong cause   550
Or at drinking from the false bottle;

89

Nam milleadh, a Rìgh! b'e 'm beud e,
'S iomadh fear bhiodh umad deurach,
Agus bean air bheagan céille,
An impis falt a cinn a reubadh,   555
Mise mar dhithis is mar thé dhiu.

Atharraich

Tha mo chion air mac na bainich,
Mac na mnatha ciùine banail,
Dh'fhuaigheadh 'n sìoda is an t-anart,
Chuireadh gràinne grinn air bhannan;   560
Bràthair nan gruagaichean glana,
As do làimh gun earbainn m'anam,
Dol timchioll rubha ri gaillinn,
Fhad 's a mhaireadh bìth 'na darach,
No buill chaola ri crainn gheala,   565
No giubhas os cionn na mara,
Le siaban 's le tràghadh mara.

Tha e ri fhaicinn gu bheil trian de'n fhonn ri ghabhail daonnan 'san
òran seo an déidh a h-uile sreath maille ris an fhonn a chantuinn dà uair
an am caochladh air an fhuaim.

XVI

Bhean ud thall, gu dé th'air t'aire?

Ró ho laoithill ó,
Ró ho laoithill ó,
Bhean ud thall, gu dé th'air t'aire?
Laoithill o ho rò,
Trom orra chó,
Fair all il ó.

Bhean ud thall, gu dé th'air t'aire?
Ró ho laoithill ó,
Ró ho laoithill ó,
Móran bròin gun cheòl fo-near dhomh.
Laoithill o ho rò,
Trom orra chó,
Fair all il ó.

If you were, o God! 'twere pity,
Many a man would shed tears for you,
Many a woman lose her senses,
Would her hair be likely rending,   555
I myself would be like sev'ral.

Change

The weaver's son's my darling,
Son of quiet modest mother,
Who'd sew silk and linen,
Who'd put a pretty knap on sashes,   560
Brother of handsome maidens,
Your hand I'd trust my life to
Rounding headland in the tempest,
While her timbers' caulking lasted,
Or the thin ropes to her mastheads,   565
Or her fir, above the water
In the seaspray and the current.

It may be seen that in this song a third of the refrain is always to be
sung after every line, besides which the refrain is to be sung twice when
the rhyme is changed.

XVI

Woman, what may be your thoughts now?

(*For tune, see pp. 284–6*)

Woman, what may be your thoughts now?
Laoithill o *etc.*

Woman, what may be your thoughts now?
Rò ho *etc.*

Much of sorrow that is songless,
Laoithill o *etc.*

Móran bròin gun cheòl fo-near dhomh.
  Ró ho *etc.*
Tha loingeas air chuan na Hearadh,   570
  Laoithill o ho rò *etc.*

'S neònach sin, 's na fir fallain,
C'àit am bheil Raghnall mac Ailein?
Stiùramaich' as fhearr ri gaillinn,
Bho nach robh i 'n làimh mo leannain,
Bheireadh sàbhailt i gu cala,   575
Fhad 's a mhaireadh beith no darach,
No giubhas os cionn na mara,
No buill chaola ri crainn gheala.

Atharraich

Tha loingeas air a' cholbh chuilce,
Siod mar a dh'òrdaichinn dut iad,   580
'S nighean rìgh 'ga pùsadh riutsa,
Le sìoda, le sròl, 's le trusgan;
Nuair théid i mach, seinnear cruit dhi,
Seinnear clàrsach nan teud druidte.

Atharraich

Bhuidhe ri m' Rìgh, tha mi sunndach,   585
Cha n-eil eagal orm mo sgiùrsadh,
No mo chur am prìosan dùinte,
No bonn a chall ris an ùmhladh,
Tha mo bhràithrean air mo chùlaibh,
Iain 'sa bheinn 's e 'na dhùsgadh,   590
Bogha an iubhair 'na làimh lùthmhor.

Atharraich

Bhuidhe ri m' Rìgh, tha mi socair,
Cha n-eil eagal orm mo dhochann,
No mo chur am prìosan cloiche,
Bho nach maireann Fionn no Oisin,   595
No Cù-Chulainn nan arm toirteil.

Tha fonn an òrain seo ri roinn 'na dhà leath, a' chiad leath ro'n chiad
rann, 's leath 'na dhéidh.

Leig mi fhaicinn anns na ciad ceithir rannan de'n òran seo cia mar as
còir a sheinn no mar a fhreagradh e bhith air a chur an clò-bhualaidh,
an earbsa daonnan gun gabh an luchd-leubhaidh agus araon sgrìobh-
adairean leithsgeul m'fhaoin oidhirp.

Much of sorrow that is songless.

Harris sea with shipping crowded,   570

That is strange if men be strong yet,
Where is now Mac Allan's Ronald?
Best to steer in tempest onrush;
Would my love the helm were holding,
Safe into port he'd steer the boatmen,   575
If her timbers birch or oaken
Or red pine wood kept unbroken
Or the white mast's slender cordage.

Change

A fleet is at . . . (?)
It is so I would have ordered   580
Princess should be your betrothed one,
Satin and silk to be her robing,
When she goes out, lute's played for her,
Harp with tightened strings entoned too.

Change

Thanks be to my King I'm happy.   585
Little fear I scourge's smarting,
Little fear I dungeon darkened
Or the loss from penance ransom.
There are brothers who will back me,
John, on hill they'll ne'er find napping,   590
Bow of yew in hand all active.

Change

Thank my King! I've fear of no one,
Nor of ill that they can cause me,
Strong prison will not hold me
Since Fionn nor Ossian live no more now,   595
Nor Cù Chulainn armed all potent.

The refrain of this song is to be divided into two halves, the first half
before the first verse, and [the second] half after it.

I showed in the first four verses of this song how it ought to be sung,
or how it should be printed, always hoping that readers and particularly writers will excuse my weak effort.

Oran Luadhaidh le Mairi Nighean Alasdair Ruaidh mhic Leoid

O ho ì ù ó,
Air fair all ill ó ho,
Ro ho ao ri rì ó.

Siuthadaibh, siuthadaibh, a mhnathan, O ho *etc.*
  Luadhaibh athaiseach liùm;
Tha sinne 'n seo ceathrar,
  Urra bharrachd air triùir,   600
Cha b'fhuilear dhuinn ochdnar,
  'S urra choltach air stiùir,
Ach ma théid sinn air adhart,
  Nì sinn tadhal 'san Dùn
Far bheil Ruairi mac Iain,   605
  Mac athar mo rùin,
Fiach am faigh sinn a' bhiaoirlinn,
  No 'm faod e a tobhairt dùinn,
Mura faigh sinn a' bhiaoirlinn,
Fiach am faigh sinn am bàta   610
  Chaidh a chàradh as ùr.

Atharraich

'Cha n-fhaigh sibh a' bhiaoirlinn,
  'S cha n-fhaod mi a tobhairt dùibh;
'S ann a gheibh sibh an coite
  'S e bu choltaiche dhùibh;   615
Nuair a dh'fhalbhas na Faoillich,
  Théid na saoir os a cionn.'

Atharraich

Gu dé nist a nì mise
  Ma bhristear mo ghlùn?
Ma bhristear 's gum bristear,   620
  Ma bhristear, 's oil liùm;

94

XVII

On, women, with vigour!

(*For tune, see pp. 287–90*)

On, women, with vigour!
  Toss the webbing with me,
We're round it a foursome,
  One more than if three;   600
'Tis eight we are wanting,
  With a captain to steer,
And if we go onward,
  To the Donjon we'll veer,
Home of Rory Mac Iain,   605
  Son of sire I loved dear,
He may give us the galley
  If his hand should be free;
If we get not the galley
Then the boat he may lend us,   610
  She was mended this year.

Change

  'You will not get the galley,
    My hand is not free—
  The skiff is much surer
    For a crew such as ye,   615
  When the midwinter's over
    She'll be sorted with gear.'

Change

  What will happen I ask you
    Should I fracture my knee?
  And sure 'twill be fractured,   620
    And a sad hap for me;

Cha dian mi ceum astair
   Gun tagsa ri m' chùl
'S mi 'm bothan gun tughadh
'S an t-snighe os mo chionn.   625

XVIII

Gura mise tha fo éislein

   Ó ho rò o hó gù,
   Hao ri ùrabh ó éileadh,
   Ó ho rò o hó gù.

Gura mise tha fo éislein, ó ho rò *etc*
Moch 'sa mhaduinn, 's mi 'g éirigh;
Chì mi 'n eilid 's a céile,
'S iad a' mire ri chéile;
Rìgh, gur buidhe dhaibh péin siod,   630
Cha n-ionann 's mar dh'éirich
Dhomh 's do Dhòmhnall mac Sheumais,
'S ann a thug e mi air éiginn,
Muigh an Gleannan na Géige,
'S mi 'nam bhanchaig air spréidh ann,   635
Aig a' bhaintighearn' òig cheutaich
Bean a bheathaich na ceudan,
Do luchd Laideann is Beurla,
Do luchd Fraingis is Gréigis.

Atharraich

'S truagh nach robh mi fad seachdain   640
'N riochd a' gheòidh no na lachann,
No na faoileige glaise,
'S mi gun snàmhadh cuan farsainn,
'S mi gun streapadh na caisteil,
Gus an leiginn a mach asd'   645
Òg ùr a Chloinn Lachlainn;
'S tu nach iarradh cra-bhata,
Dh'fhóghnadh gilead do chraicinn,
Agus deirge do leacann,
Agus bòichead do phearsa.   650

96

I can't walk a step then,
 If help be not near,
My hovel needs thatching
 With its drip o'er my ears.   625

XVIII

I am sad and mournful

(*For tune, see pp. 291–3*)

I am sad and mournful
Rising early in the morning;
I see the hind and her fellow
As they play and sport together.
O God, may they enjoy it!   630
'Twas not thus that has befallen
To me and Donald, son of Hamish:
He forcefully did take me
Out in the Glen of Branches,
When I was there milking cattle   635
For the lady young and graceful,
The lady who supported hundreds
Of scholars of French and Latin,
Of scholars of Greek and English.

Change
Alas that for a week's space   640
I was not wild goose or mallard,
Or in the shape of seagull,
I'd swim the widespread ocean,
I'd climb up to castles
Until I had releaséd   645
The young man of Clan Lachlan.
Cravat you'd not be needing,
Suffices your skin's whiteness,
Suffices your cheeks' redness,
And th' comeliness of your person.   650

XIX

Mi dualach, mi donn

Ò ho i o hì ò,
Hao ri o hù ò,
Ro ho i o hì ò.

Mi dualach, mi donn, Ò ho i *etc.*
Mi gu biorshuileach, binn,
Mi mar smeòraich an craoibh
Mi mar chuthaig an coill';
Mi torrach, mi trom, 655
Cha le balach mo throm—
Ach leis an lasgaire dhonn,
Mac Fir Bhaile nan Long,
Leis an éireadh na soinn,
Leis an diante 'n toll trom. 660

Atharraich

Galair goirteas is cràidh,
Aiceid chuim gun bhith slàn,
Air a' bheul a thuirt à—
Gu robh mi bhuat làn.

Atharraich

'S ionann sin 's mar atà 665
Tha mi lìonte le d' ghràdh,
Bho m' mhullach gu m' shàil.

Atharraich

Gu bheil mis' air mo chlisgeadh
Mu chùl fàinneach nan riobain,
'S càch ag ràdha nach dig thu; 670
Tha do phreasain am chistidh,
Cùis as cruaidhe, do litir.

Atharraich

Gaol ise, luaidh ì,
Gaol air Anna nighean Nìll,

98

XIX

My hair's curling and brown

(*For tune, see p. 294*)

My hair's curling and brown,
Keen my eyes, sweet my voice,
Like a thrush on a tree,
Like cuckoo in a wood;
I am heavy with child,   655
By no mere lad is my babe
But by hero dark-haired,
Son of laird of the ships
With whom warriors would rise
Who would give heavy wounds.   660

Change

Sickness, misery and pains,
Consumption without cure
On the mouth which told that—
That my babe is by you.

Change

Indeed it is so   665
I am full of thy love
From my head to my heel.

Change

I am sorely troubled
For the head in ribboned ringlets,
Others say that you will come not;   670
In my kist still lies your present,
What is harder yet, your letter.

Change

My love is she, my love is she,
My love Anna nic Neill,

99

Miar as grinn air an t-snàth,
'S air an anart chaol bhàn.

Mar ann 's gach òran luadhaidh eile, tha gach rann do'n òran seo ri'n cantuinn dà uair 's am fonn leis gach uair, gus e bhith buan agus feumail air son na h-obrach.

XX

'S mise 's daor a cheannaich

Tha an t-òran luadhaidh a leanas air a roinn 'na dhà earann, leath de'n fhonn ro' aon de na ceathramhnan, agus leath eile 'na dhéidh, 's gach rann ri ghabhail no ri chantainn dà uair.

> Ì ù ru rù bhi u o,
> Hó ì abh ó.

'S mise 's daor a cheannaich
Air bainne nighean Dòmhnaill;

> Chalainn éileadh ò hi ò,
> Ró ho leathag.

Cha n-e miad mo shine
Chuir mi mhilleadh m'òige,

> Ì ù ru rù bhi u o,
> Hó ì abh ó.

Cha n-e mìod mo shine
Chuir mi mhilleadh m'òige,

> Chalainn éileadh ò hi ò,
> Ró ho leathag.

'S mi 'm bothan beag cumhag
Air àirigh am ònar,

Tha mo bhràiste briste,
Tha mo chrios 'na òirnean;

Mo ghruag anns na tollan,
'S mo phlaide 'na stròicean

Neatest finger at the thread, 675
And at linen white and fine.

As in every other waulking song, each line of this song is to be sung twice, and the refrain with it each time, so that it may last, and be useful for the work.

XX

Dearly did I purchase

The following waulking song is divided into two parts, half the refrain before one of the verses, and the other half after it, and every verse is to be sung or recited twice.

(*For tune, see p. 295*)

Dearly did I purchase
Milk for Donald's daughter;

It was not my age that
Caused my youth's spoiling. 680

It was not my age that
Caused my youth's spoiling.

When I was alone at the sheiling
In a wretched little bothy.

Now my brooch is broken
And my belt's in pieces;

My hair is torn out 685
And my plaid's in tatters

Aig fear a Chloinn Mhuirich
'S Mac Muire 'na thòrachd!

Chionn mo thoirt an asgaidh,
Gun tochradh gun chòrdadh.   690

Nam faicinn do bhiaoirlinn
Fo h-aodach a' seòladh,

Gun dianainn a h-aithne,
'S gun rachainn 'na còmhdhail;

Gun dianainn mo ghearain   695
Ris an t-seabhag eòlach,

Bhiodh Raghnall mac Ailein
Air thoiseach mo thòrachd,

'S ged chanainn e rithist
Bhiodh Iain mac Dhòmhnaill,   700

Ceist nam ban a Lathaig
'S aighear bhan a Mórair,

Troma-cheist nam ban Ìleach,
'S iad Sìne agus Seònaid;

Gun aithnichinn do bhuidheann   705
Air shiubhal na mòintich,

Air ghilead an léintean
'S air deirgead an còta,

Air ghuirmead an triubhais,
'S air dhuibhead am brògan,   710

Le 'm mosgaidean fùdair,
Trom dùmhail le 'm mórshluagh.

[*Atharraich*]

Nam faicinn mo leannan
Le ghealladh do'n bhuailidh,

Gun glacainn an cuman,   715
'S gun lunnainn a' bhuarach,

Gum faighinn leat cadal
An leaba bhig luachrach,

By one of Clan Currie,
  May Mary's Son avenge it!

For taking me for nothing
  Without troth or dowry.   690

If I saw thy galley
  Under her canvas sailing

I would recognise her,
  I would go to meet her.

I would tell my story   695
  To the hawk of wisdom,

Ranald son of Allan
  Would lead my avenging.

And though I repeat it,
  So would Iain, son of Donald,   700

Beloved of Laig women,
  Joy of Morar maidens,

Beloved of Islay women,
  They are Jane and Janet,

I would know your clansmen   705
  By their moorland walking,

By their shirts' whiteness,
  By their coats' redness,

By their trousers' blueness,
  By their shoes' blackness,   710

With their firing muskets
  Thickly throng their numbers.

[*Change*]

If I saw my sweetheart
  Coming to the cowfold

I would take the milk pail,   715
  I would pin up the fetter,

I would sleep beside thee
  On a small bed of rushes,

103

'S ann fodhad a sgaoilinn
  An t-aodach, 's air m'uachdar,   720

A chuid nach biodh tioram
  Gum filleamaid uainn e,

Chuir iad thu 'n taigh glaiste
  Far nach faic mi bhuam thu,

Fhir an aodainn shoilleir   725
  Fo thaghadh na gruaige,

Sgrìobhadair, ceannachadair,
  Leubhadair, aithneadair duaise;

A Mhoire 's mo chùradh
  Chuir mi 'n lùib nan tuathach,   730

Na Sgitheanaich dhubha
  'S iad buidheann a b'fhuaire,

Chuir iad thu 'n taigh glaiste
  Far nach faic mi bhuam thu.

Cha do rinn nighean Raghnaill   735
  An fhoghluim bu dual di,

Cha dug i dhomh anart
  Gu ceangal mo ghruaige,

Ach sgòdan beag salach
  De'n anart bu shuaraich',   740

Eagal mi bhith an asgaidh
  O'n mhasla seo fhuair mi,

Iomlaid na bà dàra
  Chuir mo ghràdh an gruaim rium,

  Ì ù ru rù bhi u o,
  Hó ì abh ó.

'S mise 's daor a cheannaich   745
  Air bainne nighean Dòmhnaill.

  Chalainn éileadh ò hi ò,
  Ro ho leathag.

With the plaid beneath thee
 And stretched upon me   720

The part that was not dry
 We would put from us.

They've put you in a prison
 Where I cannot see you,

O thou of countenance clearest   725
 Under hair that's choicest.

Writer, connoisseur,
 Reader, knowing the prizes;

Marry! it pains me
 To be amongst northmen,   730

Among the black Skyemen
 Of people the coldest,

They've put you in a prison
 Where I cannot see you

Ranald's daughter did not show   735
 The knowledge she ought to,

She gave me not linen
 To bind up my tresses,

But a little rag, dirty,
 Of linen the poorest,   740

For fear I'd go freely
 From the disgrace I'd come by.

Barter of breeding cattle
 Made my love displeased with me,

Dearly did I purchase   745
 Milk for Donald's daughter.

XXI

Dhòmhnaill òig mhic Dhòmhnaill mhic Ruairi

Hoireann ó o ho i ù o,
Hi ùrabh ó ro hug éileadh,
Hoireann ó o ho i ù o.

Dhómhnaill òig mhic Dhòmhnaill mhic Ruairi,
   Chunnaic mi dol suas an dé thu.
      Hoireann ó, *etc.*

Dol a dh'iarraidh toil do chàirdean,
   'S tu 'm màireach a' dol a réiteach.   750

Ghabh thu seachad orm gu gruamach,
   'S bha mi cho suarach mu d' dhéidhinn.

Dh'earalas gum faicte fhathast
   Cheart cho aighearach riut fhéin mi.

Shaoil mi nach robh thu cho carach   755
   'S gun dianadh tu gealladh bréige.

Shaoil mi nach robh thu cho meallta
   'S gun gabhadh tu banntrach mar chéile.

Cliù do'n Tì aig am bheil m'fhortan,
   O nach do choisinn thu 'm bréid domh.   760

'S o nach do choisinn thu stòl domh,
   Di-Dòmhnaich am fianuis cléire.

'S cha mhó choisinn thu dhomh seasamh
   Anns an t-seisein air là féille.

Mo cheist fear an leadain bhòidhich,   765
   'S tric a fhuair mi pòg le streup uat.

'S gur tric a bha mi 's tu beadradh,
   'S gun bhith eadrainn ach na léintean.

Gur tric a bha mi 's tu brìodal,
   'S cha n-innseamaid air a chéil' e.   770

XXI

Donald, son of Donald MacRory

(*For tune, see pp. 296–8*)

Donald, son of Donald MacRory,
    Yesterday I saw you passing.

Going to seek goodwill of kindred
    On the eve of your betrothal.   750

You passed me with looks so churlish,
    No less surly felt I towards you.

I shall yet be seen as happy
    As you are yourself, take caution.

Once I thought you not so tricky   755
    As to make a lying promise.

I knew not such guile was in you
    That with widow you would marry.

To Providence I give my praises
    That to you I am not wedded.   760

That for you I did no penance
    Sunday morn before the clergy.

That for you before Kirk Session
    I never stood upon the Sabbath.

My love's the youth of handsome tresses   765
    Oft from you I'd playful kisses.

Often you and I were sporting
    Without aught but shifts between us.

Often you and I were talking
    And we'd not tell it on each other.   770

Tha mi sgìth ri siubhal beinne,
Ri là doilleir 's i gun ghréin oirr'.

Atharraich

Chì mi 'm bàta seach an rubha,
'S i 'na siubhal fo làn-éideadh.

'S àrd a chluinntear fuaim a daraich,   775
'S i 'na deannaibh tro'n chaol Shléibhteach.

'S àrd a chluinntear fuaim a cupla,
Air muir gucagach ag éirigh.

Bidh i an tìr Mhic Nìll fo latha,
'S fir 'ga caitheamh as an léintean.   780

Bidh an stiùir an làimh mo leannain,
Òganach deas fearail feucannt.

Bidh an stiùir an làimh nan gillean,
O, 's iad fhéin as binne dh'éibheas.

Bidh an stiùir an làimh an Leòdaich,   785
Air am bu shuarach òl sinéabhar.

Suidheamaid 's faigheamaid botal,
'S òlamaid deoch air a chéile.

Suidheamaid 's gabhamaid òran,
'S biomaid ag òl air a chéile.   790

Gur ann orm tha sgrìob na pòige,
'S cha n-eil sòlas orm mu déidhinn.

Bho nach faighinn pòg mo leannain,
Ge b'e cala an dian e éirigh.

I am tired walking the moorland,
When the day is dark and sunless.

Change

I see the ship go past the headland,
She is moving 'neath full canvas.

Loudly sounds her oaken planking   775
As through Sound of Sleat she races.

Loudly sound her shrouds
On the foaming sea a-rising.

She'll reach by dusk MacNeil's country
Her crew rowing in their shirt-sleeves.   780

My sweetheart's hand is on the rudder,
A manly, handsome youth, and clever.

The young man's hands are on the rudder,
Most melodious sounds their crying.

MacLeod's hands are on the rudder   785
Who little cared to drink Geneva.

Let us sit and get a bottle
And drink toasts unto each other.

Let us sit, and start a-singing,
And let's drink to our fellows.   790

Of kissing I have premonition,
And about it I'm not happy.

Since I'd not get my sweetheart's kisses
In whatever harbour he happens.

XXII

Marbhaisg air a' mhulad, 's buan e

E ho ì ùrabh ò rò ho chiù,
E ho ì rì rì,
E ho ì ri sa bhó hu ò,
E ho ì ùrabh ò rò ho chiù.

Marbhaisg air a' mhulad, 's buan e   795
'S tric ugam e, 's ainneamh bhuam e,
  E ho ì ùrabh ò, *etc.*

'S tric ugam e, 's ainneamh bhuam e,
Dh'fhairlich orm a chur air fuadach,
  E ho ì ùrabh ò, *etc.*

Dh'fhairlich orm, *etc.*
Chur a deas no chur a tuath bhuam,
  E ho ì ùrabh ò, *etc.*

Chur a chuideachda nan uaislean,
Chur a choimhideachd an guaillean;   800
Thug e 'n latha 'n diu fo ghruaim dhiom,
Gun òl cupa, gun òl cuaiche,
Gun òl fìon a pìosan luachmhor,
Aig an loch mu'n robh mi suarach;
Dh'fhalbh mo rùn air giùlan uainn as,   805
Mac an fhir bu mhath 'sa chruadal,
Thilleadh dhachaigh crodh na tuatha;
'S truagh 's gun choille 'n taobh-s' a tuath dhiom
Ach an fhairge ghlas 'na cluainean,
'S bheirinn gnothach do'n Leith-Uachdraich,   810
'S as a sin do dh'Achadh Luachrach
Far a bheil mo rùn an t-uasal;
Gheibhinn cadal leat air cluasaig,
'S cùl do chinn air bhac mo ghuaille,
Ge b'fhad' an oidhche, cha ghluaisinn.   815

XXII

A curse on sorrow, it is lasting

(*For tune, see pp. 299–300*)

A curse on sorrow, it is lasting,   795
Oft 'tis with me, seldom absent,

Oft 'tis with me, seldom absent,
I have failed to drive it from me,

I have failed, *etc.*
To send it south or northwards from me,

To keep company with the gentry,
To overlook their shoulders;   800
It took today for me to sorrow,
Without cup or quaich a-drinking,
Or wine from costly vessels,
At the loch which I don't care for;
My darling has been carried from me,   805
The son of bravest father,
Who would return the tenants' cattle;
Sad am I no wood lies northwards,
But the grey sea in its billows,
I would go to the Upper District,   810
And from there to th' Field of Rushes
Where is my noble lover;
I'd sleep beside thee on a pillow,
With thy head upon my shoulder,
Though the night were long, I'd move not.   815

'S truagh 's gun fhàrdrach air mo chomas,
Sgiobadh innte dh'fhearaibh foinnidh,
Dh'òladh am fìon dearg 'na thonnan,
Sheòladh i gu Tobar Mhoire,
Far am bheil mo rùn an comunn;   820
Cha b'e luchd nan curraicean croma,
Ach luchd nan leadan 's nan cùl donna,
'S nan calpannan geala troma,
Dhianadh an danns' air am bonnaibh,
Dhianadh an ùmhlachd le'm boineid,   825
Dòmhnallaich a' bhrollaich shoilleir,
'S gruagaichean òga mu'n coinneamh.

Lig mi fhaicinn anns na ciad shia rainn de'n òran roimh-sgrìobhte,
mar is còir da bhith air a sheinn.

XXIII

'S muladach mi 's mi air m'aineoil

"'S muladach mi 's mi air m'aineoil,
     Hì rì ri rì ri abh ó,

'S éisleineach mi 'sa chluain rainich,
       Ho ró ho ao ri o ho,
       Hu ru bhi ù ho ro ho.

'S éisleineach mi 'sa chluain rainich,
     Hì rì ri rì ri abh ó

Coimhead uam air chuan na Hearadh,   830
       Ho ró ho ao ri o ho
Coimhead uam air chuan na Hearadh,
       Hì rì ri *etc.*
'S nach faic mi tighinn mo leannan,
Geugaire fionn foinnidh fearail,
Mala chaol gun chaochladh seallaidh,
Sùil ghorm 'san aodann nach greannach,
Fiacaill bhàn is bial dearg tana.   835

Change

Pity no ships 'neath my order
With a crew of valiant sailors
Who'd drink red wine in gallons
Who'd sail her to Tobermory,
Where my love is with his fellows;   820
Not the folk of caps all crooked,
But the folk of brown locks flowing,
Whose calves are white and sturdy,
Who would dance upon their foot-soles,
Who'd politely doff their bonnets,   825
MacDonalds of fine figure,
And young maidens along with them.

I showed in the first six verses of the aforewritten song, how it should
be sung.

XXIII

In this strange land I'm not happy

(For tune, see pp. 301–4)

'In this strange land I'm not happy

Wearying in these fields of bracken,

Wearying in these fields of bracken,

Gazing o'er the sea of Harris,   830

Gazing o'er the sea of Harris,

Yet my lover's form I scan not.
Well bred, gentle, manly, winsome,
Slender brow o'er eye unflinching,
Eye so blue on face unwrinkled,
Teeth of snow, of thin lips crimson.   835

Atharraich

''S truagh nach fhaighinn siod air m'aineachd—
Mac 'ic Ailein bhith 'san fheamain,
Bhaintighearna a bhith aig an sgalaig,
An tighearna òg a' bruich an arain,
Mac Nìll a' feitheamh na fallaid.'   840

A h-aon eile freagairt:

'Éisd a chaile, sguir ad sgeòdal,
Cuim nach d'fhoighneachd thu 'm bu bheò mi?
No 'n do chuireadh ùir no fòd orm?
Tha mo theanga fallain còmhnard,
Chaidh i ri cloich air a bhòndé;   845
Tha trì rainn is faobhar ghleòis oirr';
'S ìseal am post thug thu Dhòmhnall,
Cha b'e beus mo thighearn' òig e,
'S ann a bhiodh tu 'n ceann do mhórshluaigh,
'S tu cur fìon an obair òircheard,   850
Do dh'iarlachan 's do Mhontròsa,
'S tu cur shaighdeirean an òrdugh.

Atharraich

'S e m'fheudail mhór Mac 'ic Ailein,
Cha b'e Mac Leòid 's mi 'na fhearann,
Na bheil beò a shliochd a sheanar,   855
'S muladach mi 's mi air m'aineoil.'

XXIV

Cha dìrich mi an t-uchd le fonn

O hi rì ill mò nigh'n donn,
Hì rì ill mò nigh'n donn,
O hi rì ill mò nigh'n donn.

[ISE]

Cha dìrich mi an t-uchd le fonn,
O hi rì, *etc.*

Change

> 'Would the power to harm I had it,
> Mid the wrack would lie Clanranald,
> And his lady with the halflin,
> While the young chief baked the bannocks,
> Leavings for MacNeil of Barra.'   840

The other one answering:

> 'Listen hussy, stop your groaning,
> Ask ye not if life still hold me
> Or if soil or sod went o'er me?
> My tongue is sound and in good toning,
> I've put it to the whetting stone too—   845
> Three blades it has with edge for goring;
> Donald's post you put too lowly,
> 'Twould become my lord but sorely,
> You will lead your clan to glory,
> Pour the wine in craft of goldsmith,   850
> For Montrose and Earls and nobles
> Range in battle-row your soldiers.

Change

> You, Clanranald, are my darling,
> Not MacLeod I live his land in,
> Nor the scions of his grandsires,   855
> In this strange land I'm not happy.'

XXIV

I'll not climb the brae with song

(*For tune, see pp. 305–7*)

[SHE]
> I'll not climb the brae with song,

115

Ceum mo choise 's truime liom,
    O hi rì, *etc.*

Bann mo chòta 's teinne liom;
Tha mi torrach, tha mi trom,   860
Cha n-ann le balach mo throm—
Ach leis an lasgaire dhonn
Nach dian seasamh air an fhonn,
No air a' mhachaire lom,
Gun a bhòtann bhith fo bhonn.   865

Tionndaidh

Mo cheist maraiche nan tonn,
Chuireadh air an fhidhill fonn,
Air an fhidhill, air an truimb,
'S air pìob mhór nam feadan toll;
'S truagh nach fhaicinn-se do long,   870
Seòladh àrd air bhàrr nan tonn,
Air a luchdachadh gu trom,
Seòladh o Cholla gu Rùm,
Steach gu Uidhist nan ian fionn,
Le òr dearg 's le airgiod pronn,   875
'S gum bu liomsa dheth 'n treas bonn.

Tionndaidh

[ESAN]

'S fada 'n sealladh chì mi bhuam,
Chì mi Uidhist nam beann fuar
Far am bi 'n eala fo'n bhruaich,
Gillean 'ga ruith, coin 'ga ruaig;   880
Soiridh bhuam do thìr 'Ill' Eathain,
Far an d'fhàg mi ghruagach laghach,
Banchaig a' chruidh-laoigh 's nan aighean,
Dhianadh a' bhó mhór a cheangal,
Dhianadh do'n laogh bheag an gamhain,   885
Dhianadh na gamhna 'nan aighean—
Cha dìrich mi an t-uchd le fonn.

Heavier my step becomes,

My coat belt still tighter grows,
I am pregnant, well I know,—   860
Not by any churl my child,
But by the youth of brown hair,
Who would never stand on soil,
Or upon the *machair* bare,
Without shoes beneath his feet.   865

Turn

I love the sailor of the waves
Who upon the fiddle plays,
On the Jew's harp, on the viol,
On hollow chanter of great pipe;
Would that I might see thy ship   870
On the wave tops sailing high,
With a cargo in her hold,
Sailing o'er from Coll to Rum,
Into Uist of white birds,
With red gold and silver coins,   875
Would that a third of them were mine.

Turn

[HE]

Far away the view I see,
I see Uist of the cold hills,
Where the swan is 'neath the brae
With lads chasing her, and dogs;   880
Farewell to MacLean's country
Where I left the pretty maiden
Tending milking cows and heifers,
Who the full-grown cow would fasten,
Who would rear the calves to stirks,   885
Who would rear the stirks to heifers;
I'll not climb the brae with song.

XXV

Nighean chruinn donn, dut is éibhinn

É ho ì hug òireann ò ro,
E hó ì 's na ù ho ì,
Na ao ri rì hug òireann ò ro.

[ESAN]

'Nighean chruinn donn, dut is éibhinn,
É ho ì hug òireann ò ro.

Na bric 's na bradain a' leum dhut,
E hó ì 's na ù ho i,
Na ao ri rì hug òireann ò ro.

Na bric 's na bradain a' leum dhut,
É ho ì hug òireann ò ro.

Na fir gheala air thì do theumadh,   890
E hó i 's na ù ho ì,
Na ao ri rì hug òireann ò ro.

Na fir gheala *etc.*
E ho ì hug *etc.*

Atharraich

Tha maraiche air thì do bhuannachd—
Cha mharaiche, ach mac duin' uasail;
'S cumha liom fhìn na chum uam thu,
Miad mo ghaoil ort, lughad m'fhuath ort,
M'athair a bhith anns an fhuarlic,   895
Mo mhàthair chaomh bhith 'n tùbh shuas di,
Gun mo bhràithrean bhith mu'n cuairt domh,
Gun mo chaoirich bhith 'sna bruachan,
'S gun mo ghearrain bhith 'san luachair,
Tainead mo chruidh-laoigh air buailidh,   900
Gun bhó dhubh ann, 's gun bhó ruadh ann,
Gun ghin idir mu'n déid buarach.'

118

XXV

Happily, o neat brown maiden

(*For tune, see pp. 308–10*)

[HE]

    'Happily, o neat brown maiden,

    For thee are trout and salmon leaping;

    For thee are trout and salmon leaping;

    Handsome men are keen to catch thee,   890

    Handsome men, *etc.*

Change

    A sailor is intent to win thee—
    No sailor he, but son of noble;
    And I lament what kept thee from me,
    My love's extent, my dislike's smallness,
    My father lying 'neath the gravestone,   895
    My kindly mother there beside him,
    My lack of brothers round about me,
    My lack of white sheep on the braesides
    And of geldings in the rushes,
    Few my milk-cows at the cowfold,   900
    There there's not a black or red cow,
    Not a beast to put on halter.'

[ISE]

'Mhic an fhir o'n Lagan Lasrach,
O Bhràighe Loch-Iall 's Loch Arcaig,
Marcraich' nan steud crùidheach seanga, 905
Bha seachd bliadhna 'n stàbull glaiste,
Chuir thu 'n cruithneachd geal 'na fhrasaich,
Thug thu fìon dha mar dheoch-mhainne,
Chuir thu crùidhean òir fo chasan,
'S chuir thu strian de'n airgiod gheal innt', 910
Nuair a lig thu 'n sin a mach i,
Muir no tìr cha d'rinn i sheachnadh,
Leum i geata nan seachd glasan,
'S an geata mór a bha faisg air,
Dh'fhoighneachd an Rìgh, "Có 'm fear tapaidh?" 915
"Dòmhnall Òg o'n Lagan Lasrach."
Dh'fhiabhaich a phéidse e do'n aitreabh,
Thug an Rìgh dha làn na h-aide
Do'n òr a chùinneadh ann an Sasann;
Sgap e siod air feadh an achaidh, 920
Eagal thoirt a dh'Alba masladh.'

Tha gach rann do'n òran seo ri ghabhail no gh-ràdha dà uair, agus a'
chiad earann an déidh a' chiad turais, 's an earann eile an déidh an
ath-turais, mar a dh'fhiach mi ri ligeil fhaicinn an toiseach an òrain.

XXVI

Gura mise tha fo mhulad air an tulaich luim fhuair

Hù, ò ro, hù ò,
Ro ho i, o hì ò,
Hù, ò ro, hù ò.

Gura mise tha fo mhulad
 Air an tulaich luim fhuair,

Cha dìrich mi bruthach,
 'S cha siubhail mi cluain. 925

[SHE]

    'Son of laird from Lagan Lasrach,
    From Brae Lochiel and Loch Arcaig,
    Rider of steeds shod and slender,   905
    Locked for seven years in stable,
    You put white wheat in his manger,
    You gave him wine for morning water,
    You put upon his feet gold horseshoes
    And harnessed him with silver bridle   910
    When you let her[1] leave the stable
    Neither sea nor land she avoided;
    She leapt the gate of seven latchets,
    And the great gate that was beside it.
    The King asked "Who's the able fellow?"   915
    "Young Donald from Lagan Lasrach."
    His page asked him into the castle,
    The King gave him of gold a hat full,
    Of gold that had been coined in England;
    He scattered it upon the paddock,   920
    Lest Scotland might be given insult.'

Every verse of this song is to be sung or recited twice, with the first part of the refrain after the first verse, and the second part after the repetition, as I tried to show at the beginning of the song.

XXVI

Truly I am filled with sorrow

(*For tune, see pp. 311–13*)

    Truly I am filled with sorrow
      On the lonely cold knoll,

    I can not climb the braeside,
      I can not pace the dell,   925

[1] *sic*

Cha choisich mi 'n t-achadh,
  No 'm machaire cruaidh,

Cha choisich mi mòinteach
  No 'n còmhnard le luas.

Cha dian mi ceum stòlda   930
  O Dhòmhnach na Luan.

Cha n-e cumha mo charaid
  Th'air m'aire 'n ceart uair.

No cumha mo leannain,
  Ged a dh'fhanadh e bhuam.   935

Ach cumha mo bhràthar,
  Cùl fàinneach nan dual.

Ge do rinneadh do bhàthadh,
  Bu tu snàmhaich' a' chuain,

Agus sgiobair a' bhàta   940
  'S muir a' gàirich ri cluais.

'S e mo ghràdh do chùl clannach
  Anns an fheamain 'ga luadh',

'S e mo ghràdh do chùl ceutach
  'Ga reubadh 'san stuaidh,   945

'S e do chluasag an fheamain
  'S fliuch do leaba 's gur fuar,

'S iad na ròin do luchd-faire,
  Liom tha 'n naidheachd ud cruaidh.

Cha n-eil bàt' thig o'n rubha,   950
  Nach ruthaich mo ghruaidh.

No eathar o'n chaolas,
  Nach caochail mo shnuadh.

Tha do phreasain am chiste,
  Nì bu mhisde mi bhuam.   955

Tha do rìobainnean sgàrlaid
  Gu deàrrsadh am ghruaig.

I can not walk the firm machair
　　Or step through the fields,

I can not walk the moorland
　　Or speed o'er the plain.

I can not make a firm step　　　　　　　　930
　　Since Sunday of doom.

'Tis not lamenting a friend
　　That fills my mind now,

Nor lamenting my sweetheart,
　　Though parted we were.　　　　　　　935

But lamenting my brother
　　With his long curling hair.

Though your death was from drowning,
　　You could swim the deep seas.

You were the ship's captain　　　　　　　940
　　When the sea sang to her sails.

The long hair that I care for
　　Midst the seaweed is toss'd,

The fine hair of my loved one
　　Is torn by the waves.　　　　　　　　945

The wrack is thy pillow,
　　Cold and wet is thy grave,

The seals are thy wake-folk,
　　For me a cruel tale.

No boat weathers the headland　　　　　950
　　But my cheek becomes red,

No boat sails through the channel
　　But my countenance pales.

In my kist are thy presents
　　Whose loss I'd bewail—　　　　　　　955

Thy ribbons of scarlet
　　To brighten my hair,

'S do lamhanan sìoda
    Gu miadachadh m'uaill.

Tha do nèapagain sìoda   960
    Cumail dian orm o'n fhuachd.

Tha do leaba 'na h-ònar
    Anns an t-seòmbar ud shuas.

Cha déid mi 'ga càradh,
    'S thusa, ghràidh, cho fad' bhuam.   965

XXVII

'S mi 'm aonaran am Beinn a' Cheòthain

Hò hi rì o ho ri ghealladh i
Ho i a bhó,
Fair all il o ho hi ri o,
Hò ri ghealladh i, ho i a bhó.

'S mi 'm aonaran, hò hi, *etc.*   'm Beinn a' Cheòthain, hò hi, *etc.*
Thog iad orm, hò hi, *etc.*   gun d'rinn mi' n t-òran, hò hi, *etc.*
Ma rinn mi h-aon,   nì mi dhà dhiu,
Nì mi tuilleadh dhiu   masa beò mi.

Tionndaidh

Gura h-e mo   ghaol-sa Dòmhnall,   970
Ort a thig na   h-airm an òrdugh,
Claidheamh is sgiath   bogha is dòrlach,
Cuinnsear caol 's a   thaobh air òradh.

Tionndaidh

Gura h-e mo   ghaol 's cha bheag orm,
Ceist nam ban bho   Eilein Bheagram thu,   975
Gu Bealach bàn   Chille Pheadair,
'S gu Cill' Amhlaidh   nam ban beadaidh,
Gu Snaoiseabhal   am biodh an t-eabar,
Gu Staonaibrig   nam ban bleideil,
Gu Ormaglaid   nam ban teisteil,   980

Thy gloves which are silken
To heighten my pride,

Thy fine silken kerchief   960
To protect me from cold.

Thy bed it is empty
In the chamber above,

I will not go to make it
While thou, love, art so far.   965

XXVII

I am alone on the misty mountain

(*Tune not recovered*)

I am alone   on the Misty Mountain,
I made the song,   or so they're telling—
If I made one   I'll make two of them,
If I survive   I'll make more of them.

Turn

My own true love   indeed is Donald   970
To thee become   arms in order,
Sword and shield,   bow and quiver,
Narrow dirk   whose side is gilded.

Turn

My love he is   my love, not little
beloved of women   From Eilean Bheagram   975
To the white pass   of Cille Pheadair
To Cill' Amhlaidh   of women wanton,
To Snaoiseabhal   where is the quagmire,
To Staonaibrig   of female gossips,
To Ormaclait   of chaste women,   980

Far am bi 'n crodh   laoigh 'san eadradh
Ligeil fìona   moch is feasgar,
Fiodhall 'ga seinn   pìob 'ga spreigeadh.

XXVIII

Chaidh mi do'n bheinn ghabhail fradhairc

Chaidh mi do'n bheinn, hì rì,   ghabhail fradhairc, hì rì,
Chunnaic mi na, o ho ao o,   long 'san fhadhail, o ho ao.   985
Chunnaic mi na, hì rì,   long 'san fhadhail, hì rì,
Struth agus gaoth, o ho ao o,   'n iar 'na h-aghaidh, o ho ao.
Struth agus gaoth, hì rì,   'n iar 'na h-aghaidh, hì rì,

Hì na hó na, o ho ao o,   Ho ro nàilibh, o ho ao.
Hì na hó na, hì rì,   Ho ro nàilibh, hì rì,

O'n thàrla dhuinn, o ho ao o,   bhith 'san fhàsaich, o ho ao.
O'n thàrla, *etc.*
C'uim' nach dugainn   greis air bànran?
Greis air mire   's air ceòl-gaire,
Sìor-chur sìos air   sìol nan àrmunn,   990
Air Torcull donn,   's air a bhràithrean,
Gun iomradh air   sìol na gràisge.

Hì na hó na, o ho ao o,   Ho ro nàilibh, o ho ao,
Hì na hó na, hì rì,   Ho ro nàilibh, hì rì,

Gura buidhe   dhutsa, Mhaighread,
Tha do leannan   air a' mhargadh,
'S leat na preasain   nach bi cearbach   995
Sgeanan beaga   nan cas cairgeach,
Sporain Gallach   nan iall almte,
Crios do leathar   féidh no earba.

Hì na hó na, o ho ao o,   ho ro nàilibh, o ho ao,
Hì na hó na, hì rì,   ho ro nàilibh, hì rì.

Gun dugainn-sa   bòid is chumainn,
Bòid am bliadhna,   bòid an uiridh,   1000
Dha'm bi màthair,   dha'm bi muime,

Where the cows are   at time of milking
Where wine is poured   late and early,
While fiddle plays   and pipe is struck up.

XXVIII

I climbed the ben to scan th'horizon

(*For tune, see p. 314*)

I climbed the ben   to scan th'horizon,
I saw the bark   on ocean riding,   985

West side a wind   against her striving.

Hì na hó na, o ho ao o,   *ho ro nàilibh, o ho ao,*
Hì na hó na, hì rì   *ho ro nàilibh, hì rì.*

Since we are out   on desert moorland

We will a while   with talk amuse us,
A while will play   till laughter moves us,
E'er singing of   the seed of nobles,   990
Of Torcull Donn,   his brothers, surely
With ne'er a word   of rabble crew then.

Hì na hó na, o ho ao o,   *ho ro nàilibh, o ho ao,*
Hì na hó na, hì rì,   *ho ro nàilibh, hì rì.*

'Tis well for thee   so happy Marg'ret
Thy sweetheart he   has hied to market
The gifts he'll bring thee   will be handsome,   995
The little knives   with rugged handles,
The foreign purse   of thong well alummed,
The winsome belt   of roe or stag skin.

Hì na hó na, o ho ao o,   *ho ro nàilibh, o ho ao,*
Hì na hó na, hì rì,   *ho ro nàilibh, hì rì.*

I'd take my oath,   and I could keep it,
An oath of last   year and of this year,   1000
To all with mother,   all with 'weema',

Chuireadh a làmh	'sa chlàr fhuine,	
Chromadh a ceann	sìos do'n chuilidh;	
B'annsa leam fear	bhreacain urad,	
Rachadh 'na bheinn	's dhianadh fuil innt',	1005
Dh'fhàgadh an damh	donn air uilinn,	
'N eala bhàn as	binne luinneag,	
Earbag bheag nan	gearrachas cuimir,	
No ròin léith bho	bheul na tuinne.	

Hì na hó na, o ho ao o,	ho ro nàilibh, o ho ao,
Hì na hó na, hì rì,	ho ro nàilibh, hì rì.

Nighean dubh, nighean dubh,	dùin an darus,	1010
Dùinidh mi e	gu fàin farasd'	
O chaidh ùir air	sùil mo leannain,	
Ùir air sùil mo	cheudghaol falaich.	

Hì na hó na, o ho ao o,	ho ro nàilibh, o ho ao,
Hì na hó na, hì rì,	ho ro nàilibh, hì rì.

Gun dug mise	bòid is gealladh	
Nach sìninn mo	thaobh ri balach,	1015
No duin' uasal	uallach falamh;	
B'annsa bhith seasg	anns na gleannain,	
Ceirb dha m' thrusgan	lùbadh farum,	
Dhol a shealltainn, o ho ao o,	air gach caraid, o ho ao,	
Dhol a shealltainn, hì rì,	air gach caraid, hì rì.	

XXIX

Dh'éirich mi moch maduinn àlainn

O ho, hi ri, nàilibh,
Ho ro, ro ho, hi ri.

Dh'éirich mi moch, o ho, *etc.*	maduinn àlainn, o ho, *etc.*	1020
Dhìrich mi suas	guala Sgàbhaidh,	
Lig mi m'uileann	air a' chàrnaich,	
Dh'amhairc mi bhuam	fad air fàireadh,	
Chunnaic mi long	mhór 'sa bhàghan.	

Who sets her hand   to board of kneading,
Who bends her hand   where stores be keeping;
I'll choose the man   with plaid up yonder
Who'd roam the hill   and there make slaughter,   1005
Who'd leave the dun   deer lowly kneeling,
The snow white swan of song the sweetest,
The little roe   with footprint neatest,
The tawny seal   that haunts the beaches.

Hì na hó na, o ho ao o,   *ho ro nàilibh, o ho ao,*
Hì na hó na, hì rì,   *ho ro nàilibh, hì rì.*

Thou blackhaired maiden, shut the door please,   1010
Please have it shut,   with noiseless motion;
For my lover's eye,   the earth is over it,
His eye who was   my first untold love.

Hì na hó na, o ho ao o,   *ho ro nàilibh, o ho ao,*
Hì na hó na, hì rì,   *ho ro nàilibh, hì rì.*

I gave my oath,   I gave my pledges.
I'd lay me not   by clownish fledgeling,   1015
Nor by noble   proud and spendthrift;
Better childless   in the glens here,
With plaid drawn over my form all slender,
Calling where I   find hearts friendly.

XXIX

Early I rose one morn of glory

(*For tune, see pp. 316–18*)

Early I rose   one morn of glory,   1020
I climbed up far   on Sgabhaidh's shoulder,
I rested my elbow   on the summit,
I cast my glance   along the skyline,
A ship I sight   in the bight before me,

Dé! ma chunnaic,	bu neo-cheàrr i,	1025
Bu lìonmhor oirre	gunna 's cànan,	
Mìle fear fionn	air a h-eàirlinn,	
'S e mo leannan	fear a b'fheàrr dhiu,	
Fear chòta ghuirm	is léine bàine.	

O ho hi ri nàilibh,   ho ro ro ho hi ri,
Nàilibh ho ro ro ho hi ri,   nàilibh ho ro ro ho hi ri.

Gura h-iad mo	rùn mo bhràithrean	1030
Dh'fhalbh a sheachdain	gus am màireach,	
Raghnall, Ailein,	Lachlann, Teàrlach	
Chuirinn geall is	[có nì m'àicheadh?]	
Geall gun sireadh,	geall nach pàighinn,	
Ge b'e cala	nochd an tàmh sibh,	1035
Gum bi mir' ann	is ceòl-gàire,	
Iomairt gu tric	air an tàileasg,	
Air na cairtean	breaca bàna,	
'S air na dìsnean	geala cnàmha,	
Ceòl le fidhill	's ceòl le clàrsaich	1040
Air pìob mhór	nam feadan àrda,	
Bualadh bòrd is	leòis air dheàrnaibh.	

O ho hi ri nàilibh,   ho ro ro ho hi ri,
Nàilibh ho ro ro ho,   hi ri nàilibh.[1]

Nàilibh ri nàil,	nàilibh ri triall	
Mo thriall, mo thriall,	mo thriall sàibhir,	
Mo thriall dachaigh	. . . . . .	1045
Gu tùr nan tùr,	gu tùr Sgàbhaidh,	
Gu tùr m'athar	fhìn 's mo mhàthar,	
Far an d'fhuair mi	gu h-òg m'àrach,	
Cha b'ann air sàil	gorm nam bàirneach—	
Air fìon 's air beòir	's air leann làidir	1050
'S air bainne cìoch	nam ban bàngheal.	

O ho, hi ri, nàilibh,
Ho ro, ro ho, hi ri.

[1] *Sic* MS.

And while I saw her   a flaw was nowhere,   1025
Cannon and guns   in number told not,
Fair men a thousand   crowd her holding;
My sweetheart is   the best aboard her,
With his coat of blue   and shirt of snow white.

O ho hi ri nàilibh,   *ho ro ro ho hi ri,*
Nàilibh ho ro ro ho hi ri, *nàilibh ho ro ro ho hi ri.*

My own brothers   are my darlings   1030
Who went a week   ago tomorrow,
Ranald, Allan,   Lachlan, Charlie,
I would wager   [and who'll gainsay me?]
Wager unsought,   wager I'll pay not,
Whatever harbour   tonight's your shelter,   1035
There'll be fun there,   sport and laughter,
Many a game   of backgammon,
And at the cards   white and speckled,
And with the dice   white and bony,
Fiddle tunes   and harps a-playing,   1040
And the great pipe   of shrill chanter,
Beating tables,   hands all blistered.

O ho hi ri nàilibh,   *ho ro ro ho hi ri,*
Nàilibh ho ro ro ho,   *hi ri nàilibh.*

Nàilibh ri nàil   *nàilibh* for going
My going, my going,   my rich departure
My going homewards   1045
To the tower of towers,   to the tower of Sgabhaidh,
To my father's tower   and my mother's
Where I early got   my rearing
Not on sickly   soup of limpets—
On wine and beer   on ale strongest,   1050
On breast milk   of white-palmed women.

131

XXX

Cha labhair mi 'n t-òran

I hoireann ó ro ho,
I hoireann ì ù o,
I hoireann ó ro ho.

Cha labhair mi 'n t-òran,
    I hoireann, *etc.*

Cha mheòraich mi 'm facal,
'S mi 'n leabaidh am ònar,
    'S mi 'g ionndrainn mo leannain   1055
Fleasgach fearail ciùin eòlach,
    Fear a chinneadh Mhic Cailein
Thig o thalla nan ròiseal;
Ach nam faighinn air m'òrdugh,
Bu leat Ceapach na Sròine   1060
Le a cnocaibh 's le leòdaibh,
    Gu corca, gu eòrna,
    Gu peasair, gu pònair.

Atharraich

Dhia, beag a' ghaoth làidir,
Gun digeadh na bràithrean,   1065
Fear Bhorghraidh 's Fear Bhàlaidh,
Fear Heisgeir an t-sàile,
Fear òg Taigh-a'-gheàrraidh,
'S Fear Ghriminis slàn duibh.

Tionndaidh air

Mìle soiridh, ciad fàilte   1070
    Bhuam gu Màiri 's a faicinn,
Gu bean òg a' chùil dualaich,
    'S nan gruaidhean dearg daithte;
'S tric a bha mi 's tu, Mhàiri,
    Air àirigh le'r martaibh,   1075
Dianamh ìm agus chàise,

XXX

I will not sing the ballad

(*For tune, see pp. 318–21*)

I will not sing the ballad,

    No word I remember,
Alone in my chamber
    Desiring my sweetheart,   1055
Manly mild youth of wisdom,
    Of the race of Mac Cailein
From the hall of the banners;
But if I had the ord'ring
Yours was Keppoch of Strone,   1060
With its hillocks and pastures,
Good for oats and for barley,
For peas and for beans.

Change

    May God the wind lessen
To let come the brothers,   1065
Lairds of Boreray and Vallay,
Laird of Heisgeir in the ocean,
Young laird of Tighgarry,
Laird of Griminish, safely.

Turn it

    To Mary a thousand   1070
    Farewells, hundred greetings
To the lass of the tresses
    And the cheeks red and rosy;
Oft were you and I, Mary,
    At the sheiling with our cattle,   1075
Making there cheese and butter,

133

Toirt na blàthcha gun cheannach,
　Muigh air àirigh na buaile,
　　Sopag luachrach 'na darus,
Muigh am bothag an t-sùgraidh,　　　　　　　　1080
　'S gun 'ga dùnadh ach barrach;
Ann an gleannan àrd fiadhaich,
　Mharbhte fiadh is laogh breac ann,
Coileach dubh air bàrr géige,
　'S moich' a dh'éibheadh ro' latha;　　　　　1085
Thigeadh féidh anns a' bhùireadh
　'Gar dùsgadh le 'n langan,
Thig gach ian anns an dùrdail
　'Gar dùsgadh ro'n latha,
Bhiodh a' chuthag 's gug gùg aic',　　　　　　1090
　Seinn a ciùil duinn air chrannaibh.

XXXI

'S moch an diu a rinn mi éirigh

Fail il o ro fail i ill o,
Fail u ill o ho ro éileadh,
Fail il o ro fail i ill o.

'S moch an diu a rinn mi éirigh,
　Fail il o ro, *etc.*

Ge moch an diu, 's moch an dé e,
'S moiche màireach e ma's éiginn;
Dhìrich mi suas gual' an t-sléibhe,　　　　　1095
Fhuair mi ghruagach dhonn gun éirigh
Phaisg mi an lùib mo bhreacain fhéin i,
Thuirt i rium gun d'rinn mi 'n eugcoir.
Thug mi bòid nach éireadh beud dhi,
Gus am faighinn toil na cléire,　　　　　　　1100
'S toil ar càirdean fhìn le chéile;
Dh'iarr i ormsa nì nach b'fheudar,
Dhol a shuirghe air nighean Rìgh Éirinn,

134

Getting buttermilk for nothing,
At the sheiling of the cowfold,
  In its door a wisp of rushes,
At the sport-making sheiling,   1080
  Only closed by a birch branch;
In the lofty wild valley
  Deer and fawns could be killed there,
Blackcock on high branches
  Which earliest is calling,   1085
Deer would come at the breeding
  Waking us with their belling,
Every bird would come murmuring
  To wake us at day break,
The cuckoo was calling,   1090
  Singing to us on the treetops.

XXXI

This morning I have risen early

(*For tune, see pp. 322–4*)

This morning I have risen early,

And yestermorn was no less early,
And so tomorrow if it may be;
I climbed up on the mountain's shoulder,   1095
The brown haired maid did not yet waken,
And in my tartan plaid I fold her,—
She said to me that I had wronged her—
No ill should come to her I swore it
Till will of clergy should betroth us   1100
The good will of our friends on both sides;
She asked of me a thing I ought not,
To woo the King of Ireland's daughter,

135

'S fàinne òir a chur m'a meuraibh,
Caisteal air gach cnoc an Éirinn,   1105
Muileann air gach sruthan sléibhe.
'S àrd a chluinntear fuaim na cléithe
Aig mnài Uidhist, 's aig mnài Shléibhte,
'S binn guth cinn mo leannain fhéin ann,
Ma's binn a guth, 's fheàrr a beusan   1110
Air chùl corrain 's air chùl cléithe;
Deoch mo chreiche do dheoch réitich,
Dh'òl an t-òigeir donn an dé i;
Siod mo chomhairle, 's dian feum di,
Na doir bean a Strath no Sléibhte.   1115

Atharrachadh fuinn

Có siod thall air stràid na meala, a?
Tha sinn ann Clann Nìll a Barraidh, a?
'G iarraidh gu farsuinneachd fearainn; a
Nam bithinnse roinn an fhearainn, a
Cha b'e ur cuid a bhith falamh dheth   1120
Bu libh Rùm is Eige 's Canaidh, a
Eilein nam Muc, 's tìr Mhic Cailein,
Àrasaig fo'r caoirich gheala,
Sléibhte riabhach fo'r cuid ghearran,
An Ceann a Tuath gu dianamh leanna,   1125
An Ceann a Deas gu dianamh arain,
'S moch an diu a rinn mi éirigh.

XXXII

Siùbhlaidh mi 's fàgaidh mi 'm fearann

Siùbhlaidh mi 's fàgaidh mi 'm fearann,
   Hì rì ill ù ill ò ho,

Falbhaidh mi air bòrdaibh daraich,
   Ho ro hu o, ho ill o.

Falbhaidh mi air bòrdaibh daraich,
   Hì rì ill ù ill ò ho,

To put a gold ring on her finger,
A castle on each mound in Ireland,   1105
A mill on every mountain streamlet.
Loud the song of waulking table
Raised by Sleat and Uist maidens,
Sweet my sweetheart's voice mid theirs is,
Sweet her voice, but none compares with   1110
Her when sickle blade she swings it;
Thy betrothal draught sore pains me
Yestere'en the brown youth drained it,
This my counsel, see ye weigh it,
Bride from Strath or Sleat ne'er take ye.   1115

Change of rhyme

Whom see I a-walking past me?
We are clan MacNeil from Barra,
Searching for a land less narrow,
If I had the land to mark off,
You should have a share instántly,   1120
Rum you'd have, and Eigg and Canna,
Muck as well as all Mac Cailein's,
Arisaig your sheep would carry,
Brindled Sleat would run your garrons,
Uist north to fill th'ale barrel,   1125
Uist south to raise the bannock;
This morning I have risen early.

XXXII

I will go, I'll leave the country

(*For tune, see pp. 325–6*)

I will go, I'll leave the country,

I will go on oaken plankings,

I will go on oaken plankings,

137

Ruigidh mi tìr-mór na Hearadh,   1130
    Ho ro hu o, ho ill o.

Ruigidh mi, *etc.*
    Hì rì ill *etc.*

Far an d'fhuair mi gu h-òg m'aran,
Ma fhuair, cha b'ann air a' ghainne,
Air bainne cìoch 's air fìon daithte,
Air bainne cìoch nam ban basgheal;
Soiridh uam gu Mac 'ic Dùbhghaill,   1135
Dhomhsa b'aithne beus do thùrlaich,
Pìob mhór 'ga spreigeadh air ùrlar,
Ruidhle mu seach air an ùrlar,
Clàrsach ghrinn 's a cruinn 'gan rùsgadh.

Atharrachadh

Ach ma théid thu do'n choill' iùbhraich,   1140
Fiosraich fhéin a' chraobh tha liùmsa,
Craobh as mìsle 's as buig' ùbhlan,
A bun a' fàs 's a bàrr a' lùbadh,
'S a cuid meangan air gach tùbh dhi,
Seileach òg 's a bhàrr a' liùgadh.   1145

Atharraich

Ach ma théid thu do'n choill' fhiosraich,
Fiosraich fhéin a' chraobh 'm bheil mise,
Chraobh a thilg a h-eàrr 's a h-iteach,
Chraobh a thilg a bàrr 's a miosan,
Chraobh a thilg a peighinn phisich.   1150

[*Atharraich*]

Seall a mach am faic thu 'n fhairge
No có sheinn an fhìdeag airgid?
Mac mo Rìgh a' tighinn do dh'Alba
Air luing a' mharaiche ghreannmhor,
Ulagan òir air gach ball dhi,   1155
Le stiùir òir is trì chrainn airgid,
'S *ruiginn* oirre 'n t-sìoda Fhrangach.
    Hì rì ill ù ill ò ho.

138

I will reach the Harris mainland,   1130

I will reach the Harris mainland,

Where I was reared in my childhood,
If I was, 'twas not on scarceness,
On breast milk and wine of colour,
On breast milk of white-palmed women;
Farewell from me to Mac 'ic Dubhghaill   1135
Well I knew your household's custom
Great pipe struck up on dance floor,
Reels in turn upon the dance floor,
Pleasant harp with its keys uncovered.

Change

But if you go to yew forest,   1140
Seek the tree of my belonging,
Sweetest tree with apples softest,
Root a-growing, top twigs bowing,
Spreading branches far around her,
A young willow its top down bowing.   1145

Change

If ye go to tended orchard,
Seek the tree whereon I'm fostered,
Tree that cast its tail and feather,
Tree that cast its leaf and produce,
Tree that cast its 'lucky penny'.   1150

[*Change*]

Look outside, do you see the ocean
Or who sounded the silver whistle?
My King's son is coming to Scotland
On the ship of the lively sailor,
Golden pulleys on each rope,   1155
Three silver masts and golden rudder,
French silk makes the rigging on her.

XXXIII

Cha déid mise, cha déid mì

O hura bhi o hi,
I a bho ho ao o hi,
O hura bhi o hi.

Cha déid mise, cha déid mì,
   O hura bhi, *etc.*

Cha déid mi do Cheann Loch Fraon
Far an dig an t-iasg air tìr,   1160
Far am beir an crodh na laoigh,
Far am fàsadh an subh craobh,
Dearcagan air bhàrr a' fhraoich.

Atharraich

Cha déid mise, cha déid mì
Cha déid mi do ghin a's tìr;   1165
Cha déid mi do mhac a' mhaoir
Gus an dig mo leannan fhìn,
Giamanach a' ghunna chaoil
Leagadh an eal' air a taobh,
'S earba bheag nan gearrachas caol,   1170
'S lacha bheag a' mhuineil chaoil.

Atharraich

Cha déid mise, cha déid mì,
Cha déid mise 's tusa 'n eilein;
'S aithne dhomh fhìn gu dé 's coireach—
Mise gòrach, 's tusa foilleil—   1175
Gun an t-eathar anns an eirthir.

Atharraich

Tha mi torrach, c'uime 'n ceilinn?
Cha n-ann bho fhear crìon no goirid—
'S math as aithne dhomh do shloinneadh,
Cha Chamshronach, cha Mhac Coinnich,   1180
Dòmhnallach deas làidir loinneil,

XXXIII

I'll not go, no, not I

(*For tune, see p. 327*)

I'll not go, no, not I,

    Where Lochbroom its bayhead lies,
    Where the fish is landed dry,   1160
    Where all fretful are the kine,
    Where there grows the sweet woodbine,
    Berries mid the heather shine;

Change

    I'll not go, no, not I,
    To one man of this land kind;   1165
    Factor holds no hand of mine
    Till my own love comes nigh—
    Huntsman he the gun can ply,
    Swan he'd fell upon its side,
    Little roe so swift and shy,   1170
    Mallard slim-neck every dye.

Change

    I'll not go, no, not I,
    Nor will you go to the Island;
    Well I know why to avoid it!
    I am foolish, you beguiling,   1175
    Boat on coast there's none to find there.

Change

    I am pregnant, wherefore hide it?
    From no puny man's beguiling;
    Well I know to tell his line too,
    No Mackenzie, Cameron before him,   1180
    But Macdonald, handsome, sprightly.

141

Bhiodh sibh air toiseach gun fhiamh,
'S bu libh toiseach a dhol sìos,
Agus deireadh tighinn a nìos,
Cha déid mise, cha déid mì.   1185

XXXIV

Cha n-eil falt orm air fuireach

Tha fonn an òrain a leanas ri chantuinn air atharrachadh dòigh, mar
a chìthear ann an rann no dhà 'na thoiseach.

            O hu ill o ho ro
     Cha n-eil falt orm air fuireach,
            O hu ill o ho,
            Hi ri ho ro,
            Hu ill o ro.

     Cha n-eil falt orm air fuireach,
            O hu ill o ho ro,
     Nach do chnàmh mar an duilleach,
            O hu ill o ho,
            Hi ri, *etc.*

     Nach do chnàmh mar an duilleach,
            O hu ill o ho ro,
     Mar challtuinn, mar chuileann,
     'S mi mar ian an cois tuinne
     Mu'n òganach chuimir;   1190
     Nuair a théid thu do'n mhunadh,
     Bu tu 'n t-ianadair fuileach,
     B'fhearr bhith triall na bhith fuireach,
         Na bhith fuireach ri d' luaidhe.
     Thog iad ormsa mar ailis   1195
         Gum bu leannan dhomh 'm buachaill',
     Cha robh ac' ach na breugan,
         Agam fhéin cha robh luaidh air.

Atharraich

     Gura càirdeach mo leannan
         Dha na falannan uasal   1200

142

You're the foremost in the onset,
First to meet the foe advancing,
Last to leave the field of carnage.
I'll not go, no, not I.   1185

XXXIV

Not a hair is remaining

The refrain of this song is to be sung in alternative ways, as will be
seen from the first verse or two at its beginning.

(For tune, see p. 328)

Not a hair is remaining

On my head, that's not withered

On my head, that's not withered

Like sea-holly or hazel,
I'm like bird on the seashore
For my young handsome lover;   1190
When you go to the hillside
You're the bloodthirsty fowler,
Better go than be waiting,
Than be waiting your gunshot.
Other folk have reproached me   1195
    That a cowherd's my sweetheart,
They only were lying
    I had naught to say of him.

Change

    My sweetheart's related
      To the noblest of families,   1200

Do Mhac Leòid anns na Hearadh,
'S dà mhac Alasdair Ruaidh leat,
Car' thu Dhòmhnall Gorm Sléibhteach,
Làmh a reubadh a' chuain ghlais;
Car' thu charaibh Mhic Dhùbhghaill,   1205
Thig o ghiùthsaich na stuaidhe.

Atharraich

Ach, a Mhàiri nighean Ruairidh,
Gura deurach, bochd, truagh thu,
Ged a théid thu do'n leabaidh,
Cha n-e 'n cadal tha thuar ort;   1210
'S beag an t-iaonadh liom fhéin sin,
B'e do chéile 'n duin' uasal;
Cha robh mais' a bh'air duine
Nach robh urad do bhuaidh air,
Bha e treubhach, treun, tapaidh,   1215
Gu ciùin, macanta, suairce—
Cha n-eil falt orm air fuireach,
Ho hu ill o ho ro.

XXXV

Craobh an Iubhair

Fonn: O chraobh an iubhair, o ho.

'S e Mac Aoidh an duine treubhach,
O, chraobh an iubhair, o ho,

Nì e sìoda dha'n chloimh cheutaich,
O, chraobh an iubhair, o ho,

Nì e sìoda dha'n chloimh cheutaich,
O, chraobh an iubhair, o ho.

Nì e fìon a dh'uisg' an t-sléibhe,   1220
O, chraobh, *etc*.

144

To MacLeod of Harris,
　　Two sons of Alasdair Roy with thee,
Friend to Donald Gorm of Sleat
　　Whose hand cleaved the grey seas
To the friends of MacDougall　　　　　　　1205
　　From the pine wood of the mountain.

Change

But, Mary daughter of Rory,
　　Thou art sad, ill and tearful,
Though you go to your bed,
　　You do not look like sleeping;　　　　1210
Little that makes me wonder
　　That thy spouse was a noble;
No man was so accomplished,
　　That he had not as much virtue,
He was valiant and clever,　　　　　　　1215
　　Gentle, modest and kindly—
Not a hair is remaining.

XXXV

The Yew Tree

(*For tune, see pp. 329–32*)

'Tis MacKay that bears him bravely,
　　O, yew tree, o ho,

Wool he'll turn to silk the fairest,
　　O, yew tree, o ho,

Wool he'll turn to silk the fairest,
　　O, yew tree, o ho,

Wine he'll turn the mountain rain to,　　1220
　　O, *etc.*

Copanan dearg air a' chréadhaich,
Lìon air bhàrr an fhraoich nam b'fheudar,
Muileann air gach sruthan sléibhe,
Tobar fìon' air bhruaich gach féithe,
Caisteal air gach cnoc 's leis fhéin 'ad.   1225

Atharraich

'S e Mac Aoidh a' chòtain eangaich
    Nach iarradh an t-earradh trom,
Chuireadh coisiche 'na dheannaibh,
    Mharcraicheadh an t-each 'na dheann.

Atharraich

Nam biodh Mac Aoidh 'san àite,   1230
No Niall anabharrach a bhràthair,
Cha bhiodh mo thochradh gun phàigheadh;
Bhiodh crodh-laoigh ann 's aighean dàra,
'S na seasgaich air chùl a' ghàrraidh.

Atharraich

Mo ghaol fhìn an cùirteir feucannt,   1235
'S tric a thog 'ad oirnn na breugan
Far nach biomaid fhìn 'gan éisdeachd.

Atharraich

Mo ghaol 's mo ghràdh an t-òg beadarrach,
Dhannsadh gu grinn lùthmhor aigeanntach;
Air ùrlar gum biomaid suigeanta,
Air chnoc àrd gum biomaid beadarrach.   1240

Atharraich

'S math thig dhut an deise chothlamaidh,
'S léine chaol dha'n anart Ghailmhinn,
Clogad cruadhach 's suaicheantas dearg ort
'S paidhir mhath phiostal air chrios nam ball airgid. 1245

Atharraich

Chraobh nan ubhal, gheug nan abhal,
Chraobh nan ubhal, gu robh Dia leat,
Gu robh Moire 's gu robh Crìosda,
Gu robh ghealach, gu robh ghrian leat,
Gu robh gaoth an ear 's an iar leat,
Gu robh m'athair fhìn 's a thriall leat.   1250

Ruddy cups he'll turn the clay to,
Heather top to linen raiment,
Mill on every rill he makes him,
Well of wine at each moor brae foot,
Castle on each knoll sun plays on.   1225

Change

Short his coat in fashion chequered
    He would ask no heavy robe,
He would set the walker running,
    He would hurry steed to foam.

Change

Were McKay still in the country,   1230
Or th'excelling Neil his brother,
Not unpaid would be my dower,
Kine with calves and heifers lowing,
Fattening beeves beyond the townland.

Change

Dainty gentle is my darling,   1235
Oft they spoke the lie of scandal
Of us lovers where we heard not.

Change

My own love's the youthful wanton,
Neat and nimble, lively dancer;
O'er the floor we'd sport and gambol,   1240
On the knowe we'd play and wanton.

Change

Garb of blended woof becomes thee,
Shirt of Galway linen fine-spun,
Helm of steel and crest all blood red,
Pistols, belt with silver studs wrought.   1245

Change

Tree of fruit and branch of apples,
Tree of apples God protect you.
Mary and her Son be with you,
Moon and sun with light assist you,
And the western wind and eastern,   1250
And my father with his means too.

147

Ach ma théid thu dha'n choill' iùbhraich
Aithnich fhéin a' chraobh as liùmsa,
Chraobh as mìlse 's as buig' ùbhian,
Chraobh mheanganach pheurach ùbhlach,   1255
Bun a' fàs 's a bàrr a' lùbadh
'S a meangannan air gach tùbh dhi,
Ùbhlan troma, donna, dlùthmhor.

[*Atharraich*]

Ach ma théid thu 'na choill' fhiosraich
Foighnich a' chraobh am bi mise,   1260
Chraobh a thilg a bàrr 's a miosan,
Chraobh a thilg a peighinn phisich.

XXXVI

Ailein, Ailein, 's fad' an cadal

Hó ró hug a bhi o,
Sìn dug a bhi nàilibh i,
Hó ró hug a bhi o.

Ailein, Ailein, 's fad' an cadal,
    Hó ró, *etc.*

'S fad' o chàirich mi do leaba,
Cha n-ann an taigh an dà chabair,   1265
'San taigh bhàn os cionn a' chladaich.

Atharraich

'S binn liom an fhoirm seo 'gam dhùsgadh,
Cha n-e stoirm nan each 'sa bhrùchda—
Mac Iain le chòmhlan sunndach
Dol a mach 's a steach ro'n dùthaich;   1270
Dol a dh'iarraidh na mnath' ùire,
'S i nighean Fir Cheann Loch Mùideart,
Do'n dian na daoin-uailse 'n ùmhlachd,
'S do'n déid an tuath air an glùinean,
Boineidean gorma 'gan lùbadh.   1275

Change

> If you go to yew tree forest,
> Know the tree of my belonging,
> Sweetest tree with apples softest,
> Branching tree with fruit a-dropping,   1255
> Root a-growing, top twigs bowing,
> Spreading branches far around her,
> Apples heavy, thick and brownish.

[*Change*]

> If you go to tended orchard,
> Seek the tree whereon I'm fostered,   1260
> Tree that cast its leaf and produce,
> Tree that cast its coin of fortune.

XXXVI

Allan, Allan, long thou'rt sleeping

(*For tune, see pp. 333–4*)

> Allan, Allan, long thou'rt sleeping,

> 'Tis long since I prepared thy pallet,
> Not in the house of the two rafters—   1265
> In the white house above the seashore.

Change

> Sweet the noise which me awakens,
> It's not horses trampling seaweed—
> MacIain with his happy Company
> Going from and to the country   1270
> Going to seek the new lady,
> Laird of Kinlochmoidart's daughter
> To whom the gentry offer homage,
> To whom the tenantry are kneeling,
> Humbly doffing their blue bonnets.   1275

149

'S binn liom an fhoirm-s' a tha mi claistinn,
An uiseag a' gairm, 's an là a' glasadh
'S an ceò dùmhail air an leacaich;
Bha mi 'n Ìle 's bha mi 'n Arainn,
Bha mi 'n Suaineart ghorm an daraich,   1280
Cha n-fhaca mi cruach no dais ann,
No pill chriathraidh, no pill fhasgnaidh,
Ach sguabag an sobhal na slataich,
Daoine tighinn beò air min ghradain,
Mnathan a' suathadh le m' basan;   1285
Bha mi 'n Leòdhas a' chruidh chaisfhinn,
'S i mo dhùthaich fhìn a b'ait liom,
Tìr an eòrna, tìr na machrach,
Tìr nan cruachan, tìr nan daisean,
Tìr nan sguaban, tìr nan adag,   1290
Far am faighte 'm biadh gun airce;
Nam bithinnsa an riochd a' ghlaisein,
An riochd a' gheòidh no 'n riochd na lacha,
Shnàmhainn an cuan 's rachainn dachaigh.

Tha am fonn ri ghabhail an déidh gach sreith 'san oran seo, 's faodar
na rainn no na sreathan fhéin a chantuinn dà uair, no dùbailte, 's ann
mar sin as buain' e 's as mò nìthear do luadhadh leis.

XXXVII

Là dhomh 's mi 'm Beinn a' Cheathaich

Fair all al ò, ro ho bhi ò,
Hoireann is ò, ho rò bhi o ho
Hi rì ho ro ho bha, o haodh ò.

Là dhomh 's mi 'm Beinn a' Cheathaich, a   1295
    Fair allal ò, *etc.*

Ruagadh nan caorach 's 'gam faighinn, a
Cha b'e caigeann an dà pheathar, a
No caigeann bheag cheann an rathaid, a

Sweet the sound which I am hearing,
The lark at song, the day at dawning
The mist thick upon the hillside;
I was in Islay, and in Arran,
In green Sunart of the oak-trees   1280
I saw neither stack nor mow there,
Nor winnowing-fan nor riddle,
But a small sheaf in a barn of withies [?],
Men living on meal of graddan,
Women rubbing with their hand-palms;   1285
I was in Lewis of whitefoot cattle
'Tis my own land I like better,
Land of barley, land of machair,
Land of cornstacks, land of haymows,
Land of cornsheaves, land of corn-stooks,   1290
Where food can be had in plenty;
If I were in shape of sparrow,
In shape of goose or of mallard,
I'd swim the sea and homewards travel.

In this song, the refrain is to be sung after each line, and the verses or
lines themselves may be sung twice, or doubled; in this way it lasts
longer, and more waulking is done with it.

XXXVII

One day on the Misty Mountain

(*For tune, see pp. 335–6*)

One day on the Misty Mountain,   1295

Rounding up the sheep to get them—
Not the pair of the two sisters
Nor the small pair of the road's end—

'S ann agam fhìn a bha an sealladh, a
Faicinn do bhàta dol seachad, a   1300
Toirt a cinn do na chuan fharsuinn, a
Mach bho dhùthaich Mhic Nìll Bharraidh, a
Mach bho Chìosamul an aighir, a
Far am faighte chuirm r'a gabhail,
Òl fìon a dh'oidhche gu latha,   1305
Caithream nam fear ag òl leanna,
Sìoda donn 'ga chur air mnathan; a
Gura mise th'air mo sgaradh, a
Ma chaidh biaoirlinn Chlann Nìll seachad, a
Bhrist i an càbla 's dh'fhàg i 'n t-acaire,   1310
Bhrist i am ball a b'fheàrr a bh'aice;
B'aithne dhomh fhìn fir 'ga fastadh, a
Gill' Eóghanain Mór an gaisgeach, a
Niall Gruamach mac Ruairi an Tartair,
Ruairi Òg an t-oighre maiseach, a   1315
Ruairi Bàn b'e 'n làmh ri tapadh e
Is Murchadh Ruadh bho cheann a' chlachain,
Is Murchadh Beag, céile nigh'n Lachlainn,
Dà mhac Iain Mhic a' Phearsain, a,
'S math thig gunna 's sgiath 'nur glacaibh,   1320
Le boineid dhùbhghorm air chùl bachlach, a.

Atharraich

Nuair bha mi 'nam nighinn fo lighe mo ghruaige,
Cha sìninn mo thaobh geal ri taobh balaich shuaraich,
B'annsa leam agam fear geal nach biodh gruaim air,
Fear buidhe donn àlainn gun àrdan gun uabhar,   1325
Dhìreadh am munadh 's a ghunna ri ghualainn,
Sealgair daimh chabraich 'san lag 'm bi 'n luachair
Sealgair a' choilich 's na h-eilide ruaidhe,
Na circeige duinne bheireadh gur as an fhuarniod,
Nach gabhadh a mhasladh a deachamh thoirt uaithe.   1330

        Fair all al ò ro ho bhi ò
        Hoireann is ò ho rò bhi o ho
        Hi rì ho ro ho bha o haodh o.

Am fonn an déidh gach rainn no sreith mar anns a h-uile òran, agus
am fonn dà uair aig atharrachadh na fuaime.

'Twas I myself beheld the vision,
Seeing thy galley going past me,   1300
Setting her head to the wide ocean
From MacNeil of Barra's country,
Out from Ciosamul's joyful castle
Where we used to be a-feasting,
Drinking wine from dawn till nightfall,   1305
Shouts of men their ale a-drinking,
With women wearing brown silk dresses;
'Tis I indeed who am afflicted
If Clan Neil's boat has passed me,
She broke the cable and left the anchor,   1310
She broke the best rope that was on her;
I knew the men engaged upon her,
Great Gill' Eoghanain the hero,
Gloomy Neill son of noisy Rory,
And the handsome heir, Young Rory,   1315
Fair Rory, apt for manly action,
Red Murdo from the end of the clachan,
Little Murdo, wed to Lachlan's daughter,
And the two sons of John MacPherson,
Gun and shield befit your handgrasps,   1320
And dark blue bonnet on curling back-locks.

Change

When I was a girl 'neath the sheen of my tresses,
I'd not lie myself down beside any mean fellow,
I'd prefer a fine man who'd never be churlish,
A handsome man, dark yellow haired, not conceited,   1325
Who'd climb on the moor with his gun on his shoulder,
Who'd hunt antlered deer in the rush-covered valley,
Who'd hunt the [black] cock and the red roedeer,
And the grey hen who'd raise her brood in the cold nest,
Who'd not be ashamed if her tenth egg were taken.   1330

The refrain after every verse or line, as in every song, and sung
twice when the rhyme is changed.

XXXVIII

'S fhada bhuam a chì mi 'n ceò

Hó i rì i liù i leò,
Hó, hó, i iù ra bhò ho,
Hó i rì i liù i leò.

'S fhada bhuam a chì mi 'n ceò, Hó i rì *etc.*
Chì mi Bheinn Bheag 's a' Bheinn Mhór,
Chì mi 'n driùchd air bhàrr an fheòir.
An cuala sibh mar dh'éirich dhòmhs'?
Bhrist an rachdan, shrac an seòl,⠀⠀⠀⠀⠀⠀⠀⠀⠀⠀1335
Dh'fhalbh na croinn 'sa chuan mhór,
Dh'fhalbh na b'fhaide leam na seòid.
Ge math leam mac m'athar beò,
Mac mo mhàthar rinn mo leòn
E bhith 'san fheamain gun deò,⠀⠀⠀⠀⠀⠀⠀⠀⠀⠀1340
'S nach giùlain a choluinn clò,
'S nach giùlain a chas a bh̀rog!
'Illean cridheil, bithibh còir,
Tadhlamaid ann as taigh-òsd'
Fair a' ghlaine, lìon an stòp!⠀⠀⠀⠀⠀⠀⠀⠀⠀⠀1345
Luadhadh nam boineidean mu'n bhòrd,
Cuireamaid air chùl am bròn,
Cha doir caoineadh daoine beò.

XXXIX

Tha 'n oidhche nochd fuar

Air fà lì leo hò
O ho ro ho hù leo,
Air fà lì leo hò.

Tha 'n oidhche nochd fuar, Air fà lì *etc.*
'S i reothadh gu cruaidh;⠀⠀⠀⠀⠀⠀⠀⠀⠀⠀1350

154

XXXVIII

Far away I see the mist

(*For tune, see pp. 337–8*)

Far away I see the mist,
I see Ben Beg, Ben More as well,
I see the dew on grassy tips.
Heard ye how my woe befell?
The traveller broke, the sail was rent,   1335
Into the sea the mast it went,
The gallant boatmen further fared.
O would my father's son were spared—
My mother's son 'tis makes my woe,
He breathes not in the wrack below,   1340
No raiment now his body needs,
His foot no covering but the weeds.
Hearty fellows be ye cheerful,
Let us prove the tavern's hoard,
Fetch the glass and fill the measure,   1345
Tossing bonnets round the board,
Banish sorrow unavailing,
The dead come not to life with wailing.

XXXIX

The night is so keen

(*For tune, see pp. 339–40*)

The night is so keen,
The frost is severe;   1350

155

Cha chadal a fhuair,
Ach a' caoi na dh'fhalbh uainn;
Cha ghillean tha bhuainn,
Ach fear gasda gun ghruaim,
Làmh stiùradh nan stuadh,   1355
I bhith deas no bhith tuath,
Le soirbheas teann cruaidh.

[*Atharraich*]

Thug mi gaol, 's cha cheil mi e,
Dha'n òigeir bhòidheach eireachdail,
Shiùbhlainn beinn is coille leat,   1360
Rachainn do thìr eile leat,
Do thìr-mór 's do dh'eileanan,
Sealgair geòidh is coilich thu.
[Creachadair niod an t-seobhaig thu]
Creachadair nan sgeireag thu,   1365
Nàmhaid an ròin sheilich thu.

[*Atharraich*]

Cha n-eil mi dheth slàn,
Tha m'aigne fo fhràmh,
Bho 'n chaidh orra 'n tàmh,
Ciste chumhag nan clàr,   1370
Air a laghadh fo'n t-sàbh,
Air a dubhadh 's cha teàrr.

XL

'S *mise chunnaic an t-iaonadh*

O ho hi o hao ri ù,
O ho hi o hao ri ù,
O ho hi o hao ri ù

'S mise chunnaic an t-iaonadh,
Maduinn mhoch 's mi 'g iarraidh chaorach,
O ho hi *etc.*

I cannot get sleep,
For who left us I weep;
Not lovers we miss—
A champion ungrim,
Who'd steer mid the reefs,   1355
Be the wind as it lists,
Blow it ever so stiff.

[*Change*]

Loved I and I'll hide it not,
Handsomest youth knightliest,
Hill and wood I'd range with thee,   1360
With thee amid the strangers live,
Be they Isle or Mainlandsmen;
Foe of cock and wild goose he,
Oft he robbed the falcon's nest,
Rocks he'd scour of cormorants,   1365
Foeman he of thick-lipped seal.

[*Change*]

I feel not well,
My spirit is quelled
Since the day that you slept
In the narrow deal bed   1370
The saw cut the shape
With blackness on spread.

XL

'Tis I who beheld the exploit

(*For tune, see pp. 341–4*)

'Tis I who beheld the exploit
At dawn while I my sheep was seeking,

Maduinn mhoch 's mi 'g iarraidh chaorach,
Chì mi bàta staigh dha'n chaolas,   1375
  O ho hi, *etc.*

Dithis air ràmh 's fear 'ga taomadh,
Fear eile a' togail a h-aodach
Bean 'na toiseach 's ise air glaodhaich,
Bean 'na deireadh 's ise air chaoineadh;
Theann mi null an càirdeas caomh dhi   1380
Dh'fhiosraich mi dhi gu dé adhbhar:—
'Cha n-e bàs nan gamhna caola,
Ged a bha 'd sa' pholl gun fhaotainn,
'S an t-earrach 'gan cur an caoilead,
'S an samhradh 'gan cur an daoiread—   1385
Cha n-e sin a tha mi caoineadh,
Ach am fear dha'n d'rug mi naonar
A bhith ri druim a' chuain gun fhaotainn,
'S mo thriùir bhràithrean gacha taobh dheth;
Fhuaras do chùl donn fo'n fhaoilinn,   1390
Craiceann chùl do chinn orr' aodann,
Craiceann do dhà chois orr' aobrann,
'S cirb dhe do bhreacan craobhach;
'S e mo làmh-sa fhuair a shaothair,
Cha chreidear mi 's mi 'nam aonar,   1395
Gus am faigh mi tuilleadh dhaoine.'

[*Atharraich*]

'Dh'fhalbh iad gu dorus bial uamha,
Bha mo bhràithrean fhéin 'nan suain ann,
Ghabh iad huca sgianan fuara;
'S e mo leaba fhéin bu chluain daibh   1400
'S e mo phlaide dhaibh bu chluasag,
Bha mi 'nam ruith huc' is bhuatha,
Tarruinn a lodanan fuara,
'S e mo bhasan fhéin bu chuach dhaibh;
Chì mi còmhlan seach an leacainn   1405
Fear air fhichead is caiftein.'

158

At dawn while I my sheep was seeking,
I see a ship enter the channel,   1375

Two at the oars, another baling,
Another yet her sails a-hoisting,
In her bows a woman wailing,
In her stern a woman crying;
With kind intent I went o'er to her,   1380
I asked of her what was the reason:—
' 'Tis not the death of lean young cattle
Though they were bogged and unrecovered
While the spring adds to their leanness
And the summer, to their dearness;   1385
'Tis not that that I'm lamenting
But the sire of my nine children
Who on the high seas is now missing,
And beside him my three brothers;
Thy brown hair was found 'neath tidemark   1390
Thy back scalp upon thy visage,
Thy legs' skin upon thy ankles,
A fold of thy plaid a-flowing;
'Twas my hand that had the trouble,
I alone folk will not believe me,   1395
Until I get other people.'

[*Change*]

'To a cave's mouth they departed,
My own brothers were asleep there,
With cold weapons they approached them;
'Twas my own bed on which they rested,   1400
'Twas my plaid that was their pillow,
Here and there I was a-running,
Drawing water from cold puddles;
For them 'twas my hands that cupped it;
I see a company the hillside passing,   1405
Twenty-one men and a captain.'

NOTES ON THE TEXT

Abbreviations

C.G.	Alexander Carmichael, *Carmina Gadelica*.
C.R.	The *Celtic Review*.
F.A.I.	Amy Murray, *Fr. Allan's Island*.
F.F.S.U.	Margaret Fay Shaw, *Folksongs and Folklore of South Uist*.
F. T.	Frances Tolmie, '105 Songs of Occupation from the Western Isles of Scotland' (*Journal of the Folksong Society*, No. 16).
G.F.B.	J. L. Campbell, Annie Johnston, and John MacLean, M.A., *Gaelic Folksongs from the Isle of Barra* (book of words and discs).
K.	The Killearnan MS. collection of Gaelic songs. This is in the Carmichael Papers in Edinburgh University Library: it is closely connected with the *MacDonald Collection of Gaelic Poetry*.
K. C. C.	K. C. Craig, *Orain Luaidh Nighean Mairi Alasdair* (Glasgow, 1949).
McD.	The Revd. A. MacDonald, minister of Killearnan, and the Revd. A. MacDonald, minister of Kiltarlity, *The MacDonald Collection of Gaelic Poetry* (Inverness, 1911).
O.	Donald MacLachlan's MS. collection of Gaelic folktales and folksongs, made around Oban in the 1890s.
T.G.S.I.	*Transactions of the Gaelic Society of Inverness.*

Note on MacCormick's Text

MacCormick's text is clearly written in a small, but always legible hand. The orthography is good, though it contains a number of peculiarities often associated with the spelling of self-taught writers of Scottish Gaelic. Thus, the apostrophe is often put in the wrong place, *'s* for *is* being frequently written *s,*; and *'ad* for *iad* 'they' being written *a,d*, a spelling which is also used for the homophone *ud* 'yonder'.

The only accent used throughout the manuscript is the grave accent. Besides being used to indicate the ordinary long vowels, this accent is frequently placed over the digraph *ao* (= ɤ:) and the diphthong *ua* (as was done in Old Irish); it is also frequently placed over vowels that are diphthongized or lengthened before final *ll, m, nn, ng*, and *rr* (or in words where such consonants are followed by another consonant), e.g. *danns*, *fonn*, *trom*, *truimb*, *fionn*, *long*, *banntrach*, etc. The word *rinn* is always spelt *reinn* or *rèinn*, corresponding to the pronunciation *röiN/*.

Cn-, *gn-*, are regularly written *cr-*, *gr-*, except in the case of the familiar word *cnoc* in one or two instances.

Throughout the whole manuscript there is a striking uncertainty about the use of single or double *l*, *n*, and *r*, whether palatal or not. Thus one finds spellings such as *Mhic Calain*, l. 1057; *Allain Dùinn*, refrain to No. 1; *òll*, l. 378 and elsewhere; *eagall*, l. 593; *gilean*, l. 423; *broileach*, l. 530; *falain*, l. 571; in the case of *n*, e.g. *faine*, l. 1104 (*fàinne*); *baine*, l. 746 (*bainne*); *annart ascaoinn*, l. 273; *ainein*, l. 4 (*aindeoin*); in the case of *r*, *corain*, l. 1111 (*corrain*); *Hearradh*, l. 7 (*Hearadh*); *bu chòrr*, l. 348 (*chòir*). *Orra* for *oirre*, e.g. l. 364, is well known in the Uist dialect. This does not distinguish between lenited and non-lenited broad *l*, lenited and non-lenited slender *n*, and broad and slender unlenited *r*; other confusions are due to uncertain spelling, not to reproduction of the dialect by the writer.

The dependent forms of the irregular verbs *thoir* (*feir* in Uist Gaelic), *thig*, *abair*, are written usually with *d-* as pronounced, e.g. *dugainn*, l. 435; *cha dig*, l. 38; *du-irt*, l. 431. This spelling in fact is preferable to writing *tugainn*, etc., and very much so to the erroneous *d'thugainn*, etc.[1]

Other forms used by MacCormick that may be noticed are *breachd*, l. 9 (but *breaca*, l. 445); *eir* for *air*, e.g. ll. 441, 933 (but not always); *dhairlich*, l. 797 (*dh'fhairtlich*); *faichte*, l. 753 (the same form was used by Alexander MacDonald in his *Aiseirigh*, 1751, p. 43, for *faicte*); *ròir*, l. 411, for *raoir* (cf. A. MacDonald *a rair*, *Aiseirigh*, p. 170); *soiridh*, l. 1134 (usual Uist form of *soraidh*, cf. *Aiseirigh*, p. 136); and *u* for *thu* throughout (cf. again *Aiseirigh*).

All in all, MacCormick's spelling gives little difficulty to an editor: any unusual eccentricities encountered are mentioned in the following notes.

NOTES

I

Ailein Duinn, o hó hì, shiùbhlainn leat

('Brown haired Allan, o hó hì, I'd go with thee')

MacCormick MS., p. 1.

Air recorded from Miss Janet MacKinnon, Northbay, Isle of Barra (J. L. C. wire no. 1134, in 1954, and again on tape on 28/1/64); and from Mrs. Archie Munro, Lochboisdale, South Uist, on 5/12/63. Also recorded from Mrs. Patrick MacCormick, Hacklett, Benbecula, and from Mrs. Campbell ('Bean Nill'), Frobost, South Uist.

[1] See T. F. O'Rahilly, *Scottish Gaelic Studies*, iii, p. 119.

Other versions: text, translation, and air, *F.A.I.* 151; *F.F.S.U.* 258; part text and air, Gesto Coll. 61; text alone, K. C. C. 105; *T.G.S.I.* xxvii. 394 (from the MacNicol MS.); Òranaiche, 124. MS., Canon MacLean, no. xv.

A Barra version of this song, sung by Mrs. Samuel MacKinnon ('Bean Shomhairle Bhig'), mother of Miss Janet MacKinnon abovementioned, is the basis of the art version published by Mrs. Kennedy-Fraser in *Songs of the Hebrides*, iv. 99. The song also occurs in *Songs of the Hebrides*, i. 128, with an authentic enough traditional version of the words collected and translated by the Revd. Kenneth MacLeod, and an air described as 'noted from the traditional singing of Frances Tolmie'; but it is, in fact, the air communicated by Frances Tolmie to the Gesto Collection transposed a third lower and given a 4/4 instead of a 2/4 time signature. See Miss Ethel Bassin's comments on this in *T.G.S.I.* xxxix–xl. 340–1. It was Miss Tolmie who noted the melody, not Mrs. Kennedy-Fraser.

The song is said to have been made by Annie Campbell, Scalpay, Harris, to her drowned sweetheart Allan Morrison in 1786. The story has been told at length by John N. MacLeod in the Gaelic column of the *Stornoway Gazette*. See also the notes in *F.F.S.U.* 260–1.

11. 'Death of stock in springtime'. Before the coming of the black-faced sheep towards the end of the eighteenth century, the main industry in the Highlands and Islands was cattle-rearing. Loss of cattle through fodder running low in a late spring after a bad winter could be a serious misfortune to a pastoral people; it is often referred to in seventeenth- and eighteenth-century Gaelic folk-songs.

MacCormick's note: *sàbhail* is used intransitively as well as transitively in South Uist: *shàbhail na daoine*, 'the men were saved'.

II

'S mise bhean bhochd chianail thùrsach

('I am a poor, sad, sorrowful woman')

MacCormick MS., p. 5.

Air recorded from Donald McIntyre ('Am Bàrd Ruadh') at Paisley on 14/12/49, wire recording no. 91.

Other versions: text, translation, air, and notes, *F.F.S.U.* 246; text and translation, *C.G.* v. 32; Fr. Allan MS., folio 63; text alone, K. C. C. 102.

50, 51. *Marcraich'*. MacCormick has *Marcaich*, but the South Uist form of the word is *marcraich(e)*.

54. This is Donald MacDonald, son of Iain Muideartach. (John of Moydart, chief of Clanranald from 1619 to 1670. He fought in the Royalist army under Montrose at Kilsythe (cf. l. 56) on 15 August 1645, and in other battles. He was lieutenant-colonel of the regiment that went to Ireland under Alasdair mac Colla Chiotaich, which fought in

the battle of Knockanoss in County Cork where the Royalist leader Lord Taafe was defeated by Murrough O'Brien, Earl of Inchiquin, on 13 November 1647.)

64. See AOINE in Fr. Allan McDonald's *Gaelic Words from South Uist*. The allusion is to a saying *Àireamh na h-Aoine ort* meaning 'may you be drowned'. *Àireamh na h-Aoine*, 'Friday's numbering', was the name of a charm; if it were recited on a Friday in the presence of people bathing, at least one of them would be drowned.

III

Nighean ud thall, bheil thu 't'fhaireachadh?

('Woman would you, if you're waking yet')

MacCormick MS., p. 8.

Translated by Fr. Allan McDonald.

This song is widely known. I have recorded it at various times from the following persons: Mrs. MacDougall ('Anna Raghnaill Eachainn'), Castlebay, Barra, on disc in March 1938; Mrs. Mary Morrison ('Bean Phluim'), Earsary, Isle of Barra, also on a disc in March 1938; Miss Kate MacMillan, Benbecula, on 21/11/49 (wire recording no. 22); Miss Mary Morrison, Earsary, Barra, on 3/1/50 (wire no. 153); Miss Kate MacDonald ('Ceit Iseabail'), at a genuine waulking at Iochdar, South Uist, on 29/3/51 (wire no. 634); and from the late Duncan MacDonald, Peninerine, South Uist, on 27/7/50 (wire no. 388).

Mrs. MacDougall's version can be heard on one of the discs in the set of Gaelic folk-songs from the Isle of Barra published by the Linguaphone Institute in 1950. Another version, text, translation, and air can be found in *F.F.S.U.*, p. 242. Text alone, K. C. C. 81. In MS., Fr. Allan McDonald, folios 35, 86; K. 198, from Nurse Marion MacLennan, printed in McD., p. 254.

There is an art version of this song in Mrs. Kennedy-Fraser's *Songs of the Hebrides*, ii. 157, under the title 'Bloweth the West Wind'. The song is said to have been collected in Benbecula from the wife of Calum Barrach.

94. MacLeod, i.e. MacLeod of Dunvegan (formerly called MacLeod of Harris).

95. Mac 'ic Alasdair, i.e. MacDonell of Glengarry.

96–100. (cf. also 1303). Compare Aodh Mac Aingil *Scáthán Sacramuinte na hAithridhe*, l. 2459 (1952 edition), of the drinking that went on in the houses of the great Gaelic nobles, *muna rabhad na póteireadha ann do ghnáth, ní bhiadh san tigh sin achd cró meathaigh agus áit gan onóir gan mhaitheas gan mhórdháil achd lán do chruas agus do ghortuighi*, 'unless drinkers were always there, that house would only be considered a wretched hut and a place without honour or bounty or grandeur but full of meanness and starvation'.

IV

Nach fhreagair thu, Chairistiana?

('Why not answer, Cairistiana?')

MacCormick MS., p. 11.

Translated by Fr. Allan McDonald.
Recorded from Mrs. Mary Morrison, Barra (disc, 1938); Mrs. D. J. MacLellan, at a genuine waulking at Iochdar, South Uist, on 29/3/51 (wire no. 653); from Miss Janet MacKinnon, Barra, on 5/4/51 (wire no. 724); from Mrs. Campbell ('Bean Nill'), Frobost, South Uist, on tape in 1957. The song is sung at a considerably quicker tempo in Uist than in Barra.
Other versions of the text: K. C. C. 87; *Gairm*, 2, p. 45 (with air). Versions of the words also occur in the manuscripts of Canon MacLean and Donald MacIntyre. The song is not connected with that called 'Caristiona' in *Songs of the Hebrides*, ii. 182, which Mrs. Kennedy-Fraser describes as a 'Clanranald Air collected by Frances Tolmie'.

127. 'Weema' is an anglicization of *muime*, Gaelic for 'foster-mother' (or 'godmother'), used here and elsewhere by Fr. Allan McDonald for the sake of the metre.

137. *Fo leaca troma na dìleann*. In *Gaelic Words from South Uist*, Fr. Allan McDonald has *leacannan troma na dìleann*, the rocky crust of the earth. (See DÌLEANN.) Dr. George Henderson noted *clach dhìlinn*, the eternal rock.

V

Cha n-eil mi gun nì air m'aire

('I'm not free from thoughts that harass')

MacCormick MS., p. 13.

Translated by Fr. Allan McDonald.
Air recorded from Mrs. Mary Steele at Bornish, South Uist, on 9/1/50 (wire no. 195).
Other versions of text: K. C. C. 27, 81; MS., Canon MacLean, no. xxvi.

148–66. A stock description of the household of a great Highland chief in the early seventeenth century.

160. 'Apple rolls'. The allusion is to an incident in folk-tales when the hero, under various penalties, has to clean out a byre so thoroughly that an apple can be rolled from end to end of it and remain perfectly clean. The Augean stable motif. In a story called 'Donnamhara' taken down by Fr. Allan McDonald from Angus MacInnes, Smercleit, South Uist, on 19 October 1896, the hero, the king's son, was threatened by his prospective father-in-law with being put under *geasa* ('tabus') '*mura bi*

*a' bhàthach mhór ud shuas air a cartadh agad as a bheil seachd mìle air
fad nuair a thig mise am bial na h-oidhche an athoidhch' air chor 's gu
ruitheadh ubhall eadar a dà cheann'*, 'unless you have that cow-shed,
which is seven miles long, cleaned out by the time I come at sunset tomorrow so that an apple would roll between its two ends'. Seonaidh
Caimbeul the Lochboisdale bard (1859–1944) in an unpublished poem
made to his wife when she was away in a hospital on the mainland, says:

> *Caileag laghach, shunndach,*
> *Tha i math gu sgùradh,*
> *'S bheir i air an ùrlar*
> *Gun ruith ùbh'l air fhathast.*

'A nice, happy lass, she is good at scouring, and she'll make the floor
so that an apple will roll on it yet.'

The apple was the ambrosial food of the Gaels in the old stories, cf.
Quiggin, *Prolegomena to the Study of the Later Irish Bards*, p. 26.

170. For goats in the economy of the Highlands in the old days, see
article by Basil Megaw in *Scottish Studies*, vii, pt. 2. Goats and sheep
were then called *meanbh-chrodh*, 'small cattle', and were considered of
little account compared with cattle. Theft of goats or sheep was a paltry
matter in a country where cattle-raiding was the traditional kind of
foray.

189. *Buaile bhó*, a fold of cattle (implying they were well-bred cattle).
One of the greatest gifts that could be bestowed in the Highlands. Cf.
the proverb *Bean a taigh mór is bó a buailidh*, 'a wife from the big house
and a cow from a cattlefold' (pedigree herd).

194. MacCormick has *Chuirinn a hiuil air a haineoil*. It is possible this
stands for *Chuirinn i shiubhal air a h-aineoil*, 'I would set her wandering
in places unknown to her'.

196. Fr. Allan McDonald has 'with white sails crowded (or gleaming)' in
his translation. The Gaelic might imply that the anchorage was crowded
with white-sailed galleys, or simply that they often visited it.

VI

Tha 'n latha 'n diu gu fliuch fuaraidh

('The day today is wet and chilling')

MacCormick MS., p. 16.

Translated by Fr. Allan McDonald.

Recorded from Mrs. MacDougall, Castlebay, Barra, in March 1938
(disc no. xxii). On wire from Mrs. Mary MacNeil, Criochan, Barra, on
2/3/50 (no. 271) and from Mrs. Morrison, Earsary, on 5/4/51 (no. 719).
Other versions: F. T., no. 61 (different tune and translation): text in

Puirt-a-beul, p. 45; text alone, K. C. C. 112. There is a version of the tune, with no words, at the foot of p. xxiii of vol. ii of *Songs of the Hebrides*, taken down from 'Isobel of Kentangaval' (in Barra), called by Mrs. Kennedy-Fraser the 'Horned Sea-Creature's Croon' though (as can be confirmed from Frances Tolmie's version) the 'creature' was hornless. There is also a version of the tune, with words, on p. vii of *More Songs of the Hebrides*. In this the chorus is not complete; and there is an art version, under the title of 'The Seal Maiden', with two airs, one from Barra and one from Frances Tolmie, in vol. iv, p. 110.

203. *Iaonadh*. This represents the South Uist pronunciation of *ioghnadh*, 'wonder, marvel' as a rule, but as the late Professor Angus Matheson pointed out in *Éigse*, viii. 249, in such contexts as this one it represents *eangnamh*, 'exploit'.

204. MacCormick accidentally omitted the second half of this line; it is supplied here from other versions.

213. Cù Chulainn was the great hero of the Ulster cycle. A version of the Táin Bó Cuailgne was known in the oral tradition of South Uist, see *Toirioc na Tàine*, taken down by Alexander Carmichael from Hector MacIsaac, Iochdar, *T.G.S.I.* ii. 25 (1872).

216. Sìol Ailein, i.e. the MacDonalds of Clanranald. Their coat of arms, as carved on the stone wall of the old chapel at Howmore in South Uist, was 'a lymphad (i.e. galley) with rudder, central mast and sail set; above this is a hand couped bearing a wheel-cross. In the sinister base is a castle and above it a lion rampant; in the centre and surmounting the whole is a bird on a thistle slip' (*Historical Monuments Commission*, ninth report, p. 106). Their badge was heather. The ship, the lion, and the hand are often referred to by Gaelic poets: e.g. Alexander Mac-Donald, *Aiseirigh* (1751), p. 54, says of the Clanranalds:

> *'S mairg naimhde do 'n nochd iad fraoch,*
> *Long, leoghann, craobh, 's laimh-dhearg.*

> 'Pity the foes to whom they show heather,
> a ship, a lion, a tree, and a red hand.'

One would therefore expect here *Le sìol Ailein nan long 's nan leómhann*, but *long leómhann* has become stereotyped, as if *leómhann* were an adjective. MacCormick here writes *Na n' Lòng Leòmhainn*. In No. VIII here, where ll. 217–22 recur (308–13), he writes *na n' Long Leòmhann*. Cf. K. C. C. 95, *Le Sìol Cholla nan long leóghann. F.F.S.U.* has here *Le Sìol Ailein mhóir na feòladh.* The occurrence of these six lines in two quite different songs is a good example of the indeterminate nature of Hebridean waulking songs.

220. Mac 'Ille Chaluim, i.e. MacLeod of Raasay. Probably Iain Garbh, who was chief of the MacLeods of Raasay from 1648 until his death by drowning (supposedly due to witchcraft) in 1671. He is still remembered in Skye tradition for his size and strength.

221. An Gruamach, i.e. Dòmhnall Gruamach, thirteenth chief of the MacDonalds of Sleat, d. 1534, son of An Gallach, who was Dòmhnall Gallach, killed in 1506.

222. Dòmhnall Gorm is probably Dòmhnall Gorm Mór, chief of the MacDonalds of Sleat from 1585 to 1617; he was involved in some notable feuds with the MacLeans of Duart and the MacLeods of Dunvegan. As he is referred to as no longer alive, these lines must have been made after 1617.

VII

Di-Sathuirne ghabh mi mulad

('Saturday I felt the gloom come')

MacCormick MS., p. 18.

Translated by Fr. Allan McDonald.

This song is (or was) widely known in South Uist and Barra. I have recorded it from Mrs. MacDougall, Castlebay, in March 1938 (disc no. xxi); Miss Mary Gillies and Mrs. James MacNeil, Castlebay, on 9/3/50 (wire no. 305); Mrs. Kate MacCormick, Benbecula, on 31/10/50 (wire no. 482); Miss Penny Morrison, Iochdar, South Uist, on 2/11/50 (wire no. 517); and at a genuine waulking held at Iochdar on 29/3/51 (wire no. 638).

Other versions: F. T., no. 75 (English translation but different tune); *Puirt-a-beul*, p. 47 (Gaelic text); K. C. C. 41; MS. versions, Canon MacLean, no. v; Donald MacIntyre, p. 23; O., p. 48.

A Benbecula version of the air of this song was used by Mrs. Kennedy-Fraser for her 'Benbecula Bridal Procession', *Songs of the Hebrides*, ii. 125, where the air is said to have been collected from Fr. John MacMillan (then parish priest of Benbecula). In the Introduction (p. xii) to this volume, however, it is said to have been got from the wife of Calum MacMillan ('Calum Barrach') in Benbecula. As will be apparent to anyone who reads the words of a genuine version, such as are given here, the song has nothing whatever to do with bridal processions; it just happened that Mrs. Kennedy-Fraser saw a bridal procession on the day the tune was written down. Use of the air in *Songs of the Hebrides* with English words composed by the collector and Gaelic ones made by Kenneth MacLeod is a typical example of many departures from authentic folksong to be found in Mrs. Kennedy-Fraser's volumes, together with the creation of a false atmosphere and the invention of imaginary song-categories.

230. *Tìr a' mhurain* is a Gaelic kenning for South Uist, where much bent-grass grows on the sandhills along the Atlantic coast.

233. Compare the saying *Oidhche Chaluinn bu mhath cuileann agus calltainn a bhith bualadh a chéile*, 'on New Year's eve it were a good thing for sea-holly and hazel to be beating against each other' (anonymous article on *Aimsirean na Bliadhna* in *Guth na Bliadhna*, v. 352). It was believed that the wind that blew at New Year would prevail throughout

the year, and that it presaged the prosperity of crops and fishing, or the reverse. See GAOTH in Fr. Allan McDonald's *Gaelic Words from South Uist*.

244. Some other versions have here *B'ionraic a' mhèirle fhuaradh agam*, 'it was an honourable theft that was found in my possession'.

249. O. has *'S i Florai bhan an fhuilt chlannaich*, ending here.

260. Duntulm was the seat of the MacDonalds of Sleat, see ll. 220–2.

265. 'Weema' means 'foster-mother'. Used by Fr. Allan McDonald for metrical reasons. Fosterage was common in the old Highlands and considered a very close relationship. Various sayings illustrate this, for example *Comhdhaltas gu ciad, is càirdeas gu fichead*, 'fostership to a hundred degrees, and kinship to twenty'.

VIII

Rinn mi mocheirigh gu éirigh

('Haste made I to rise all early')

MacCormick MS., p. 23.

Translated by Fr. Allan McDonald.

Recorded from Mrs. MacDougall, Castlebay, Barra, March 1938 (disc no. xxv); Mrs. Sinclair ('Ealasaid Iain Dhunnchaidh'), Vatersay, on ediphone in June 1949; Mrs. Mary Steele, Bornish, South Uist, on 9/1/50 (wire no. 198); Miss Mary Morrison, Earsary, Barra, on 2/3/50 (wire no. 281); Miss Kate MacDonald ('Ceit Iseabail') at a genuine waulking at Iochdar, South Uist, on 29/3/51 (wire no. 642).

Other versions: tune, text, words, and notes, *F.F.S.U.* 250; text alone, K. C. C. 94. In MS., Canon MacLean, no. ii; D. MacIntyre, p. 1; K. 19, from Mary MacDonald ('Màiri nighean Dhòmhnaill 'ic Thormaid'), Baleloch, North Uist, printed in McD., p. 242, with alteration in the order of lines.

This song makes two appearances in *Songs of the Hebrides*, the first on p. xvi of vol. iii, where it is described as a 'slow waulking song' heard in North Bay, Barra, in the summer of 1920. The air alone is given and the middle phrase of the chorus, for which no words are supplied, is called the 'verse'. An art version of the song is printed in vol. iv, p. 55, with 'Air and Gaelic Words from Mrs. McKinnon, North Bay, Barra', under the title 'Sea-wandering'. Two lines of the text and the chorus are all that is given, and readers might well be left with the impression that it was a rowing song. The air is closely connected with that printed in vol. iii and both may have the same origin: possibly recordings made at different times were involved.

The Barra versions I have heard bring in a passage about Uisdean Mac 'Ille Easbuig Chléirich, cf. Craig, p. 23.

276. i.e. to keep the cattle out of the young oats and barley.

285. K. C. C. *dùinte*; D. McI., *F.F.S.U. Dùnain(n)*; K. *chùmhnaidh*.

302. i.e. the chiefs would rise with their clans.

307. This line was not translated by Fr. Allan McDonald. Donald Mac-Cormick's transcription of the text originally ended with this line, following which he wrote the note that is printed at the end of the poem; later he added the last fifteen lines of the song (308–22 here) on the next page of his manuscript.

308–13. Compare ll. 217–22, and notes thereon. MacCormick annotated *Dòmhnaill Ghuirm* as follows: *Donull Grùamach s Donull Gallach s, Donull gorm, triuir Do chloinn Raonaill Tighearnan Uist a Chinn a Deas*, i.e. 'Donald Gruamach and Donald Gallach and Donald Gorm, three Clanranald lairds of South Uist'; but they were MacDonalds of Sleat.

321. K. C. C. *cothrom coimhlidh*; D. McI., *cothrom coimhliont*; *F.F.S.U. Cothrom Chainnleam*. The late Professor Angus Matheson suggested these are corruptions for *Coire Chainglidh*, a place in Lochaber.

IX

Dh'éirich mise moch Di-Dòmhnaich

('I rose early Sunday morning')

MacCormick MS., p. 26.

Translated by Fr. Allan McDonald.

Recorded from Duncan MacDonald, Peninerine, South Uist, on 11/4/51 (wire no. 768); and on tape for me by the late Captain D. J. Mackinnon from Mrs. Archie Munro, Lochboisdale, on 14/11/61. Apparently not now widely known.

Other versions: text, K. C. C. 66.

341. Sgorabreac, in the Isle of Skye.

X

'S fliuch an oidhche 'n nochd 's gur fuar i

('Wet the night is, full of coldness')

MacCormick MS., p. 30.

A different version, containing many identical lines, was translated by Fr. Allan McDonald. His translation is followed as far as possible.

Recorded from Mrs. Kate MacCormick, Benbecula, on 31/10/50 (wire no. 484).

Other versions: tune, text, and words, F. T., no. 76; *F.F.S.U.* 208; text alone, K. C. C. 43; MS., Fr. Allan McDonald, folio 88; K. 202, from Nurse Marion MacLennan, printed in McD., p. 263.

The first eleven lines here occur also in a very well-known waulking song beginning *Coisich, a rùin* which is the basis of 'Shoreless Seas' in *Songs of the Hebrides*, iv. 84.

As the text preserved by Fr. Allan McDonald is of some interest, I give it here:

O hù ŏ-hŏ
Hèileadh 's na hù-ro bhŏ-hŏ.

Fliuch an oidhche	*nochd 's gur fuar i*	
Cha n-eil cùram	*orm na buaileadh*	
Na cùram chruidh	*'s laoigh 'gan uallach*	
Ach do chùramsa	*a ghaoil a Ruairidh*	
Thug am bàta	*bàn an cuan orra*	5
'S mo leannan fhéin	*air bhòrd an fhuaraidh*	
Cha n-eil cùram	*orm mu fuadach*	
Cha n-fhear cearraig	*bheireadh bhuat i*	
'S cha b'fhear làimhe	*deis' is fuachd air*	
Làmh cheangal	*nam ball 's 'gam fuasgladh*	10
Gum bu slàn	*dha'n t-saor a dh'fhuaigh i*	
Dh'fhàg e dìonach	*làidir luath i*	
Aigeannach air	*siubhal cuain i*	
'S ioma sgeir dhubh	*bodha 'm buail i*	*(a bhuail i)*	
Agus liaghan	*liath a ghluais i*	15
Agus duilleasg	*donn a bhuain i*	
Agus bàirneach	*ghlas a shuath i*	
Nam bu chuimhne	*'n oidhche bha sinn*	*(bhàth?)*
'N cuan a sheas sinn	*('N Coire Bhreacain) . . . .*	
B'fheudar dhuinn	*na siùil a bheagadh*	20
Bha struth mór ann	*. . . .*	
Saoil sibh fhéin	*nach mór an truaigh' e*	
Dha m' leithid fhéin	*de gheala-ghruagaich*	
Bhith 'm bothaig bhig	*an gleannan uaigneach*	
Fo dhìolanas	*ri mac duin' uasal*	25
Gun òl cupa	*gun òl cuaiche*	
—Fliuch an oidhche.		

I recorded another version of this song from Mrs. David Patterson, Benacadie, Cape Breton, in 1937, with a different chorus: *Fire, faire hó ro ho.* This supplies the missing half of l. 21 here: *bha struth bras ann.* But the truth is that there are several songs of this type in existence, and their words are inextricably confused.

In l. 23, Fr. Allan McDonald has *dheala-ghruagaich*; and a note at the foot of the page gives the second half of l. 24 with a question mark.

XI

Thug mi gaol do'n nighinn duinn

('A brown maiden I wooed')

MacCormick MS., p. 32.

Translated by Fr. Allan McDonald.

Recorded from Mrs. Campbell ('Bean Nìll') and her daughter Mrs. Patrick MacPhee on tape on 30/1/64.

Other version of text: K. C. C. 123. Apparently not now widely known.

XII

Gura mise tha fo mhulad, 's mi air tulaich na buaile

('I am full of sorrow, on the mound of the cowfold')

MacCormick MS., p. 35.

Air recorded from Mrs. Campbell ('Bean Nìll') and Mrs. Patrick MacPhee on tape at Frobost, South Uist, on 30/1/64. Duncan MacDonald, Peninerine, recorded this song on 11/4/51 on wire no. 765, but with a different tune and chorus, which he insisted was the correct one for this song, but they go with another, that in K. C. C., p. 54. Apparently not now widely known.

Other versions of text: K. C. C. 52; Donald MacIntyre MS., p. 64.

415. i.e. a Campbell.

429. It is assumed from the rhyme that a line has been lost here.

435. MacCormick has *air òr u*.

442. MacCormick *Anns an ts-euis*. But metre and sense, and the version in K. C. C., support the reading *anns an t-seisein*, 'in the kirk session'. The reference is to the early Presbyterian discipline for fornication.

XIII

Gura mise tha làn airteil

('Truly I am full of sorrow')

MacCormick MS., p. 36.

This fine song was popular and widely known. I have recorded it from Roderick MacKinnon ('Ruairi Iain Bhàin'), brother of Mrs. MacKinnon ('Bean Shomhairle Bhig'), who sang for Mrs. Kennedy-Fraser at Northbay in 1920, on ediphone on 3/6/37, and on disc in March 1938; from Janet

MacKinnon, daughter of Bean Shomhairle Bhig, in 1954 (wire no. 1135); from Miss Kate MacDonald (daughter of Duncan MacDonald, Peninerine) on wire no. 206 on 10/1/50; from Mrs. John Galbraith, Barra, at Castlebay, on wire no. 274 on 2/3/50; from Mrs. Fanny MacIsaac, Torlum, Benbecula, on wire no. 474 on 31/10/50; from Mrs. Norman MacInnes, Eriskay, on wire no. 678 on 1/4/51; from Mrs. James Mac-Dougall ('Flòraidh Alasdair'), a native of Eriskay, at Castlebay, Barra, on wire no. 730 on 5/4/51; and from Miss Annie MacDonald, who was born and brought up in South Uist, on Canna, on wire no. 1129 on 4/6/55. Singers sometimes begin with l. 447, sometimes with the first few lines of No. XXXI.

Other versions: tune and text, *An Gàidheal*, iv. 184 (1874); text alone, *C.R.* v. 91; K. C. C. 59; MS., Fr. Allan McDonald, pp. 25, 33, 110; Canon MacLean, no. xxxvi; J. L. Campbell, words taken down from Mrs. Geoghegan ('Mairi Seasaidh na Caillich') at Bruernish, Isle of Barra, on 28/6/48; tune alone, M. F. Shaw, *Studia Memoriae Belae Bartók Sacra*, p. 440.

An art version of this song is printed in *Songs of the Hebrides*, iii. 72, the air and refrain from the singing of Marion MacLeod, Isle of Eigg, with words written by Kenneth MacLeod substituted for the real text.

447. The *An Gàidheal* version has *Bheinn Cruachan*.

455. If the song was made in South Uist, *té thuathach* would mean a North Uist woman.

464. Up to this line MacCormick writes the lines down in the form AB, BC, CD, etc.: from l. 465 to the end he writes couplets of the form AA, BB, CC, etc. This is probably a slip.

470. *orr 'o* i.e. literary *air do*, 'on thy'.

XIV

Gura mise tha fo ghruaman

(' 'Tis I who am melancholy')

MacCormick MS., p. 39.

Recorded from Mrs. Marion MacInnes ('Bean Dhòmhnaill Iain') on Eriskay on 6/7/50 (wire no. 323A); and from Miss Anna MacDonald, daughter of Duncan MacDonald, Peninerine, on 30/10/50 (wire no. 465). Other versions of text: K. 16, from Mary MacDonald, Baleloch, North Uist, printed in McD., p. 238; Donald MacIntyre MS., p. 18.

480. MacCormick *m'feilleadh*.

484. MacC. *air pagsa*.

495. i.e. she could not praise him adequately without knowing his family tree.

498. MacC. *na n' seairean*.

506. MacC. *do-altramachd.*

511. MacC. *dug s, nach t-obhair.*

527. MacC. *Muig m Bàthaich.*

530. MacC. *Broileach.*

XV

'S i nochd a' chiad oidhche 'n fhoghair

('Tonight's the first night of the autumn')

MacCormick MS., p. 41.

First ten lines translated by Fr. Allan McDonald.

Recorded from Mrs. A. J. MacLellan, Hacklet, Benbecula, on 21/11/49; from Miss Kate MacDonald, daughter of Duncan MacDonald, Peninerine, on 30/10/50; from Miss Penny Morrison, Iochdar, on 2/11/50; from Miss Kate MacDonald ('Ceit Iseabail') at a genuine waulking at Iochdar on 29/3/51 (wire nos. 24, 473, 514, and 645); and from Mrs. A. Morrison, Milton, on tape.

Other versions: text and translation, *C.G.* v. 36; text alone, K. C. C. 99; in MSS., Fr. Allan McDonald, folio 121; K. 206, from Nurse Marion MacLennan, not printed in McD.; Canon MacLean, no. xxx; Donald McIntyre, p. 52. Some lines from this song occur in F. T., no. 68, but the tune is different.

533. MacC. *ròir.*

551. MacC. *Na ma òll.*

558. MacC. *Mac na mra.*

563. MacC. *gailinn.*

XVI

Bhean ud thall, gu dé th'air t'aire?

('Woman, what may be your thoughts now?')

MacCormick MS., p. 49.

Translated by Fr. Allan McDonald.

Recorded from Miss Annie Johnston, Castlebay, Isle of Barra, on disc in March 1938.

Other versions: text, K. C. C. 114.

There is an art version of this song in *Gaelic Songs of the Isles of the West* by Fr. John MacMillan, Dr. Patrick McGlynn, and F. W. Lewis, ii. 20. Only six lines of text are given.

568. MacC. *gu de th-orr h-aire.*

572. It is possible that 'Mac Allan's Ronald', *Raghnall mac Ailein,* is *Raghnall mac Ailein 'ic Iain Òig,* MacDonald of Benbecula, uncle of John of Moydart mentioned in ll. 53, 77. Ronald died in 1636. He was a well-known person in his time. In 1631 he rescued the Irish Franciscan missionary Fr. Patrick Hegarty, who had been captured in South Uist by the men of the Protestant bishop of the Isles.

576–8. Cf. ll. 564–6.

579. The meaning of *colbh cuilce* here is uncertain. Literally it means 'a pillar of reed'. Fr. Allan McDonald did not translate this line. It is apparent from the entry in his *Gaelic Words from South Uist* that he could not find anyone who could explain the meaning of these words to him. Probably a corruption is involved. Cf. Irish *colbha cúain,* 'the entrance of a harbour'.

584. MacC. *na' n' tèud druit-te.* Fr. Allan McDonald translated *druidte* 'tightened', but it seems more likely it means 'close together' of the strings of a harp.

595. Fionn, i.e. Fionn mac Cumhail.

596. Cf. ll. 214, 218, 309.

'The refrain of this song', etc. MacCormick actually wrote the first part of this note before the song in his manuscripts, the second part after it.

XVII

Siuthadaibh, siuthadaibh, a mhnathan

('On, women, with vigour!')

MacCormick MS., p. 50, where it is called 'Oran Luaidh Le Mairidh Nigh'n Alasdair Ruaidh Mhic Leoid'.

Translated by Fr. Allan McDonald.

Recorded from Mrs. Angus John MacLellan, Hacklet, Benbecula, on 21/11/49; and from Mrs. Nicolson, Iochdar, on 2/11/50 and 29/3/51, the second time at a genuine waulking at Iochdar (wire nos. 16, 503, 637). Also on tape in May 1958 from Mrs. Morrison ('Bean Alasdair Mhóir'), at Milton, South Uist.

Other versions: F. T., no. 58 (tune, 14 lines of text and translation); text alone, K. C. C. 37; Fr. Allan McDonald MS., folios 15, 65; O., p. 5 (24 lines).

This song was overlooked by the late James Carmichael Watson when compiling his edition of the *Gaelic Songs of Mary MacLeod* (for which printed sources were used). See the Revd. W. Matheson, *Notes on Mary MacLeod . . . her Forgotten Songs (T.G.S.I.* xli. 16). Singers always ascribe this song to Mary MacLeod, the seventeenth-century poetess; it is one of the very few waulking songs attributed to a definite author. In his manuscript collection Fr. Allan McDonald heads it *Oran nighean Alasdair*

Ruaidh (Dùn Dhalabrog) san dùnan sìos am machaire 's Màiri Dhubh còmhla rithe. Cha chanadh ise facal 's nuair a bha i ullamh dhiubh bha h-uile facal aicese riamh air a teangaidh, 'a song by the daughter of auburn-haired Alasdair [i.e. Mary MacLeod] (Dùn Daliburgh) in the little dùn down on the links, while black-haired Mary was along with her. She [i.e. black-haired Mary] would not say a word, and when she [i.e. Mary MacLeod] was finished with them [i.e. her songs as she composed them], black-haired Mary had every one of them on her tongue.' His informant was 'Bean Iain 'ic Dhòmhnaill na Càrnaich' in Eriskay.

Elsewhere Fr. Allan McDonald wrote that 'Màiri nighean Alasdair Ruaidh though popularly so called was not "Màiri" at all but Fionnaghal. The delusion crept in owing to a certain "Màiri Dhubh nan òran" [black-haired Mary of the songs] always accompanying her, who sang her songs for her and committed them to memory, as Fionnaghal herself was defective both in memory and singing. The Revd. Alexander Campbell [a native of South Uist who lived from 1820 to 1893] frequently told me that he had a grand aunt who was named after Nighean Alasdair Ruaidh and consequently named "Fionnaghal". This poetess lived for some time in Eriskay, at the spot where Prince Charlie afterwards landed, when he first set foot in Scotland. The site of the house is that now occupied by the house of two sisters McInnes at Coilleag a' Prionnsa' (ii. 15).

'A stream in Smerclet is so called [Struthan a' Bhàird], and the people of the township say the name was derived from the fact of Nighean Alasdair Ruaidh the poetess, having fallen when crossing on horseback. The horse had a leg broken in the fall' (ii. 14).

Fr. Allan McDonald says an Eriskay family was called 'Clann 'ic 'Ille Threubhaich' because 'a story is told that (Màiri) nighean Alasdair Ruaidh the poetess (my informant doesn't call her "Màiri" and never heard a Christian name for her) was crossing Struthan a' Bhàird in Smerclet and was carried across by an ancestor of this tribe and she said "Bu tu fhéin an Gille Treubhach" [you were the valiant fellow] and his descendants were ever after called Clann 'ic 'Ille Threubhaich'.

'The poetess once lost a horse at this stream and she said:

'S beag ioghnaidh mi bhith gun stòras
'S ioma dòigh air a thoirt bhuam
Chosg mi mo leathdusan botal
Tarruinn do chlosnaich gu uaigh.'

(v. 40, 41.)

The late Revd. Dr. Kenneth MacLeod told me (J. L. C.) that a girl called 'Nighean dubh nam fonn' 'the black haired girl of the tunes' used always to accompany Mary MacLeod, and composed the tunes to which her songs were sung, and that an interval leading to a high note such as occurs in the third bar of the tune of this song was characteristic of her tunes. It is likely that she was the same person as 'Màiri Dhubh'.

597. The Revd. William Matheson quotes (*T.G.S.I.* xli. 22) a version of this song printed in 1908 in the *Celtic Monthly* which begins *Siùdaibh, siùdaibh so fhearaibh,* 'come on, fellows', from which he infers that the

song was probably originally a rowing song. If that is so, the persons mentioned in ll. 599 and 601 would be rowers. But in its present form I am told by Mr. John MacInnes that these lines are taken to refer to women at the waulking-board. 'An everyday type of team was four women on each side' as visualized in this song, the persons referred to in l. 601 being the women at the ends of the board, the ones who pulled the cloth across the board and who were always the strongest and the best at the songs.

604. *'San Dùn.* In spite of what Fr. Allan McDonald says about Dùn Dhalabrog, this is usually taken to refer to Dunvegan Castle, seat of the chiefs of the MacLeods.

605. Ruairidh mac Iain was the son of Iain Breac, and was chief of the MacLeods from 1693 to 1699. If he is the person referred to here, the poem can be dated within narrow limits, as the Revd. W. Matheson points out. The metre suggests it was originally *Ruairi mac Sheathain.*

607. MacC. *bhiòrlainn.*

608. MacC. *to-irt.*

609. Fr. Allan McDonald omitted this line in his translation.

614. *Coite* is a derogatory term for a boat. Glossed 'a canoe' in O.

XVIII

Gura mise tha fo éislein

('I am sad and mournful')

MacCormick MS., p. 52.

Recorded from Mrs. A. J. MacLellan, Hacklet, Benbecula, on 21/11/49; from Miss Kate MacDonald ('Ceit Iseabail'), Iochdar, at a genuine waulking, on 29/3/51; and from Norman MacMillan at Lochboisdale on 11/4/51 (wire nos. 25, 639, 778). Mr. MacMillan's air for this song is different from the usual one, and bears a resemblance to that to which Mr. Duncan MacDonald sung the waulking song *'S mór an dùldachd th'air an latha*, K. C. C., p. 107 (wire no. 942).

Other versions: tune, text, words, and notes, *F.F.S.U.* 216; text alone, K. C. C. 47; MSS., Fr. Allan McDonald, folio 79; Donald MacIntyre, p. 94; Canon MacLean, no. xxiv.

A version of the air taken down from A. Nicolson, Braes, Isle of Skye, is printed in *Songs of the Hebrides*, IV. xi.

633. MacC. *mi r' èiginn.*

635. The *banchag* was a person of some importance on old Highland farms, the woman in charge of the dairy, not a mere milkmaid.

XIX

Mi dualach, mi donn

('My hair's curling and dark')

MacCormick MS., p. 54.

Recorded from Miss Kate MacMillan, Torlum, Benbecula, on 21/11/49 (wire no. 17).

Other versions of text: K. C. C. 57; Donald MacIntyre MS., p. 66.

663. MacC. *a thu-irt à. Á* is the stressed form of *e* 'he'.

XX

'S mise 's daor a cheannaich

('Dearly did I purchase')

MacCormick MS., p. 56.

Recorded by Miss Kate MacDonald, daughter of Duncan MacDonald, Peninerine, on 10/1/50 (wire no. 210).

Other versions of text, K. C. C. 98. Two manuscript versions exist in the Carmichael Papers in Edinburgh University. One, which with some other material must have been sent to Carmichael by someone living in South Uist, is headed *Oran Luaidh rinn Boirenach mhuintir a Chinne deas* South Uist *Chaidh gu ruige* North Uist *Agus dhfhuair i paiste diolain Sann na Banchaig Bha i aig nidhan dhomhuill mhic Sheumais*, 'a waulking song which a woman from South Uist made. She went to North Uist and got an illegitimate child. She was a dairymaid for the daughter of Donald, son of James'. This version has thirty-nine couplets. The other version is in the Killearnan manuscript collection of songs from Uist. It is headed: 'This song is by Nighean Aonghuis 'ic Dhomhnuill Bhain 'ic Dhomhnuill Oig [the daughter of Angus, son of fair-haired Donald, son of young Donald]. She was a near relative of Donald MacDonald (Mac Iain 'ic Sheumais) the hero of Blàr Chàirinis. She was buried in the Churchyard of Sand, North Uist.' In the list of contents the compiler states that it came from the manuscript collection of the Revd. J. N. MacDonald, minister of Harris. This version has thirty-four couplets. Unlike most of the songs in the Killearnan collection, it was not printed in the MacDonald Collection of Gaelic Poetry.

There is also a version in Donald MacIntyre's MS., p. 49, and in O., p. 13 (36 couplets).

678. It is clear from all the five other versions referred to here tha
MacCormick has omitted the second couplet of the song, which is:

Chan e mhìod sa dh'ith mi,
Dh'imir mi no dhoirt mi   (K. C. C.)

Cha 'n e mheud sa dhith mi
Dhidir mi no dh'òl mi   (Killearnan MS.)

Cha 'n e mhiod sa mhillinn
Dh'iomair mi na dhoirt mi   (Oban MS.)

Cha meod mo mhillidh
dhimer mi na dhoirst mi   (Carmichael)

Cha n e mheud is a mhill mi
Na a dh imir na dh'ol mi   (MacIntyre)

i.e. it is not the amount (of milk) that she consumed or drank (or
spoilt or spilt) that has cost her so much, but the fact that she has been
raped and is now pregnant.

679. The other versions have here:

Chan e mìod mo shìnead
Mura millinn m'òige   (K. C. C.)

Na ro mheud mo shinead
Ach mi mhilleadh m'òige   (Killearnan MS.)

No mithead mo shinead
Mar a millinn m'oige   (Oban MS.)

Cha be meud mo shinead
ach mi mhillead moigeadh   (Carmichael)

Cha an e meud mo shinead
Mar a millean m oige   (MacIntyre)

MacCormick wrote *mhìad* first and then *mìad* above it.

691. 'Thy galley'—presumably that of her chief or lover.

697. See note on l. 572.

700, 701. MacC. *Laaig.* Laig, a well-known farm on the Isle of Eigg.
The MacDonalds of Laig were connected with the MacDonalds of
Morar; but none of them is a 'John, son of Donald' in the genealogies
printed in *Clan Donald.* O. has *Raonull mac Dhomhuill.*

702. O. has *Athair bean Fear Mor-thir,* 'the father of the wife of the laird
of Morar'.

712. The words *trom dùmhail* are underlined in MacCormick's manuscript.

716. Two couplets follow here in Carmichael's Uist informant's version:

> *Cha be do dheoch chaisge*
> *deoch a uis(g)e an fhuarain*
>
> *Ach baine na tanaich*
> *is fear anns a Bhuailidh*

'The drink to quench your thirst would not be a drink of spring water, but milk of the best cattle in the cowfold.'

726. See under CEANNACHADAIR in Fr. Allan McDonald's *Gaelic Words from South Uist*.

732. MacC. *b'fhùaile*. K. C. C. has not got this line; Carmichael's informant has *siad buidhen a uaire* (? *uaine*); MacIntyre has *S iad buidhean dhomh b'fhuaire*. The couplet is not in K. O. has *'Siad buidheann a b'fhuaire*.

736. For *fhoghluim* (which must be pronounced *fhaoluim* here), O. has *faolainn*, glossed *faoilidheachd*, 'hospitality'. K. has *An fhoghlum* and Carmichael apparently *An fhaolum*. The couplet is not in the other versions.

XXI

Dhòmhnaill òig mhic Dhòmhnaill mhic Ruairi

('Young Donald son of Donald MacRory')

MacCormick MS., p. 58.

Ll. 747–52 and 755–64 roughly translated by Fr. Allan McDonald: revised here.

Recorded from Mrs. Kate MacCormick, Hacklett, Benbecula, on 21/11/49; and from Miss Penny Morrison with chorus at a genuine waulking at Iochdar on 29/3/51 (wire nos. 33 and 652).

Other versions: text alone, K. C. C. 114. A version of the air, taken down from Marion MacKay, Obbe, Harris, was printed by Mrs. Kennedy-Fraser on p. iv of *More Songs of the Hebrides*.

750. *Réiteach*, a formal betrothal, considered binding and nearly as important as the marriage ceremony itself.

753. MacC. *faichte fathast*.

759. MacC. *Cliùth do'n' T-Sìth*.

760. *Bréid*, a kertch, head-dress formerly put on by women in the Highlands the morning after marriage, considered a symbol of wifehood.

761–4. Compare ll. 439–42, and note thereon.

786. Geneva, i.e. gin.

791. *Sgrìob*, a premonitory itch. See *sgrìob* in *Gaelic Words from South Uist*.

XXII

Marbhaisg air a' mhulad, 's buan e

('A curse on sorrow, it is lasting')

MacCormick MS., p. 60.

Recorded from Miss Kate and Miss Anne MacDonald, daughters of Duncan MacDonald, Peninerine, on 30/10/50 (wire no. 472); and from Mrs. Campbell ('Bean Nìll'), Frobost, on tape in the winter of 1958–9 by the Revd. John MacLean for the writer.

Other versions of text: K. C. C. 70; Donald MacIntyre MS., p. 41.

807. i.e. he would return the cattle from the marauders who had stolen them.

808. There is an Achadh Luachrach in Lochaber.

820. In the seventeenth century men in the Highlands still wore their hair long. There are many references to this in waulking songs, see under *cùl*, *falt*, in the glossary here.

823. MacC. has *càlapannan tròma geala*. But the rhyme requires *geala troma*. The conception of white calves of the legs as a sign of nobility is very old in Gaelic literature. Cf. the story of Cath Maige Mucrama, in which Mac Con was recognized at the battle of Cend Abrat by his enemy Eogan by his 'legs (*colptha*) white as snow', wounded, and defeated. See Myles Dillon, *The Cycles of the Kings*, p. 18 n. The expression *calpa geal* occurs a number of times in waulking songs, cf. l. 468 here. The ordinary folk working in the fields would have swarthy sunburnt legs as compared with the nobly born.

XXIII

'S muladach mi 's mi air m'aineoil

('In this strange land I'm not happy')

MacCormick MS., p. 63.

Translated by Fr. Allan McDonald.

Recorded from Mrs. MacDougall ('Anna Raghnaill Eachainn'), Castlebay, Isle of Barra, on ediphone in January 1937; from Miss Kate MacDonald, Peninerine, on 10/1/50; from Duncan MacDonald, Peninerine, on 27/7/50; from Miss Annie Johnston and Calum Johnston at Castlebay, Barra, on 7/8/50 (wire nos. 204, 386, 441); and from Mrs. Campbell ('Bean Nìll'), Frobost, on tape in November 1957.

Other versions of text: K. C. C. 80; McD. 249; MS., Canon MacLean, nos. viii, xxiii, and xxxix; Donald MacIntyre, p. 27; O., p. 1 (44 lines).

An art version of this song is printed in *Gaelic Songs of the Isles of the West*, i. 8. Only four lines of text are given.

The song is in the form of a flyting between a follower of MacLeod of Harris and a follower of MacDonald of Clanranald.

836. *air m'aineachd*. MacC. had *air m'ainneach* (first time) *air m'aineach* (second time). To both of these a *d* has been added in pencil, possibly by Fr. Allan McDonald. O. has *aineachd*. See AINEACH in *Gaelic Words from South Uist*.

841. This line, and also 842 and 843–6, occur in another flyting waulking song, between a follower of MacNeil of Barra and MacDonald of Clanranald, beginning *Cha déid Mór a Bharraidh bhrònaich*, see F. T., no. 73, where only the first part is printed. The respective opponents are said to have been Nic Iain Fhinn and Nic a' Mhanaich. The song was known in Cape Breton but not allowed to be sung at concerts as it could provoke a row between Barramen and Uistmen.

851. MacC. *Mhuntroos*. The well-known Marquis, Royalist commander in Scotland in the Civil War.

XXIV

Cha dìrich mi an t-uchd le fonn

('I'll not climb the brae with song')

MacCormick MS., p. 67.

Recorded from Mrs. Kate MacCormick, Hacklet, Benbecula, on 21/11/49. There is also a tape recording made for me by the Revd. Fr. John MacCormick from Mrs. Effie Monk in Benbecula in 1953.

Other versions: K. C. C. 13. The song is apparently not widely known, today anyway.

Chorus. K. C. C. has *ó hi rìl Mór nigh'n donn*.

876. MacC. *dheith*.

881. MacC. *thir ,n Leathain*.

XXV

Nighean chruinn donn, dut is éibhinn

('Happily, o neat brown maiden')

MacCormick MS., p. 69.

Recorded by Duncan MacDonald, Peninerine, on 27/7/50 and on 11/4/51 (wire nos. 385 and 773); on tape for me from Effie Monk in

Benbecula by the Revd. Fr. John MacCormick in 1953; and by myself from Mrs. Campbell ('Bean Nill'), Frobost, in 1957.

Other versions of text: K. C. C. 89; McD. 273. Not in K.

Apparently not now widely known. Another dialogue song.

893–902. These lines occur in other songs where they are usually attributed to a young woman lamenting that her lover has deserted her because she has no dowry.

903–21. The remainder of this song appears to be connected with the folk anecdote in which the unknown rider of the rough-looking horse wins the race (and the king's or chief's daughter's hand) in the contest held before the king (or chief) and his court. Duncan MacDonald himself recorded such a story for me on 14/2/50 (*Mac 'ic Ailein agus nighean Mac-a-Phì*, 'Clanranald and MacPhee of Colonsay's daughter').

906. K. C. C. *an stàbla*, McD. *air stapull*.

911. *a mach i.* The horse is masculine in ll. 907–9, but feminine thereafter.

XXVI

Gura mise tha fo mhulad air an tulaich luim fhuair

('Truly I am filled with sorrow on the lonely cold knoll')

MacCormick MS., p. 71.

Recorded from Duncan MacDonald, Peninerine, on 31/7/50; from Mrs. Kate MacCormick, Benbecula, on 31/10/50; from Miss Kate Monk, Benbecula, on 27/3/51; from Miss Mary Gillies, Castlebay, Barra, on 5/4/51 (wire nos. 408, 481, 628, 741), and from Mrs. Campbell ('Bean Nill') on tape on 3/6/58.

Other versions: tune, text (15 couplets), and translation, F. T., no. 46; text alone, K. C. C. 48; MS., Fr. Allan McDonald, folio 59; K. 26, from Anne Morrison, taken down at Cladach Kirkibost in 1883, printed in McD., p. 174.

There is a fair copy of a closely similar version in Fr. Allan McDonald's manuscript, with a rough translation on the opposite page, but I have not used this translation.

Art versions: six couplets of this song are given in *Songs of the Hebrides*, II. xvi, followed by a literal translation and a 'singing adaptation'. The song is there called 'Sea-keening' and a four-bar tune, different from Miss Tolmie's or those that are printed here, is given on the preceding page. On p. 237 of the same volume the air of this song, described as an 'old rowing measure' collected by Kenneth MacLeod from Mrs. Malloch, Loch Maddy, North Uist, is used in an arrangement of 'Ye Highlands and ye Lowlands' by Mrs. Kennedy-Fraser.

The song is poetical and has a greater unity of theme than most waulking songs.

XXVII

'S mi 'm aonaran am Beinn a' Cheòthain

('I am alone on the Misty Mountain')

MacCormick MS., p. 72.

Other versions of text: O. 57.

Though this is obviously a song that was made in South Uist, all the places mentioned in it being there, we have been unable to find anyone who knows it or who can remember having heard it, in spite of extensive inquiries. The Oban MS. is the only other source for the text; it is very close to MacCormick's version. In O., the refrain is

> *Fa ral dal ò*
> *Ho hi rì o*
> *Ho ri ghealadh i*
> *O hì a bhò*

In the School of Scottish Studies archives there is a recording of a song sung by Kirsty Munro on the Isle of Skye, which has the first three lines in common with this; the refrain, sung after each half-line, is *O hi ri ó/Fair al al leó/O hi ri ó*; this has something in common with the third line of the meaningless refrain as given by MacCormick. Mr. John MacLeod recorded a few lines of this song sung by Miss Penny Morrison, Iochdar, South Uist, to the air and refrain of No. XXIX here.

966. O. has *'S mi aonaran   'M beinn a cheo na*

969. O. *thuilleadh*

975. O. *Eilein Bheatrum*

977. O. *Cill-Fhionnlaidh*

979. O. *Nam ban teisteil*

980. O. *Gu Ormacleit am   Biodh am beadradh*

the lines here then follow in the order 983, 982, 981.

XXVIII

Chaidh mi do'n bheinn ghabhail fradhairc

('I climbed the ben to scan th' horizon')

MacCormick MS., p. 74. Titled *Oran Sunntach Luaigh.*

Translated by Fr. Allan McDonald.

Recorded from Mr. John MacLean, M.A., from Isle of Barra, at Mallaig on 16/12/49; and from Mrs. Duncan MacDonald, Peninerine, on 30/10/50 (wire nos. 101 and 471).

Other versions of text: K. C. C. 22; MS., O. 37 (31 lines). In O. it is titled *Torcul Donn*.

990. 'Ever singing of'. So Fr. Allan McDonald. In Scottish Gaelic *cur sìos air* usually means to deprecate or run down. But cf. Dinneen, *cuirim síos ar*, 'I describe, descant on'.

1001. 'Weema' is Fr. Allan McDonald's anglicization of the Gaelic *muime*, foster- or god-mother.

1004. Fr. Allan McDonald translated *urad* (O. *urrad*) as 'equal'; but the Revd. William Matheson has pointed out to me that it must mean 'up yonder', and that the line should probably read *B'annsa fear a' bhreacain urad*. O. has *Nach taobhainn fear Bhreacain urrad*.

1010. The rhyme here and in l. 1079 shows the pronunciation must have originally been *darus*, though MacCormick wrote *dorics*.

1011. O. has *Gu fail farasd*. The Revd. William Matheson has pointed out that *fàin* is a form of *faoin*.

XXIX

Dh'éirich mi moch madainn àlainn

('Early I rose one morn of glory')

MacCormick MS., p. 45 and p. 78.

Fr. Allan McDonald translated a different version. Ll. 1020–1 and 1024–9 here are from his translation.

Recorded from Mrs. MacDougall, Castlebay, Isle of Barra, on disc in March 1938. Also from Miss Penny Morrison, South Uist, see p. 183.

Other versions: *F.F.S.U.* (but to a different tune and chorus); K. C. C. 38; MS., Fr. Allan McDonald, folio 81; Donald MacIntyre, p. 78.

Art versions: there is a version of this song in *Songs of the Hebrides*, ii. 199, under the title 'Mingulay Sea Rapture', described as having been collected from Mary MacDonald, Mingulay. Twelve lines of the text are given. In *Songs of the Hebrides*, iii. 98, the words (eight lines this time) are used again with two alternating airs, one from Frances Tolmie and one from Barra, under the title of 'A Barra Love Lilt'.

The version on p. 78 of MacCormick's manuscript is printed here. MacCormick wrote down a very slightly differing version of the same song on pp. 45–47 of his manuscript. Variants are noted here, the versions being referred to as 'B' and 'A' respectively.

1022. A *chàrnan*.

1025. A has *atharraich* before this line.

1027. A *eàirlinn*, B *eirlinn*.

1030–2. These lines are not in B.

1033. The second half of this line is missing in MacCormick's manuscript, here supplied from Donald MacIntyre's manuscript version.

1034. A has *geall a phàighinn*, 'a wager I would pay'.

1036. A *cluic a's gàire.*

1040–3. These lines are not in A.

1042. *Bualadh bòrd* in this line (which is not in any of the other versions referred to) may be a corruption for *Bualadh bhròg*, beating with a shoe, the forfeit formerly paid by the loser in card games in the Highlands, see Derick Thomson, *Scottish Gaelic Studies*, ix. 84.

1045. The rhyme indicates that a half-line is missing here.

1048–51. Compare ll. 238–41.

XXX

Cha labhair mi 'n t-òran

('I will not sing the ballad')

MacCormick MS., p. 80.

Recorded from Miss Kate MacDonald, daughter of Duncan Mac-Donald, Peninerine, South Uist, on 30/10/50; from Miss Penny Morrison, Iochdar, South Uist, on 2/11/50; from Miss Kate MacDonald ('Ceit Isea-bail'), Iochdar, at a genuine waulking at Gerinish on 29/3/51; and from Catriana Caimbeul at Loch Carnan on 10/4/51 (wire nos. 470, 505, 654, and 823).

Other versions: text, translation, and tune, *F.F.S.U.* 232; text alone, K. C. C. 14; Fr. Allan McDonald MS., folio 68; Donald MacIntyre MS., p. 84.

Mrs. Kennedy-Fraser gives a version of the tune from Lexie MacRae, Harris, on p. xiv of vol. iv of *Songs of the Hebrides*, calling it 'an old Harris salute'. The transcription is obviously an incorrect one: the last two words of l. 1070 here (which is sometimes sung as the first line of the song) are given as if they comprised a whole verse, and the verse is described as 'the shortest on record'. Possibly a defective phonograph recording was used for the transcription. The 'verses' actually consist of seven-syllable lines as here printed. She gives another version of the tune on p. vii of *More Songs of the Hebrides*, with no mention of the source, and no reference to the version she had already published in vol. iv.

1053. MacC. *faca.*

1054. MacC. *'S mi leabaidh.*

1057. MacC. *Mhic calain. Mac Cailein Mór* is the Gaelic patronymic of the chiefs of the Campbells of Argyll, the dukes of Argyll.

1058. MacC. *thalla na'n rò sheol.*

1060. Keppoch, in Inverness-shire.

1066–9. Boreray and Vallay and Heisgeir are islands in the neighbourhood of North Uist; Tighgearry is in North Uist, and Griminish is in Benbecula. The lairds of Boreray were MacLeans, a branch of the Ardgour family. The tacksmen of Vallay were MacLeans until 1727, according to *The Clan Donald*, and thereafter MacDonalds. The tacksmen of Heisgeir (which lies in the Atlantic west of North Uist) were MacDonalds until 1748.

1071. MacC. *mairidh*.

1077. MacC. *to'irt*.

XXXI

'S moch an diu a rinn mi éirigh

('This morning I have risen early')

MacCormick MS., p. 83.

Ll. 1107 to end translated by Fr. Allan McDonald.

Recorded from Miss Annie Johnston (disc no. 33); from Mrs. James MacNeil, on 9/3/50; from Mrs. John Galbraith, in every case at Castlebay, Isle of Barra, on 5/4/51 (wire nos. 302 and 726); and from Mrs. Campbell ('Bean Nìll'), Frobost, on tape.

Other versions: different tune, text, and translation, *F.F.S.U.* 226; text alone, K. C. C. 46; MS., Fr. Allan McDonald, folios 32, 66; Donald MacIntyre, p. 56.

1106. Cf. l. 1221.

1110–11. The literal translation is 'sweet as her voice is, her qualities at the sickle and at the waulking-board are better'.

1116. The tempo of the song quickens here. Some singers begin at this line. Some versions have *stràid na h-eala*.

1119. MacC. *bithimse*.

1122. *Tìr Mhic Cailein*, i.e. Argyll.

XXXII

Siùbhlaidh mi 's fàgaidh mi 'm fearann

('I will go, I'll leave the country')

MacCormick MS., p. 84.

Recorded from Mrs. MacDougall, Castlebay, Isle of Barra, on disc in March 1938; and from John MacKinnon, Borve, Isle of Barra, on wire no. 605 at Castlebay on 27/2/51.

Other versions: an Eriskay version of the tune was printed by Amy

Murray in the *Celtic Review*, ii. 201 (January 1906). A Barra version of the text was printed by Ella Carmichael in the same journal, i. 147 (October 1904). Also K. C. C. 35; MS., Fr. Allan McDonald, folio 111; Canon MacLean, no. xvii.

Art versions: Mrs. Kennedy-Fraser put the words published by Ella Carmichael to an arrangement of the air 'noted in Eriskay from the singing of Peggie MacInnes', *Songs of the Hebrides*, i. 134. The tune as given (and the key) is the same as that published by Amy Murray, except that it is given in *alla breve* time instead of 2/4 time.

There is another art version of this song in *Gaelic Songs of the Isles of the West*, i. 4, based on the traditional version sung by the Revd. Fr. John MacMillan, Isle of Barra.

1136, 1137. Compare ll. 147, 157. A similar passage is found in a song in the MacLagan MS., which was written in the latter half of the eighteenth century. This song, which the editor says must be from Lochaber, is printed in *T.G.S.I.* xxii. 186. The first verse is:

> *Eoghain mhic Iain mhic Ailein*
> *Dhomhsa b'aithne beus do bhaile;*
> *Piob ga spreigeadh, long ga tarruing,*
> *Bhi 'g òl fion, a piosaibh glaine.*
> > *O i oirinn, O i o u, O i oirinn, O i o ro,*
> > *O i oirinn, O i o u, Thog u oirinn, O i o ro.*

'Ewen, son of John, son of Allan, I knew the custom of your township; pipes struck up, ship pulled ashore, the drinking of wine from vessels of glass.'

1141. MacC. *tha leamsa. Tha* is used with *le* colloquially in South Uist; but in l. 1251 MacCormick has *a's leamsa.*

1150. See note to l. 1262.

Ella Carmichael calls this 'A Jacobite Waulking Song' and says: 'This song is known, in versions more or less imperfect, in the Hebrides. I took down this and other forms in Barra, my father has taken down versions which differ in several details, and I know other collectors who have yet other variations. All reciters, however, agree that 'Mac mo rìgh' is Prince Charlie. 'Mac 'ic Dhu[bh]ghail[l]' is the patronymic of MacDonald of Morar.'

I have not seen any of the other versions collected by Alexander Carmichael. The Barra versions of the song I have heard begin with the same line as Ella Carmichael's—*Có sheinneas an fhìdeag airgid?*—'Who will sound the silver whistle?', a version of l. 1152 here, and the song has a greater artistic unity than the Uist versions, such as MacCormick's, which appear to be made up from pieces of at least two songs, for ll. 1140–50 here are nearly identical with ll. 1250–60 of the song *Craobh an Iubhair* here, to which they seem to be much more appropriate, and the beginning and end portions of the Barra version are reversed. Ll. 1131–9 are the stock description of the entertainment afforded in a great chief's house. The 'silver whistle' may have been a badge of rank.

XXXIII

Cha déid mise, cha déid mi

('I'll not go, no, not I')

MacCormick MS., p. 87.

Translated by Fr. Allan McDonald.
Recorded from Miss Kate MacDonald, Peninerine, South Uist, on
10/1/50 (wire no. 205).
Other versions of text: K. C. C. 17; Donald MacIntyre MS., p. 96.

The textually very similar song with chorus ending *hó hi iù a hó hug ó*,
of which printed versions can be found in K. C. C., p. 19, and McD.,
p. 266, has been much more widely recorded than this one. In K. C. C.
the first twelve lines of the two songs are almost identical: but the songs
are different songs, not versions of the same song. Miss Annie Johnston
used to sing the other song, *Mìle marbhphaisg air a' ghaol*, very attrac-
tively.

1162. *Subh craobh* means a raspberry bush, or any bush bearing berries.

1163. *Bharr 'n fhraoich* is what MacCormick first wrote, and Fr. Allan
McDonald translated; later MacCormick substituted *chaoil* for *fhraoich*.
The latter is also the reading in K. C. C., but Donald MacIntyre has
air bharr a chaol [*sic*].

1170, 1171. There are no words in the text corresponding to 'shy' and
'every dye' of Fr. Allan McDonald's translation.

XXXIV

Cha n-eil falt orm air fuireach

('Not a hair is remaining')

MacCormick MS., p. 89.

Recorded from Duncan MacDonald, Peninerine, on 11/4/51 (wire no.
760); and on tape from Mrs. Effie Monk, Benbecula, by the Revd. John
MacCormick for me in 1953.
Other version of text: K. C. C. 26. This song is not now widely known.

1203. Donald Gorm, see note to l. 222.

1205. K. C. C. here has *Thig o thùr nan trì stuagh thu* (perhaps we should
read *stuaghaibh*), 'Who comes from the tower of three gables'.

1206. Kingussie? but it is unlikely a person from there would be mentioned along with island chiefs.

XXXV

Craobh an iubhair

('The Yew tree')

MacCormick MS., p. 94.

Translated by Fr. Allan McDonald.

Recorded from Roderick MacKinnon ('Ruairi Iain Bhàin'), Northbay, Isle of Barra, on disc in March 1938; and from Calum Johnston ('Calum Aonghais Chaluim'), Barra, in Edinburgh on 11/12/49 (wire no. 76); a fragment was also recorded from Mrs. Steele at Bornish on 9/1/50. Also from Roderick MacKinnon's niece Janet MacKinnon, daughter of 'Bean Shomhairle Bhig', on tape at Northbay, Barra, on 28/1/64.

Other versions: text, translation, and gramophone recording, *G.F.B.* 36 (sung by Roderick MacKinnon); text and translation, *C.G.* v. 2 and v. 6, two versions, the first from Marion MacNeil ('Mór nighean Alasdair mhic Ruairi Bhàin'), Kentangaval, Isle of Barra. The song does not seem to be now widely known.

1220. *Mac Aoidh.* Carmichael says 'it was his sweetheart who made this song to MacKay of the Rinns in Islay'. The MacKays or Magees of the Rinns of Islay were a prominent family in the days of the MacDonalds of Islay. The MacDonald historian says that they sat on the Council of the Lords of the Isles (*Highland Papers*, i. 24). The only extant charter in Scotland written in Gaelic was granted by Donald, Lord of the Isles, to Brian Bicaire Magaodh, conveying lands in the Rinns of Islay to Brian for his service to Donald and to his father before him, on 6 May 1408. This document was retained by the Magees, who later settled in Antrim under Somhairle Buidhe, until 1852, when their descendant reluctantly sold it to the National Register House in Edinburgh. (*Book of Islay*, 16.)

Another MacKay or Magee of the Rinns of Islay who is mentioned in historical documents is Neil, who was 'officer' or 'crunair' of the Rinns of Islay at the end of the sixteenth century. He was the first signatory of a petition to the Privy Council of Scotland in favour of the MacDonalds as superiors of the tenants of Islay, that was written *c.* 1600. In February 1606 he was named as the second of four cautioners for the non-molestation of the Government troops stationed in Dunivaig House, seat of the MacDonalds of Islay. (*Book of Islay*, 451, 117.) It is very interesting to find a song connected with Islay preserved in the tradition of the Isle of Barra. The Neil MacKay abovementioned could be the subject of it.

1223. Compare l. 1106.

1243. *Gailmhinn* is Galway in Ireland.

1252–62. Compare ll. 1140–50, and see note thereon.

1246. 'Apple tree' was a kenning for a chief. The apple was the ambrosial food of the Gaels, see Quiggin, *Prolegomena to the Study of the Later Irish Bards*, p. 26.

1258. Fr. Allan McDonald did not translate this line.

1262. According to Alexander Carmichael 'in some districts old and young kept a coin in their pocket to hail *rìoghain na h-oidhche*, "the queen of the night". The coin was called *peighinn phisich*, "propitious penny", and was turned thrice in the pocket when the new moon was seen.' (J. C. Watson, *Yorkshire Celtic Studies*, i. 37.)

XXXVI

Ailein, Ailein, 's fad' an cadal

('Allan, Allan, long thou'rt sleeping')

On loose leaf in MacCormick's manuscript, headed *Oran Laigh eile* [*sic*], the page being numbered 45.

Recorded from Duncan MacDonald, Peninerine, on 11/8/51 (wire no. 931).

Other versions: tune, text, and translation, F. T., no. 64; *F.F.S.U.*, p. 253; text alone, K. C. C. 7.

1268. 'It's not the noise of horses in the decayed seaweed.' *Brùchda*— decayed fermenting seaweed lying at the top of high-water-mark along the shore, where presumably the horses were grazing.

The meaning 'noise' for *stoirm* is not given in the dictionaries, but it is attested from other waulking-song contexts: K. C. C. 41, *Stoirm a' challtainn ris a' chuileann* (in a context where MacCormick has *fuaim*, see l. 233 here); K. C. C. 47, *An cuala, an cluinn sibh stoirm na cléitheadh?*, 'Did you, do you hear the noise of the waulking-board?'; K. C. C. 59, *Far am bi na h-eich ghorma, Chluinn' an stoirm gam marcrachd*, 'Where there are the dark-grey horses, the noise of their being ridden used to be heard'; K. C. C. 25, *stoirm nan gobhar ri taobh na h-abhann*, 'the noise of the goats beside the river'. Peggy MacRae once said to me of some trees that had been planted beside her house in South Uist, *dheanadh iad a leithid a stoirm ris a' ghaoith*, 'they would make such a noise in the wind'. The idea seems to be the kind of noise made by trees or bushes beating against each other in the wind, or by animals galloping. Cf. Old Norse *stormr*, which can mean 'uproar, tumult', as well as 'storm'. Cp. A. MacDonald, *Ais-eiridh*, p. 55, '. . . *iomad bochdan fuilteach, foirmeil, Theid le stoirm go bás*'.

1269. *Mac Iain* was the Gaelic patronymic of the MacDonalds of Ardnamurchan, and of the MacDonalds of Glencoe. It means 'John's son', and explains the question put to Dr. Samuel Johnson by MacLaine of

Lochbuie on 21 October 1773, when as Boswell records 'Lochbuie bawled out to Mr. Johnson "Are you of the Johnstons of Glen Croe [*sic*], or of Ardnamurchan?" Mr. Johnson gave a curious look. Sir Allan and I told Lochbuie that Mr. Johnson was not John*ston*, but John*son*, and that he was an Englishman.' (1962 edition of Boswell's *Journal of a Tour to the Hebrides*, edited by Frederick A. Pottle and Charles H. Bennett, p. 343. The allusion is not explained. 'Glen Croe' must be a mistake for 'Glen Coe'. Some of the dispossessed Mac-Donalds of Ardnamurchan had anglicized their name as Johnston.)

1272. Few of the names of the wives of the MacDonalds of Glencoe or the MacDonalds of Ardnamurchan are given in *Clan Donald*, so it is impossible to say if either ever married a lady from the house of Kinlochmoidart.

1283. K. C. C. has *Sguabag sobhail no slataich.*

1284. 'Graddan' was meal made from oats which had been prepared for grinding in the quern by burning the ears, the method formerly used by the poorest people in the Highlands.

1288. *Tìr an eòrna* can be a kenning for the Island of Tiree, which is considerably more fertile than most parts of the Highlands.

XXXVII

Là dhomh 's mi 'm Beinn a' Cheathaich

('One day on the Misty Mountain')

On loose sheet in MacCormick manuscript, the page being numbered 46.

Recorded from Mrs. John MacInnes (a daughter of Roderick Mac-Kinnon), Northbay, Barra, on ediphone on 21/5/37; from Mrs. Morrison ('Bean Phluim'), at Castlebay, Barra, on 3/1/50; from the late Captain Donald Joseph MacKinnon (a son of Roderick MacKinnon) on 22/1/50 (wire recordings nos. 159, 213). In Nova Scotia recorded from Mrs. MacLean, Beaver Cove, Cape Breton, and from Mrs. Neil MacInnes ('Anna Néill Ruaidh'), MacKay's Crossing, Glace Bay, Cape Breton (both of Barra descent), on ediphone on 1/10/37 and 8/10/37 respectively.

Other versions: apparently none has been printed apart from the art version in *Songs of the Hebrides*, i. 80. This has become famous under the title of 'Kishmul's Galley'. The words are said to have been obtained from Mrs. MacLean, Barra, and the air from the singing of Mary Mac-Donald, Mingulay. In all the versions I have heard the tempo of the song is about twice as fast as that indicated by Mrs. Kennedy-Fraser; it begins fairly slowly, and gradually gathers speed, and the last nine lines here (or similar passages in other versions) are sung very fast.

In Barra where the song is popular and widely known, its composition is attributed to Nic Iain Fhinn ('The Daughter of Fair-haired John') the poetess from the island of Mingulay who lived in the seventeenth century, and is also said to be the Barra poetess involved in the two flytings with the Uist woman, which begin *A bhradag dhubh a bhrist na glasan* and *Cha déid Mór a Bharraidh bhrònaich.*

1297–8. i.e. it was not an insignificant little band of sheep.

1303. Kishmul Castle, built on a rock in Castlebay harbour, the ancestral stronghold of the MacNeils of Barra.

1313. Gill' Eóghanain Mór was chief of the MacNeils of Barra from about 1655 to about 1670.

1314. Ruairi an Tartair was chief of the MacNeils of Barra from 1594 until about 1620. He was well known as the unruly product of an unruly age. In 1613 he complained to the Privy Council of Scotland that he and his lawful son 'Gilleruan Oig' by his wife Moir, sister of MacDonald of Clanranald, had been seized and imprisoned by his illegitimate son by Mary MacLeod, Neill Oig, who had seized Castle Kishmul and kept his father and half brother in irons. This 'Neill Oig' may be the same person as Niall Gruamach here.

In November 1625 the Irish Franciscan Conchobhair Mac an Bháird (Cornelius Ward) visited Barra and reported that he had celebrated the marriage of the lawful heir of the island, remarking that a younger brother had previously seized the castle by force and kept his father imprisoned until he died, and his brother until he made an oath renouncing his inheritance. See J. L. Campbell, 'The MacNeils of Barra and the Irish Franciscans', *Innes Review*, v. 33.

1315. Ruairi Òg was the son of Gill' Eóghanain Mór. He and his brother James were tried in Edinburgh in 1679 for the deforcement of a King's Messenger sent to Barra in 1675 to collect a debt owed to MacLeod of Dunvegan. See the *Book of Dunvegan*, i. 180, and the *Scottish Genealogist*, vi. 9.

1317, 1318. In 1703 *A List of the children under Popish parents* printed in vol. iii of the Miscellany of the Maitland Club, p. 424, mentions the following Murdos as Catholics then living in Barra: Murdo McNeile brother to the Lairde of Barra (Ruairi Òg here); Murdo McNeile in Vattersai; and Murdo McNeile in 'Grim' (presumably a misreading of 'Greian').

1322. MacC. *fo Lia.*

1328. MacC. *choillich.*

1330. MacC. *deachaibh.* Originally *deachamh* meant 'tithe' but *ugh deachamh* acquired the meaning of 'addled egg' possibly because the worse animals, etc., used to be put into the tithe. See under *DEACH-AMH* in Fr. Allan McDonald's *Gaelic Words from South Uist.*

XXXVIII

'S fhada bhuam a chì mi 'n ceò

('Far away I see the mist')

From Fr. Allan McDonald's MS., folio 58, fair copy. The singer was Catherine MacIntyre, Eriskay. Translated by Fr. Allan McDonald.

Recorded from Mrs. Duncan MacInnes, Eriskay, on 2/4/51 (wire no. 686); and from Mrs. Alec Johnston, Castlebay, Barra, on 5/4/51 (wire no. 722). Also recorded in Cape Breton from Jonathan G. MacKinnon, formerly editor of *Mac Talla*, at Whycocamagh on ediphone on 10/9/37.

Other version of text: K. C. C. 100.

This song is unusual in that the same refrain and words are sung to two quite different tunes. Usually a meaningless refrain denotes a single tune.

Art version: 'A Birlinn Health-drinking Chant' in *Songs of the Hebrides*, iv. 60, gives the first four lines of a version of this song, 'ancient Gaelic from Kenneth MacLeod' set to an air from Mrs. MacKinnon ('Bean Shomhairle Bhig') of Northbay, Barra. The air and chorus appear to belong to some other song.

The chorus of the version recorded by Mrs. Johnston resembles the tune of 'The Christ Child's Lullaby' printed in *Songs of the Hebrides*, i. 26, said to have been noted from Mrs. John MacInnes on Eriskay. 'Words from Fr. Allan McDonald.' The words were, indeed, printed in the Gaelic hymnal Fr. Allan published in 1893, but they are not traditional, as Kenneth MacLeod suggests. They were written by Fr. Ranald Rankin of Moidart in 1855, and printed in *An Gàidheal* in 1873, and in vol. xv of the *Transactions of the Gaelic Society of Inverness* in 1889.

XXXIX

Tha 'n oidhche nochd fuar

('The night is so keen')

Fr. Allan McDonald MS., folio 97.

Recorded from Mrs. John MacInnes ('Màiri Raghnaill 'ic Alasdair Mhóir'), Eriskay, on 1/4/51, and from Mrs. Campbell ('Bean Nìll') on tape on 30/4/58.

Words apparently not published elsewhere. Fr. Allan McDonald wrote a Christmas hymn to the tune, *'S i Moire tha truagh*, and this was printed in the *Mercat Cross* of December 1952, with a transcription of the tune; it is reprinted in *Bàrdachd Mhgr. Ailein*.

1364. This line occurs only in the translation in the manuscript.

1366. The translation (which is not a fair copy) is difficult to read here.

1372. *Air a dubhadh*: coffins used to be blackened with black-lead in the Highlands.

XL

'S mise chunnaic an t-iaonadh

(' 'Tis I who beheld the exploit')

Text on a loose sheet in Fr. Allan McDonald's papers; apparently taken down from 'Bean 'ic Dhomhnaill na Carnich' in 1904; refrain from Widow J. MacIntyre, Roshinish, Eriskay.

Recorded from Mrs. MacDougall ('Anna Raghnaill Eachainn'), Castlebay, Barra, on disc in March 1938; from Mrs. Angus John Mac-Lellan, Hacklett, Benbecula, on 21/11/49; from her again on 31/10/50 (wire nos. 20, 483); and from Miss Penny Morrison, Iochdar, on 2/11/50 (wire no. 504).

Other versions: translation and different air, F. T., no. 52; text and translation, *C.G.* v. 28; text alone, K. C. C. 96. The *C.G.* version is from Mary MacRae, Harris, and is to a different chorus, resembling the F.T. version's chorus. MS., Canon MacLean, no. xxxi.

1374. *Iaonadh* is the South Uist pronunciation of *ioghnadh*, 'wonder', but the late Professor Angus Matheson pointed out that in such contexts as this it represents *eangnamh*, 'exploit', see *Éigse*, viii. 249.

1390. *Orr' aodann—air t'aodann.*

1401. The word *dhaibh* is not in Fr. Allan McDonald's text, but is needed metrically, and is found in other versions.

NOTES ON THE SINGERS

THE recording of traditional Gaelic folk-songs and folk-tales which the writer has undertaken began early in 1937 with a clockwork ediphone which was used during that year in Barra and in Nova Scotia, continued in March 1938 with a Presto J-6 disc recorder at Northbay, Barra, and after the war was restarted with a Webster wire recorder in 1949 which was used until 1955 when it was replaced by a Grundig tape recorder. Tape recorders have been used since 1956. Owing to the quality of ediphone recordings, none of these has been used for the making of transcriptions printed in this book. In any case, nearly all the material recorded in Scotland by ediphone in 1937 has been re-recorded since on more suitable apparatus.

The disc recordings made in 1938 (the first electrical recordings of traditional Gaelic folk-songs made in the field in the Outer Hebrides) are of considerable interest, most of the songs having been recorded from four very good folk-singers, the late Roderick MacKinnon ('Ruairi Iain Bhàin') (XIII and XXXV here), Mrs. MacDougall ('Anna Raghnaill Eachainn') (III, VI, VII, VIII, XXIII, XXIX, XXXII, and XL), Miss Annie Johnston ('Anna Aonghuis Chaluim') (XVI, XXXI, and XXXIII here), and Mrs. Mary Morrison ('Bean Phluim') (III, IV, VI, and XXXVII—but these from re-recordings made on wire after 1949). Ten of the songs recorded on discs from Roderick MacKinnon, Mrs. MacDougall, and Miss Annie Johnston, were published as a set of twelve-inch discs with book of words by the Linguaphone Company in 1950.

The bulk of the recordings from which transcriptions have been made for this book were made on wire from the middle of November 1949, however. As it is usual in Britain to deprecate the quality of wire recordings it is necessary to say here that the quality of those made by the Webster wire recorder, an American product, were considerably better than any I have heard made by British wire recorders, and what is even more important, appear likely to keep their quality better than tape recordings do. Their quality would be better still had it been possible to buy wire in Britain which had not obviously been previously used and demagnetized again.

In the making of these transcriptions, priority has been given to those of songs sung at an actual waulking at Gerinish in South Uist on 29 March 1951. The MacCormick manuscript had not been recovered by that date, and no particular request was made for particular songs, but quite spontaneously versions of Nos. III, IV, VII, VIII, XV, XVII, XVIII, XXI, and XXX of the MacCormick collection were sung by the following ladies who sang as soloists in turn: Mrs. Kate Nicolson, Miss Kate MacDonald

('Ceit Iseabail'), Miss Penny Morrison, and Mrs. D. J. MacLellan, all of Iochdar, South Uist, the chorus at the waulking-board consisting of Miss Mary Margaret Hunter, Miss Marion MacPhee, Miss Marion Mac-Eachen, Miss Mary MacKay, and Miss Kate Beaton.

Apart from this waulking there were a good many occasions when a number of singers were brought together, and the songs with their choruses sung in a natural way, though no cloth was waulked, particularly in Benbecula and Barra. In Benbecula the first such session was arranged by the late Dr. Calum I. MacLean, and singers recorded then and later included Mrs. Patrick MacCormick (I, VII, X, XXI, XXIV, XXVI, XXXIII), Mrs. Fanny MacIsaac (XIII), Mrs. Angus John MacLellan (XV, XVII, XVIII, and XL), Miss Kate MacMillan (III and XIX), and Miss Kate Monk (XXVI).

In Castlebay, Barra, very successful sessions were arranged by the Barra Folklore Committee, particularly Miss Annie Johnston, and held in the chapelhouse by the kind consent of the Rt. Revd. Mgr. Ewen Mac-Innes (himself a native of South Uist)—this being one of the few houses in Barra where electric power was available. The singers recorded included Mrs. John Galbraith (XIII, XXXI), Miss Mary Gillies (VII, XXVI), Mrs. Alex. Johnston ('Mairi Choinnich', from Mingulay) (XXXVIII), Mrs. James MacDougall (XIII), Miss Janet MacKinnon ('Seonaid Shomhairle Bhig', a daughter of Mrs. MacKinnon who sang for Mrs. Kennedy Fraser) (I, IV, XIII, XXXI, XXXV), John MacKinnon (from Borve) (XXXII), Mrs. James MacNeil (VII, XXXI), Mrs. Mary MacNeil ('Màiri Ruarachain') (VI), Miss Mary Morrison, Earsary (III, VIII), Mrs. Mary Morrison ('Bean Phluim', who had been recorded on discs in 1938) (III, IV, VI, XXXVII), and Miss Annie Johnston herself (XVI, XXIII, XXXI, XXXIII), and her brother Calum (XXXV).

In a similar session in the chapelhouse on Eriskay on 1 April 1951, arranged by the Revd. Fr. John MacCormick, singers recorded included Mrs. John MacInnes ('Màiri Raghnaill 'ic Alasdair Mhóir') (XXXIX) and Mrs. Norman MacInnes ('Flòraidh Raghnaill 'ic Aonghuis') (XIII); and at Loch Carnan, in South Uist, Catriana Campbell (XXX).

The remaining singers were mostly recorded at the fireside, in their or my homes. Sometimes one or two persons present took up the chorus.

Mrs. *Neil Campbell* ('Bean Nìll, Mór Aonghais 'ic Eachainn'), sister of the late Angus MacLellan, M.B.E.,[1] Frobost, South Uist, recorded versions of the Nos. I, IV, XI, XII, XXII, XXIII, XXV, XXVI, XXXI, and XXXIX. Sometimes her daughter Mrs. MacPhee assisted with the refrains. Mrs. Campbell, who has now passed her 100th year, has an excellent knowledge of waulking songs, and has recorded many others, for the School of Scottish studies and for the Revd. Fr. John MacLean as well as for myself.

Miss *Annie MacDonald* ('Anna Raghnaill'), a native of South Uist now living on Canna, recorded a version of No. XIII on 4/6/55.

---

[1] See translations of some of his tales in *Stories from South Uist* (London, 1961) and of his autobiography *The Furrow Behind Me* (London, 1962).

The late *Duncan MacDonald* ('Dunnchadh mac Dhòmhnaill 'ic Dhunn-chaidh') and his wife and daughters Anna and Kate, formerly living at Peninerine, South Uist. This family was one of the greatest upholders of the Gaelic tradition in South Uist, if not the greatest. Duncan MacDonald was a great storyteller and the style and purity of his Gaelic were classical.[1] Though not possessed of a good voice he knew an immense number of songs, and recorded Nos. III, IV, IX, XII, XXIII, XXV, XXVI, XXXIV, and XXXVI on visits to Canna. His wife recorded No. XXVIII, his daughter Anna Nos. XIV and XXII, and his daughter Kate Nos. XIII, XV, XX, XXII, XXIII, XXX, XXXIII. Their contribution towards the preservation of the airs of the songs in this book, like Mrs. Campbell's, was outstanding.

Mrs. *Donald MacInnes* ('Bean Dhòmhnaill Iain') recorded a version of No. XIV in the chapelhouse on Eriskay on 7 July 1950.

The late Mrs. *Duncan MacInnes*, Ru' Bàn, Eriskay, widow of a well-known storyteller, recorded a version of No. XXXVIII in the chapelhouse on Eriskay on 2 April 1951.

The late *Donald MacIntyre*, the well-known Gaelic poet, brother-in-law of Duncan MacDonald already mentioned, recorded a version of No. II at Paisley on 14/12/49.

The late Captain *D. J. MacKinnon* of the R.M.S. *Lochmor*, a son of Roderick MacKinnon ('Ruairi Iain Bhàin') whom I recorded in Barra in 1938, recorded a version of No. XXXVII in my house on 22 January 1950.

Mr. *Norman MacMillan*, South Uist, recorded a version of No. XVIII at Lochboisdale Hotel on 11 April 1951.

Miss *Effie Monk*, Benbecula, recorded versions of Nos. XXIV, XXV, and XXXIV for the Revd. Fr. John MacCormick, using my machine, in 1953.

Mrs. *Alex. Morrison* ('Bean Alasdair Mhóir'), Milton, South Uist, recorded versions of Nos. XV and XVII on tape at her home at Milton, South Uist.

Miss *Penny Morrison*, Iochdar, South Uist, who took part in the waulking at Gerinish referred to earlier in these notes, also recorded for me at other times versions of Nos. VII, XV, XXIX, XXX, and XL.

Mrs. *Archie Munro* (*née* Mary MacRury), Lochboisdale, South Uist, recorded a fine version of No. IX for Captain D. J. MacKinnon on my machine on 14 November 1961, and recorded a version of No. I for me on 5 December 1963, at her home at Lochboisdale, South Uist.

Mrs. *Mary Steele*, Bornish, South Uist, recorded versions of Nos. V, VIII, and XXXV in 1950.

Owing to their inferior qualities of reproduction, ediphone recordings made in 1937 have not been used in the transcription of airs for this collection. It is worth noting, however, that in the autumn of that year versions of the following songs which occur in the MacCormick Collection were recorded from singers of Barra and Uist descent in Cape Breton, Nova Scotia: No. I, from Mrs. MacLean, *née* Catherine Nicholson, Beaver Cove; XIII from Mrs. David Patterson, *née* Katie MacNeil, Benacadie; XXXI from Mrs. Neil MacInnis, *née* MacDonald, Glace Bay;

[1] See K. C. Craig, *Sgialachdan Dhunnchaidh* (Glasgow, 1944).

xxxvii in versions from Mrs. MacLean and Mrs. MacInnis; and xxxviii from Jonathan G. MacKinnon, Whycocamagh, formerly editor of the Gaelic paper *Mac Talla* (the last of Skye descent). These, and many other waulking songs, were then recorded by ediphone in Cape Breton, and the words transcribed, proving that the changes in subject in the songs take place at the same points on both sides of the Atlantic, although the Gaelic-speakers of Nova Scotia had been separated from those of Scotland by then for a hundred years.

NOTES ON THE METRES

THE METRICAL STRUCTURES OF WAULKING SONGS

The structure of waulking songs is more complicated and varied than might be at first expected. The variations involve differences in the number of syllables in the lines or 'verses', which may be repeated to identical or different musical phrases; in the length of the refrains; and in the relationships of the refrains to the verses.

The word 'verse' is used here for what the singers themselves call a *ceathramh*, the normal word for 'verse' in Scottish Gaelic. The 'verse' of a waulking song may be as short as four syllables. But such verses are really half-lines, the full line being one of eight syllables with penultimate rhyme, but without internal assonance or alliteration as a rule. This type of metre, which is very common in waulking songs, is known in Gaelic as *caoine*, and is that used e.g. by Seán Ó Conaill in his *Tuireamh na h-Éireann*, which was probably written between 1655 and 1659.[1]

The verse of a waulking song can take the following forms:

1. A half-line verse of four syllables. (Irregularly the eight-syllable line is divided into 'halves' of three and five syllables.) Songs of this type here are Nos. III, VI, X, XXVII, XXVIII, and XXIX.

2. A whole-line verse of from five to twelve syllables, but most frequently of eight, as described above, the rhyme being either on the ultimate, penultimate, or prepenultimate syllable. Nos. II, IV, V, VII, VIII, XI, XV, XVI, XVIII, XIX, XXIII, XXIV, XXV, and XXXI–XL inclusive are of this type.

3. Couplets of the type AB, BC, CD, etc., without internal rhyme. Usually the lines are of eight syllables, as above. Songs of this type here are Nos. I, IX, XIII, and XXII.

4. Couplets of the AB, CD, EF type, with internal rhyme within the couplets, and the even numbered lines having the same final rhyming vowel throughout the song. Songs of this type here are Nos. XX, XXI, and XXVI. This kind of waulking song gives the impression of being the most modern: the poems composed by Alexander MacDonald and Duncan Ban MacIntyre in the eighteenth century in waulking-song form are of this type.[2]

[1] See Cecile O'Rahilly, *Five Seventeenth-Century Political Poems*, p. 50.

[2] e.g. *A Mhórag chiatach a' chùil dualaich* and *Òganaich ùir a' chùil teudaich* by MacDonald and *Togamaid fonn air luadh' a chlòlain* by MacIntyre.

Three songs here, Nos. XII, XVII, and XXX are peculiar in that their metrical structures, 7^2+7^2, 6^2+5^1, and 6^2+6^2, in the last case irregularly, suggest that they were originally composed as couplets, but as sung now as waulking songs, each line is sung separately. Probably, as the Revd. William Matheson has suggested, No. XVII was originally composed as an *iorram*.

As my collaborator points out in his chapter on the form of the tunes, there is also a fundamental division of waulking songs into types with divided and undivided refrains, the later class being subdivided into two types, one of which has refrains that end with a repetition of their first phrase (music and meaningless syllables being identical), and the other has refrains that do not.

The refrains of waulking songs, as Mr. Collinson says, are of much more importance musically than are the verses. They are usually longer (and certainly never shorter) than are the verses, and they carry the main part of the melody, including the most striking cadences of the tunes, that are often reminiscent of the rise and fall of waves surging on the shore. Furthermore, the refrains, which are nearly always sung to fixed[1] meaningless syllables, are what serves to identify the songs in the minds of the singers, as the opening 'verse' or first line can be quite different in different versions of the same song. Indeed, if a song is asked for by the title of the first line as sometimes sung, the folk-singer is likely to reply with the question *Dé 'm fonn a th'air?*, 'What is its refrain?'. The part of the melody given to the verse in many waulking songs is little more than a recitative.

Waulking songs may therefore be conveniently classified according to the form of the refrain and its relationship to the verse.

Type 1A. Songs with refrains of three (or occasionally four) phrases, the last being identical with the first. Each verse (except sometimes the first) is sung twice to an identical melody. The formula is therefore *A* plus *a, b, a,* or sometimes plus *a, b, c, a*. The type 1 can be subdivided according to the length of the verse. Such songs here are:

(i) With half-line verses: Nos. VI, XXVII.

(ii) With whole-line verse: IV, VIII, XI, XII, XVIII, XXIV, XXX–XXXIII inclusive, XXXVI, XXXVIII–XL inclusive.

(iii) With couplets of the type AB, BC, CD, etc.: I, IX, XIII, XXII.

(iv) With couplets of the type AB, CD, EF, etc.: XXI, XXVI.

Type 1B. Songs with refrains of three (sometimes two or four) phrases, the last phrase of the refrain not being identical with the first. The formula is *A* plus *a, b, c* (or *a, b,* or *a, b, c, d*).

Such songs here are:

(i) With half-line verses: III, X, XXIX.

(ii) With whole-line verses: II, XVII, XIX, XXXVII. (XVII has its own

---

[1] Fixed with regard to the particular song in which they occur, that is. Within this, there is no liberty to vary them at all.

peculiarities, as has been noted above; in XIX the third phrase of the refrain very closely resembles the first.)

(iii) With couplets of the type AB, CD, etc.: XIV.

Type 2. Waulking songs with divided refrains.

These can be quite intricate. There is often an archaic feeling about them, as compared with songs of types 1*A* and 1*B*. Their classification involves two variables: first, the length of the verse (which is nearly always sung to a different musical phrase on repetition), and secondly, the proportions into which the refrain is divided. This is usually as 1 : 1, 1 : 2, or 1 : 3. Taking the shorter part of the refrain first, the formula for such songs can be therefore

	a, A, b, A, a, B, b, B, a . . . etc.
or	*a, A, b,c, A, a, B, b,c, B, a* . . . etc.
or	*a, A, b,c,d, A, a, B, b,c,d, B, a* . . . etc.

but it must be borne in mind that fairly often in these songs, the first line is not repeated.

This collection contains the following songs of Type 2:

(i) With verses of half-lines: No. XXVIII. This is a peculiar song of formula *A, a*; *B, a*; *C, b*; *D, c*; *C, a*; *D, a*; *E, b*; *F, c*; and so on, where *A, B*, etc., represent half-lines. The song is also unusual in that special meaningless syllables are sung at the dividing points between the different sections.

(ii) Songs with verses of whole lines, the refrain phrases being of equal length: V, XXXV (in the latter the different phrases of the refrain are sung to the same words).

(iii) Songs with verses of whole lines, the refrains being divided into sections of one and two phrases: VII, XXIII, XXV.

(iv) Songs with verses of whole lines, the refrains being divided into sections of one and three phrases: XV, XXXIV.

(v) Songs with couplets, the refrain being divided into two equal phrases: XX.

These are the types of structures illustrated by the songs in the present collection: it goes without saying that a survey of waulking songs as a whole, if it were practicable, would certainly show other subdivisions.

III

THE MUSICOLOGY OF
WAULKING SONGS

FRANCIS COLLINSON

THE SCALES OF THE TUNES

In determining the scale upon which a folk-tune is constructed, standard musicological practice is to accept the last note of the tune as the keynote or *final* of the mode or scale, and to name it accordingly. This was the method of assessment used by Bela Bartók, based upon the work of Ilmari Krohn, the Finnish folk-musician. With Scots folk-music, however, both Gaelic and Lowland Scots, though the great majority of tunes do yield to this analysis, the rule occasionally needs qualifying. Sometimes the tonal centre or 'feel of the key' of a tune is found to centre upon another note than the last one. Such tunes are to be seen in this collection in Nos. xviia, xviib, and xxxva.

The tunes of the waulking songs in the MacCormick Collection will be found to be constructed upon five-note, six-note, and seven-note scales, with a few exceptional examples of scales of four notes. The five-note or pentatonic scale, though ordinarily not the scale most often found, may be said to be the basic scale of Scots music from which the six- and seven-note scales have developed. One is tempted on this account to look upon the pentatonic tunes as older in origin than the six-note, and these older than the seven-note tunes; but there is no concrete evidence for this, and though such may have been the case in an era of musical prehistory, so many pentatonic tunes must certainly have been composed both contemporaneously with and subsequently to hexatonic and heptatonic ones, that it would be rash to read any antecedence in a tune now on account of its scale. One has only to look at the composed tunes of Niel Gow (1727–1807) to realize the mastery of pentatonic as well as of other Scots idiom possessed by such composers in the traditional style—not to mention the school of professional exiles from 'The Lone Shieling of the Misty Island' (many resident in Glasgow) who have turned out so much musical rubbish, mostly pentatonic, to the debasement of Gaelic song, in the early years of the present century.

What one may say with some confidence is that the origin of the pentatonic scale was almost certainly a vocal one, for it is the only one which the older type of traditional singer can sing in what the academic musician would call 'in tune' with consistency and certainty, by reason of the fact that the smallest interval in it, the full tone, is, as experience shows, the smallest interval which the average untrained traditional singer can negotiate with unvarying certainty of intonation without the aid of instrumental accompaniment. The interval of a semitone, in the traditional singer's performance, is liable to be either greater or smaller than the half-tone of the 'true scale' of the academic musician, and often contains quarter-tone shadings. The remark of Helmholtz[1] is worth quoting in this connexion. He says: 'It seems that in the first stages of the development of music, many nations avoided the use of intervals of less than a tone, and hence formed scales which alternated in intervals from a tone to a tone and a half.'

When the traditional singer comes to split the minor third of the pentatonic scale with an intermediate note, that note will generally be found to be unstable and liable to variation in pitch, often according to whether the melodic progression is upwards or downwards. The resulting intonation, though strange to the academic ear, is characteristic of the folk-singer, and particularly so of the singers of the Hebrides from whom these tunes have been recorded. In this connexion the remark of Patuffa Kennedy-Fraser may be worth quoting, that it was difficult to take down the music from the Hebridean singers because the time and scale were so different from modern music;[2] as may also be quoted the following paragraph from the same source.[3]

'A curious result of our long stay in the Isles and our obsession with the ancient music there, was that when Patuffa returned to London and to her pianoforte studies at the Matthay School, she felt her sense of tonality temporarily out of step, so to speak, especially with Beethoven.'

Such deviations from the theoretically 'true' scale in the tunes in this collection are indicated by the symbols ↑ and ↓ according to whether they are sharp or flat.

---

[1] On the Sensations of Tone, p. 257 (English translation by Alexander J. Ellis, London, 1885).
[2] Cf. Marjorie Kennedy-Fraser, A Life of Song, p. 126.
[3] Ibid., p. 140.

The Classification of the Pentatonic Scales

In the classification of the various inversions of the pentatonic scale, opinions differ as to which position should be regarded as the basic one. It will generally be found convenient, however, to set down the position CDE–GA as such; or, if one thinks of it in the terms of the black keys of the pianoforte, G♭A♭B♭–D♭E♭, i.e.

By accepting each of these five notes as a possible starting note or 'Final of the mode' (keynote) in turn, five scale positions are possible, though some are less often used than others. The five positions as they are numbered throughout this collection are therefore:

1st position, CDE–GA–(C) (with gaps at nos. 4 and 7)
2nd   ,,   DE–GA–C   (with gaps at nos. 3 and 6)
3rd   ,,   E–GA–CD   (with gaps at 2 and 5)
4th   ,,   GA–CDE–(G) (with gaps at 3 and 7)
5th   ,,   A–CDE–G   (with gaps at 2 and 6)

The Six-note (Hexatonic) Scales

These are in theory a development from the pentatonic scales by the insertion of an intermediate note in one of the gaps of that scale. Though they should therefore strictly speaking be related to the pentatonic scales for purposes of classification, it will in practice be found more convenient to relate them to the seven-note scales of the 'church' modes, and so to label them as in a sense heptatonic or seven-note scales with one note missing or 'gapped', rather than as pentatonic scales with a note added. For this reason it will be better to treat of the heptatonic scales first, and to return to the hexatonic scales after dealing with these.

The Seven-note (Heptatonic) Scales

These correspond in their intervals to the 'ecclesiastical' or 'church' modes, and may therefore be conveniently labelled by the customary modal titles, namely, Ionian, Dorian, Phrygian,

Lydian, Mixolydian, and Aeolian modes, corresponding to the scales on the white keys of the pianoforte, beginning in turn on C, D, E, F, G, and A, with the 'inadmissible' but nevertheless existent Locrian mode beginning on B. Examples of all these with the exception of the Lydian mode[1] are to be found in the tunes of the MacCormick Collection. It may be observed, however, that though there is no tune actually in the Lydian mode, No. xxxv*a* is an example of a tune which, though Ionian by the 'rule of the last note' mentioned above, possesses the quality of the Lydian mode in its general sound and feel, a condition of mixed or indefinite modality not infrequently to be found in Scots music.

In considering the theoretical development of the heptatonic scale from the pentatonic by the insertion of intermediate notes within the gaps of the latter, it will be seen that, as the intermediate note in either gap of the pentatonic scale may proceed either by a step of a semitone followed by one of a full tone, or vice versa, and as there are two such 'gaps' in the scale, it is possible *theoretically* to construct four different heptatonic scales on each position of the pentatonic scale. These four possible pairs of intermediate notes are, to take them in the 'key of C', obviously, (1) F and B; (2) F sharp and B; (3) F and B flat; and (4) F sharp and B flat. Not every such scale so formed is an acceptable 'mode', however, and it will in fact be found that while the first three of these pairs of intermediate notes do form one or other of the 'church' modes, the pair F sharp B flat does not do so, and so must be excluded.

To take the five positions of the pentatonic scale:

First position (CDE–GA–C)

Intermediate notes F natural and B natural give the Ionian mode (the ordinary major scale) CDE (f natural) GA (b natural) C.

---

[1] It may be of interest to quote the following remarks about the rarity of the Lydian mode by Cecil Sharp, the English folksong collector. He says: 'So far as I am aware, no English collector has yet found a folk tune in the Lydian mode. I have however occasionally noticed a tendency, more particularly amongst fiddlers, to sharpen the fourth note of the major scale, and it is possible that this may be due to Lydian influence. The English folksinger, to judge by his tunes, is very sensitive to the harsh effect of the tritone, which of course is the characteristic interval of the Lydian mode. Lydian tunes are occasionally found in Irish and Scottish folk-music' (*English Folk Song; Some Conclusions*, p. 54 (Novello, London, 1907)).

Intermediate notes F natural and B flat give the Mixolydian mode, CDE (f natural) GA (b flat) C.

    ,,   ,,   F sharp and B natural give the Lydian mode, CDE (f sharp) GA (b natural) C.

    ,,   ,,   F sharp and B flat give the unacceptable scale CDE (f sharp) GA (b flat) C (not included in the 'church' modes).

Second position (DE–GA–C)

Intermediate notes F natural and B natural give the Dorian mode.

    ,,   ,,   F natural and B flat give the Aeolian mode.

    ,,   ,,   F sharp and B natural give the Mixolydian mode.

    ,,   ,,   F sharp and B flat—not recognized as a mode.

Third Position (E–GA–CD)

Intermediate notes F natural and B natural give the Phrygian mode.

    ,,   ,,   F natural and B flat give the Locrian mode (only theoretically admitted as a mode).

    ,,   ,,   F sharp and B flat—not recognized as a mode.

    ,,   ,,   F sharp and B natural give the Aeolian mode.

Fourth position (GA–CDE–(G))

Intermediate notes B natural and F sharp give the Ionian mode.

    ,,   ,,   B natural and F natural give the Mixolydian mode.

    ,,   ,,   B flat and F natural give the Dorian mode.

    ,,   ,,   B flat and F sharp—not recognized as a mode.

Fifth position ((A)–CDE–G)

Intermediate notes B natural and F natural give the Aeolian mode.

    ,,   ,,   B natural and F sharp give the Dorian mode.

    ,,   ,,   B flat and F natural give the Phrygian mode.

    ,,   ,,   B flat and F sharp—not recognized as a mode.

It will therefore be seen that in each position of the pentatonic scale, three out of the four possible pairs of intermediate notes give scales corresponding to the 'church' modes, while the remaining pair, the intermediate notes of F sharp and B flat, result in a scale which is not recognized as a mode.

The Six-note (Hexatonic) Scales (resumed)

To return to the hexatonic scales, which we postponed for consideration of the heptatonic as mentioned above; Professor Bertrand H. Bronson has pointed out[1] that each of the church modes contains the same series of intervals as the mode commencing a fourth below it, except for the numerical position in the scale of one of the two semitonal steps. This may be clearly shown if the first of the two modes is transposed a fourth downwards so that their starting notes coincide. To take the Ionian and Mixolydian modes as an example:

Ionian Mode (transposed down a fourth) (upper stems)

Mixolydian Mode (lower stems)
⌐¬ ∟⌐ indicates the step of a semitone

It will be noticed that while the first semitonal step occurs in both modes between notes 3 and 4, the other of the two semitonal steps occupies a different position in each of the two scales, i.e. between 7 and 8 in the Ionian and between 6 and 7 in the Mixolydian mode. If therefore we omit the note F, which contains the semitone (F natural in the one case and F sharp in the other) we will now have a six-note (hexatonic) scale in which all the notes are common to the two modes, i.e.

Ionian Mode with gap at 7 (upper stems)

Mixolydian Mode with gap at 7 (lower stems)

[1] Cf. *The Traditional Tunes of the Child Ballads* (Princeton University Press—in progress).

Lacking the distinguishing seventh note (the note F) we now find that the notes of this hexatonic scale may be considered either as in the Ionian mode commencing on G, or in the Mixolydian mode commencing on the same note, with the distinguishing note 'gapped' in each case. The same correspondence will be found between the Mixolydian mode and the mode a fourth below that, i.e. the Dorian mode, the distinguishing note to be similarly omitted being now the third degree of the scale, i.e.:

Mixolydian Mode (upper stems)

Dorian Mode (lower stems)

Here then is a basis of classification of the hexatonic scales, the formula in the first example above being 'Hexatonic: Ionian-Mixolydian with gap at 7', and in the second example, 'Hexatonic: Mixolydian-Dorian with gap at 3'.

It must be stated, however, that a few of the tunes on six-note scales in the collection will not submit to this system, in that they can only be related to *one* of the church modes. Such an example is to be seen for instance in the scale of the tune of No. XII:

Here, if the gap be filled with a D natural, the resulting seven-note scale will be Mixolydian: if, however, D flat be substituted as the intermediate note, we get a scale which is not recognized as a mode. Hence the scales of Nos. X and XII can only be classified as 'Mixolydian with gap at 6'. Versions by different singers of such tunes may sometimes show the gap to be filled up, albeit with a 'weak' note, which would seem to indicate that the true scale of the tune is possibly a seven-note one, and that the weak note has been dropped by a particular singer or singers, resulting in the gapped scale in question. Other examples of such gapped scales which do not yield to the two-mode classification may be seen in the tunes of Nos. VIII*e*, XIII, XIV, and XXXVIII*b*.

Four-note Scales

Though tunes constructed on a scale of four notes do exist, and are to be found in this collection, it cannot be suggested that the four-note scale ever existed as a primary stage from which the five-note scale was developed.[1] Two explanations of such four-note scales may be suggested: one, that the melody is a rudimentary one, like some of the simpler labour-tunes such as the 'reaping song', *Oran Arabhaig*, in the Tolmie Collection (No. 74); or alternatively, that a four-note tune may have had originally a scale of five notes, of which one, possibly a weak note, has been dropped.

This dropping of one of the five notes of the pentatonic scale may be seen also, though in a special way, with some of the Ossianic Ballad tunes. Here, however, we see what may in effect be a practice borrowed from ecclesiastical plain-chant, where a particular Gregorian 'tone' may make use of only a part of the complete seven-note 'church' mode upon which it is based. In similar fashion a four-note part of the full pentatonic scale may sometimes be used for certain verses of the Ossianic ballad, while the full five notes appear in other verses.[2]

There are four tunes in the MacCormick Collection which are based upon four-note scales. They are:

Tune No.	Scale	Remarks
III*a*		Pentatonic 1st position with note no. 5 (D) missing
VIII*a* & VIII*c*		Pentatonic 3rd position with note no. 3 (D) missing
XXVIII		Pentatonic 3rd position with note no. 4 (C) missing
XXXIII		Pentatonic 1st position with note no. 5 (D) missing

[1] Cf., however, Anne Gilchrist's comment on the germ or symbol of Scottish Highland music being contained in the four notes CDFG (Tolmie Collection, p. 151).

[2] Cf. the tune for the Ossianic ballad *Duan na Ceàrdaich*, as sung by

It should be added that tunes on four-note scales have also been recorded of which the scales cannot be related to the pentatonic, notably from Miss Nan Mackinnon of the Isle of Vatersay. See also *Folksongs and Folklore of South Uist* by Margaret Fay Shaw, p. 191, for a tune constructed on the four conjunct notes F, G, A, B natural. Other four-note tunes may be seen in the introductions to *Songs of the Hebrides*, vol. i, p. xxvii, and vol. ii, pp. xi and xiii.

Other systems of classification of the modes and scales in Gaelic folk-music may be found in *F.F.S.U.* by Margaret Fay Shaw, p. 77 (based upon the system devised by A. H. Fox Strangways) and in the more complicated system proposed by Miss Anne G. Gilchrist in her introduction to the Tolmie Collection (*Journal of the Folksong Society*, vol. iv, p. 152, insert). See also 'Folksong and the Modes' by Professor B. S. Bronson, first published in the *Musical Quarterly*, vol. xxxii (January 1946), and used in substance in his *Traditional Tunes of the Child Ballads*, vols. i and ii, Introduction (Princeton University Press).[1]

Many folk-musicologists seek to indicate modal classification by numerical or other formulae, most of which require a greater or lesser degree of mental calculation on the part of the reader to arrive at the exact musical meaning. In this collection, the scale, in addition to being named, is set out for greater clarity in musical notation, the *final* or 'keynote' of the mode being indicated by a minim and the rest of the scale by crotchets. This is followed by a separate indication of the compass of the melody, also in musical notation, the position of the final being again expressed by a minim. This makes it unnecessary to use the terms *authentic* and *plagal* in describing the range of a tune (for a plagal tune seldom coincides with its text-book definition, which is that it should extend from the lower to the upper dominant of its particular mode): and the method used here shows exactly the extent of the tune in relation to the position of its final.

Mrs. Archie Macdonald of South Uist, in *The Traditional and National Music of Scotland* (Francis Collinson, Routledge & Kegan Paul, London, 1966). For an example of a waulking tune of five-note scale with the fifth note similarly dropped in some verses, see Marjorie Kennedy-Fraser's *Songs of the Hebrides*, vol. iii, Introduction, p. x.

[1] Some modern musicologists would deny the principle of a development of the six- and seven-note scales from the pentatonic. Much would seem to depend on whether the process, in the national culture concerned, has been a vocal or an instrumental one.

THE FORM OF THE TUNES

In the musical transcriptions of the songs, the phrase divisions of the tunes are indicated by the symbol ». The number of phrases is summarized at the end of each tune, and correspondence or difference of phrase is indicated by capital letters in the usual way.

The number of phrases making up the tunes in the collection will be found to vary from two to eight. Difference of interpretation as to the length of a phrase in certain of the tunes is, however, possible, and the summary of phrase construction in some examples may well be open to argument. Some of the tunes of two phrases for instance will be found to cover only half a line of the text. From this point of view, if the verse (i.e. line of text) be held to be the minimum metrical unit, and to that extent to govern the musical construction, such a two-phrase tune could be held to be only half the tune, a repetition of the two phrases being necessary to complete the verse line. If this be so, the number of phrases making up the tune must of course be regarded as doubled, that is four instead of two. In the single example of a tune of eight phrases (xviic), on the other hand, it is possible to regard the divisions there marked as phrases, as being rather *sections*, with two sections to a phrase, in which case the number of phrases will be halved, i.e. from eight to four phrases of two sections each.

Two main musical forms are to be found in the waulking-song tunes. In the simpler of these, the tune may be regarded as being of two short *strains*, that of the verse (often consisting of no more than one bar of 2/4 time) and that of the refrain. Of these, the refrain will usually be found to be melodically the more important of the two, that of the verse being in a sense preparatory, and leading up to, the tune of the refrain; in much the same way, though in a greatly compressed form, as the verse of the popular song of the earlier part of the present century led up to the main tune, the chorus. In the waulking tunes of this type, the refrain will almost always be found to be in ternary, ABA form, the first phrase being identical or closely similar to the last. Most such refrains are of three phrases, conforming to the ABA pattern above mentioned. A few will be found of four phrases, in which the last phrase is the same as the first, the two middle phrases being either different from or corresponding to each other. To see this ternary construction of the refrain the more easily in these two-strain tunes in the transcriptions, the letters representing the phrase or phrases of the verse are separated from those of the refrain by two perpendicular strokes, e.g.:

	VERSE	REFRAIN
No. VIII*c*. Four phrases;	*A*	*bcb*

	VERSE	REFRAIN
No. XXII*a*. Six phrases;	*AB*	*cdec*

	VERSE	REFRAIN
No. I*a*. Six phrases;	A^1A^2	$b^1c^1c^2b^2$

The other main form of waulking-song tune, which appears to be the older, could be said to be a binary structure—a short verse (half-line) with a refrain (marked in the transcriptions Verse A and Refrain A) followed by another half-line verse and refrain (marked B), each of these four sections usually being different, and one of the refrain sections normally being *longer than the other*, a feature which has an important bearing upon the correct formal interpretation and transcription of the tune.

It has frequently been said by collectors and annotators of Gaelic songs that such 'circular' (i.e. repetitive) tunes as the waulking-song tunes have no definite starting or finishing point, and that the point of commencement and of ending of all such songs is purely arbitrary.[1] A study of the examples recorded at an actual waulking, however, reveals established conventions as to both the point of commencement and of ending.[2] The song begins with the refrain; (in those types which have both solo and chorus sections of the refrain, the point of commencement is the *chorus* refrain). This is sung first by the soloist, in order to indicate to the other women at the waulking-board what song she has chosen to sing. In passing, it may be mentioned that the traditional singers always identify these waulking songs by their meaningless refrains. The

[1] Cf. Marjorie Kennedy-Fraser, *Songs of the Hebrides*, vol. i, p. xxxi; Frances Tolmie Collection, p. 149; Anne Gilchrist, ibid., text and footnote, p. 153.

[2] These are clearly indicated by Donald MacCormick in all his transcriptions.

query 'do you know such and such a song' will nearly always be answered with the words *Dé 'm fonn a th'air?*, 'What is the refrain?'. It is the refrain that is constant and that identifies the song; the 'first line' can be quite different in different versions.[1]

The soloist having first sung the refrain (after the pounding of the cloth on the board has proceeded for a few moments in silence), this is repeated by the chorus; and then the soloist continues with the first line or 'verse' of the song, following it with the solo refrain, and the chorus follows with the rest of the refrain. As an example of this, the way song No. xxx here would be sung at the waulking-board is set out here:

1. Soloist: *Hi hoireann, hi hiù o,*
Hi hoireann, ó ro ho.

2. The chorus repeats this.

3. Soloist: *Cha labhair mi 'n t-òran,* (verse)
Hi hoireann, ó ro ho. (solo refrain)

4. The chorus completes the refrain:

Hi hoireann, hi hiù o,
Hi hoireann, ó ro ho.

5. The soloist then repeats the first verse-line, with the solo refrain, each line of the song being sung twice.

When the singers arrive at the end of one section of the song, and before they go on to the next, where there will be a change of subject and usually a change of rhyme (sometimes with the substitution of a long rhyming vowel for a short one, or vice versa, with a corresponding slight variation in the tune), the soloist indicates this change of subject, which MacCormick marks in his text with the word *atharraich*, 'change', in the margin, by repeating the chorus refrain instead of singing the next line of the song:

6. Soloist: *Gu peasair, gu pònair.*
Hi hoireann, ó ro ho.

Chorus: *Hi hoireann, hi hiù o,*
Hi hoireann, ó ro ho.

Soloist: *Hi hoireann, hi hiù o,*
Hi hoireann, ó ro ho.

[1] See p. 200.

The chorus repeats this, resulting in a threefold singing of the refrain at this point. Then the soloist sings the next line:

7.
> *Dhia, beag a' ghaoth làidir,*
> *Hi hoireann, ó ro ho.*

The chorus completes the refrain, and the song continues as before, and ends with the refrain sung twice as above (6), sometimes after the repetition of the first line of the song, as in XXXI here. It will be seen that by this method the soloist has complete control over what song is chosen, where the changes from one section to another are made, and where the song is brought to an end. The ending, as in most Scots traditional music, is abrupt, and without any suggestion of the customary *rallentando* of sophisticated music; and even the rhythmic thumping on the waulking-board ends at full tempo about two bars after the singing has ceased with an equal suddenness.[1]

In the binary form of the waulking-song tune, in which one of the two refrains is longer than the other, the song ends, surprisingly enough, with the *shorter* of the two refrains. To the academic musician this may be felt to be at variance with the general pattern of music, which is for the shorter of two musical sections to come first, and the longer, more elaborate section second. From the *a priori* musical point of view, therefore, the sequence of some of these tunes may seem to be inverted; nevertheless this is how they are sung, and the practice, being consistent, must be accepted. It is, of course, important to determine the real point of conclusion in order to establish the last note of the tune—for upon that the correct classification of the scale or mode of the song depends.

In its purely formal aspect, though the song begins with the *refrain* in performance, the fact that it also ends with the refrain allows the actual form of the tune to be determined.

It must be realized that the repetition of each line of the song to the same or different melody, the division of the refrain into solo and chorus sections, and the formality of indicating the changes of subject within the song and its final ending, can only be set down

---

[1] This abruptness of conclusion is perhaps more noticeable in *pìobaireachd* (pibroch) than in any other form of Scots traditional music, where a long and intricate movement of air and variations is brought to a cessation with a suddenness that to the sophisticated musician is almost disconcerting.

with complete certainty from an actual waulking performed in the true traditional style, or a recording of one. Next in authoritative rendering comes the purely musical performance by a group of women with knowledge of the waulking, but without any cloth being actually waulked. Much less reliable, it need hardly be said, is the impromptu chorus gathered together perhaps by chance for the sake of making a recording of the song, in which one may even hear male voices joining in, an element entirely foreign to true waulking tradition.

When the song is sung at the fireside without any chorus at all, unless the singer, like Mrs. Neil Campbell, is very conscientious, a good deal of the process may well be omitted. The singer may leave out the introductory refrain (1)[1] and only sing the complete chorus refrain once or twice, probably at the beginning and end of the song, otherwise omitting the chorus refrain (2) completely— a thing that has more than once misled transcribers of Gaelic folk-music. Thirdly, the singer may only sing each line (5) once, instead of twice; and fourthly, she will probably omit the extra refrains (6) sung between the changes of subject. What the collector is therefore liable to get is the lines of the song sung once each followed only by the solo chorus. In this way the considerable effort needed to sing these long songs through their entire length as at a waulking is lightened when they are sung at the fireside, especially if the singer perceives that the collector is ignorant of the Gaelic language. It is always necessary to be on one's guard against recording what may be only an incomplete form of the song in this way, but from analogy and experience the structure of the songs as they would actually be sung at a waulking should usually be apparent. Of course, if the fireside singer sings both verse and complete refrain, there may be doubt which part of the refrain would be sung by the soloist and which by the chorus at an actual waulking; though even here, if the singer sings the verse and part of the refrain *in one breath*, it is a reasonable inference that that part of the refrain belongs properly to the soloist.

In the same way it is only in the recording of an actual waulking, or of the singing of these songs by women experienced in waulking, or from the careful and accurate transcriptions of such a collector as Donald MacCormick, that the points of the beginning and ending of the songs can be accepted as authoritative. Here the

[1] Numbers refer to divisions of song as described on p. 216.

transcriptions of the tunes have been set down exactly as the songs were recorded, though the beginning and ending of some of them would certainly differ when sung at an actual waulking. For this reason the circumstances of each recording have been carefully noted; but in any case the last word on this matter can be safely left with MacCormick's text.

THE WAULKING PULSE

THE thumping of the cloth on the board is, of course, primarily functional to the process of shrinking the cloth; but it also forms such a strong rhythmic element or pulse in the musical performance of the song that it would be a palpable omission not to touch upon it from this point of view. The thumping invariably commences before the singing of the song, and this preliminary rhythmic pulsing may vary in duration from the equivalent of a bar or two of the succeeding tune, to perhaps nearly a full minute before the song begins. Such a setting up of pure rhythm becomes almost hypnotic in its insistence and excitement, accumulating in its intensity to the point when one feels that it positively *demands* a song to go with it; and the spectator has the feeling that the soloist calculates the psychological moment to raise the tune with a sense of 'timing' that forms an artistic element of performance. The standard rhythm of the waulking-song tune is of two pulses to a bar of 2/4 (or alla-breve) or of 6/8 time. The most frequent accentuation is that of a strong beat followed by one less strong. Sometimes, however, a bar of 3/4 time is introduced into the tune, most often at the last bar, which has the deliberately calculated effect of reversing the position of the accents in the bar in the next repetition of the tune, the accent reverting to the normal on the succeeding rotation, and so on—a sure indication that the singers feel the pulse of their thumping to be of musical as well as functional effect. In some songs the elaboration of further bars of three instead of two pulses are introduced, throwing the accents into a series of cross-rhythms.

Other forms of accentuation in the waulking pulse are to be found besides that of the strong followed by a lesser accent. The following have also been recorded:

$$\| \begin{array}{c} > \\ \frac{2}{4} \ \times \end{array} \ \underset{\times}{\mid} \ \mid \underset{\times}{\mid} \ \begin{array}{c} > \\ \times \end{array} \ \mid \underset{\times}{\mid} \ \underset{\times}{\mid} \ \mid \underset{\times}{\mid} \ \underset{\times}{\mid} \ \| \ \text{etc.}$$

$$f \quad pp \quad p \qquad f \quad pp \quad p$$

Here the second pulse is scarcely audible, giving almost the effect of a musical rest, i.e.:

$$x \quad \ulcorner \quad | \; x \quad x \; | \; x \quad | \quad | \; x \quad x \; || \text{ etc.}$$
$$f \qquad p \qquad f$$

Other rhythmic patterns are:

$$|| \; {}^2_4 \; x \quad x \; | \; x \quad x \; | \; x \quad x \; | \; x \quad x \; || \text{ etc.}$$
$$f \qquad\qquad p \quad f \qquad\qquad p$$

and:

$$|| \; {}^2_4 \; x \quad x \; | \; x \quad x \; | \; x \quad x \; | \; x \quad x \; || \text{ etc.}$$
$$mf \qquad f \quad mf \qquad\qquad f \quad mf$$

A curious pulse sequence was recorded in the performance of song No. xv*d* at a genuine waulking at Iochdar, where four loud pulses or thumps during the singing of the *verse* are followed by four much softer pulses during the singing of the *refrain*, the pattern being maintained throughout the song, thus:

Verse   Refrain

$$|| \; {}^2_4 \; x \quad x \; | \; x \quad x \; | \; x \quad x \; | \; x \quad x \; || \text{ etc.}$$
$$f \qquad\qquad\qquad p$$

Whether or not these patterns of pulsation and rhythm are constant in the performance of certain songs and belong to them by tradition is something yet to be ascertained. The unanimity with which the singers perform them in particular songs would seem to indicate that such may well be the case. The question also arises as to whether or not such differences of pulsation and accent result from a modification or difference in the actual movements at the waulking-board. Such differences of hand movements are indeed said to exist, but have been described as a variation between one locality and another rather than within the course of the same waulking. The statement of Nan Mackinnon of Vatersay, a traditional singer and an intelligent informant on the subject, is worth quoting. In a tape recording made in the autumn of 1964 she says: 'They had a different way in every place, even in the island of Barra—the west and the east end, and the north end—they had ways of their

own of moving the cloth.'[1] It may be observed that where the song
is sung with a proper chorus supporting the soloist, the tempo of
the chorus is often slightly quicker than that of the soloist.

Where the accentuation of the pulse into main and subsidiary
accents has been ascertained from an actual waulking, the signs
▽ and △ are used to indicate main and subsidiary accents respectively. When these accents become reversed in alternate cycles of
the melody by reason of an odd number of beats in the tune, the
signs are superimposed thus, ⅄ ⟠, the top line of signs indicating
the accents in the odd-numbered cycles, and the lower line the
accents in the even-numbered ones.

When the pulse has not been verifyable from an actual waulking, the downward-pointing sign ▽ only is used, solely as an
indication of the position in the bar at which the pulse would
occur, without reference to main or subsidiary accents, as these
could only be tentative.

[1] Too much must not be read into this statement. It is doubtful whether
Nan MacKinnon had attended waulkings outside Barra and Vatersay.

MUSICAL VARIATION IN THE TUNES

VARIATIONS occur most frequently in the airs of the verses of waulking songs, often in accordance with the usual liking of folk-singers for varying their melodies. However, in the case of waulk-ing songs, the words of the songs are so intimately linked with the tunes that it can be said that any variation in the prosody of the verse lines is likely to produce a variation in the tune. Often these variations are consistent within different sections of the same song; that is to say that if the rhyming vowels are short in one section of the song, and long in another (e.g. as in No. XVIII here), or if the rhyming words are disyllabic in one section of the song and tri-syllabic in another (as in No. XXXV here), the tune is naturally varied to accommodate itself to these metrical variations. Other-wise, the tunes must accommodate themselves to the stress system of the Scottish Gaelic language, which is strongly on the first syllable, except in the case of true compounds, which are stressed on the second[1] syllable; to the occasional occurrence of epenthetic or svarabhakti vowels, which though not metrically counted or written, have to be sung;[2] to inconsistencies in the position of the stressed syllables in the lines; these are normally the odd syllables, but trisyllabic words and unstressed particles have also to be accommodated. Furthermore, vowels in corresponding positions in the lines may be either long or short, and the tunes have to accommodate themselves to this, though they sometimes resist doing so. But at times variations may occur in almost every line of a waulking song.

Some examples of these variations may be given from No. XXXV here. The normal line in this song consists of eight syllables, ending in a disyllable, the penultimate vowel rhyming, and the stresses

[1] The tendency of the first syllable to attract the stress is so strong that there are many instances of such compounds becoming stressed on the first syllable. (This and following paragraph, information from J. L. Campbell.)

[2] Such vowels are inserted here in brackets when they occur in words printed below the music.

falling on the odd numbered syllable in the line. The fundamental metrical structure is therefore

— ᴗ — — ᴗ — ᴗ — ᴗ
Nì e fìon a dh'*u*isg' an t-sl*é*ibhe   (l. 1220)

However, in the next line we get

— ᴗ ᴗ — — — ᴗ — ᴗ
Copanan d*ea*r(*a*)g *a*ir a' chr*é*adhaich

the line beginning with a trisyllable, followed by *dearg* with a svarabhakti vowel that attracts equal stress with the original vowel of the word. Later on we have (l. 1231)

ᴗ — — — ᴗ ᴗ ᴗ ᴗ — ᴗ
No N*ia*ll *a*nabharrach a bhr*à*thair

while there is a short section later where the rhyming words are of three syllables:

ᴗ — ᴗ — ᴗ — — ᴗ ᴗ
Mo gh*ao*l 's mo ghr*à*dh an t-'*ò*g b*ea*darrach

The tune must be accommodated to these, and to other similar variations.

As variations in the meaningless syllables of the refrains of the songs are non-existent within any one particular version of the song, so variations in the melodies of the refrains occur only exceptionally. Occasionally the melody of a refrain may be varied, perhaps by one particular singer in the chorus. When such a thing happens, one finds that the rest of the chorus singers will either adopt the variation, or else stubbornly stick to their own version against it, so that the two versions of the tune may be heard in concert throughout the rest of the song, making an unintentional and untraditional two-part effect, such as occurs in the recording of the chorus of No. xxxvii, *Beinn a' Cheathaich*,[1] transcribed here.

Often, also, the true version or 'norm' of a Gaelic folk-tune does not appear immediately at the beginning of the performance, and the singers, whether soloist or chorus, may take several verses to sing themselves into the 'correct' version as they begin to settle down and recollect the air more surely. This last is characteristic of most Gaelic singers.[2] In the transcriptions, all such variations

[1] Incidentally, this was the traditional waulking-song melody upon which Mrs. Kennedy-Fraser arranged or composed her 'Kishmul's Galley'.

[2] One cannot help feeling that it is a weakness of some of Mrs. Kennedy-Fraser's transcriptions that they are based on the opening verse and chorus

of interest have as far as possible been noted down. Verse lines requiring adaptation of the tune by the singer owing to different numbers of syllables or different lengths of rhyming vowels have also been set down.

For practical reasons the songs have been transcribed at a pitch at which the melody lies conveniently within the confines of the stave. The actual pitch of the singer's opening note has, however, been set down in the form of a diamond-shaped note-head.[1] A word may be said of the remarkably low pitch of the women's voices, of which the pitch so indicated in the transcriptions might seem incredible to the reader and therefore wrongly set down. Such extremely deep tessitura is, however, characteristic in actual fact of the women singers of the Outer Hebrides, notably in Barra, Eriskay, and South Uist, where E and D in the *bass stave* are commonplace, and even notes as low as B flat, the second bottom line of the bass stave, are not unknown. Tunes Nos. IV*d*, V, VIII*e*, XIII*c*, XXII*a*, XXII*b*, XXIII*b*, XXXIX*a*, and XL*b* are interesting examples. The tessitura of singers in the isle of Lewis, at the north end of the island chain of the Outer Hebrides is, on the other hand, a peculiarly high one.

It will be found that the pitch rises often in the course of a long song. This is a normal feature of the performance of many unaccompanied traditional singers, and has not been noted in the transcriptions. The indicated pitch is that of the singers at the commencement of the songs.

only. In *A Life of Song* (p. 136) she says that 'in order to get records of as many songs as possible, we generally made a practice of taking only one verse and chorus on the [dictaphone] cylinder'.

[1] It should be noted that this indication refers to the pitch of the note at which the song begins (usually the refrain), and not necessarily to the first note of the transposition.

CHARACTERISTIC RHYTHMS

CHARACTERISTIC of much Gaelic song is a dotted rhythm which is neither the dotted quaver of 2/4 rhythm, e.g. ‖ 2/4 ♩. ♪ ♩. ♪ ‖, nor the more flowing long-short rhythm of 6/8 time, e.g. ‖ 6/8 ♩ ♪♩ ♪ ‖, but which is something between the two.[1] In the course of a single song, dotted rhythms will seem to vary in approximating more nearly to the one figure than to the other, and in such cases it is convenient to use the mixed time signature of 2/4 (6/8) or 6/8 (2/4), of which examples will constantly be found throughout the transcriptions.

[1] It is a rhythm approximating to the dance-band interpretation of dotted rhythm, particularly by the saxophone team, in popular dance 'numbers', about which there was some interesting correspondence in the musical periodicals of some years ago. It actually consists of a slight lengthening of the short note at the expense of the longer.

THE MEANINGLESS REFRAIN-
SYLLABLES AND THEIR SIGNIFICANCE

(J. L. Campbell and Francis Collinson)

It is well known that waulking songs and other traditional Gaelic labour songs have refrains that consist of meaningless syllables occasionally interspersed with meaningful words or expressions. Most of these meaningless vocables are open monosyllables, i.e. monosyllables ending in a vowel. A few are di- or even trisyllables, though these could be broken down into monosyllables for the most part.

Occasionally meaningful phrases occur in the refrains, for example the first and last lines of that of No. 1 here;[1] but more usually meaningful words are limited to interjections, e.g. *nàilibh*, 'yea!'; *bheir mi*, 'I'll say'; *trom orra* (xvi) perhaps meaning 'hard at it!' (i.e. the work); *falbh orra seinn*, 'get on with it, sing!'. Occasionally apparently meaningful expressions such as *ghealladh i* ('she would promise') are sung in quite meaningless contexts.

An exhaustive analysis of the phonetic structure and the mnemonic and musical significance of the meaningless refrains of traditional Gaelic songs is something that has not yet been undertaken. It would demand a careful study of a great deal more material than the forty songs that are contained in this book. It may be said, however, that the evidence contained in these songs and in others known to the writers does seem to point in a certain direction, and that this is worth indicating, with the qualification that many of the observations made in this chapter must at present be considered tentative.

A prime purpose of these refrains is obviously mnemonic, to fix the tune and the version of the song known to the reciter in her or his mind. As has already been pointed out, the traditional singer identifies this kind of song by the refrain, not by the title or any possible first line—one reason being that waulking songs usually

[1] In this case they may have been substituted for original meaningless syllables, as the words of this song are of comparatively recent origin.

have no titles and different versions of the same song often have different opening lines. The importance of the refrain to the traditional singer may be shown by the fact that while a person who has learnt Gaelic may not find it difficult to learn some of these songs and their melodies, he or she will often find it difficult to memorize the meaningless refrains, and may be tempted to think that their exact reproduction is not a matter of great importance: whereas with the traditional singer precisely the opposite is the case; the singer cannot remember the song properly unless she or he can recall the refrain exactly, and deviations from its 'correct' form are immediately noticed and corrected.

The importance of the refrains is emphasized by the fact that there is no standard version of any of these songs, and that most of them embody different sections on different topics, many of which are part of a floating oral tradition that could be drawn on for the purpose of extemporization at will.[1] One may therefore compare the refrain of a waulking song to a thread upon which differently coloured beads, i.e. different sections on different subjects, have been strung at different times by various improvisors. The order in which the beads occur is not a matter of great importance: what is important, is that the thread should not be broken.

So much is certain. A more difficult question is whether the meaningless syllables used can have a musical significance akin to that of *canntaireachd*, the system whereby players of *pìobaireachd* memorize the bagpipe scale and even complicated rhythmic figures and grace-notes by means of meaningless vocables based on meaningless monosyllables representing the nine notes of the bagpipe scale, *em, en, o, o, a, e, ve, di*, and *i*—allowing for the fact that the rigid standardization of this system is a comparatively modern development.[2] But before one can attempt to answer such a question, it is necessary to investigate the phonetic structure of the meaningless syllables occurring in the refrains of waulking songs, and the manner in which they are used.

An examination of these meaningless refrains reveals that their phonetic structure is by no means a haphazard one. It is fundamentally vocalic, like that of the Finnish language,[3] being based

[1] See p. 22, n. 1.

[2] See Francis Collinson, *The Traditional and National Music of Scotland* (Routledge and Kegan Paul, 1966).

[3] It may not be impossible that these refrains embody fragments of a forgotten language. Compare the use of the Hebrew *alleluia* in English choruses

on the long and short forms of the stressed vowels of the language as described by Professor C. Hj. Borgstrøm in *Dialects of the Outer Hebrides*, p. 11, with the exception that the sounds *ö:* and *æ:* (long open *e*) are either very rare or absent. Counting long and short vowels as independent phonemes in this case, this gives 16 vowel sounds as available for the formation of such syllables, to which must be added the diphthongs *eo* (with open and close *o*), *iu*, and *ua*. The favourite vowels are short *a*, long or short close *e*, *i*, and *u*, and open and close *o*, the last being considerably more frequent in these refrains than it is in everyday speech. Moreover, back and front vowels are preferred, the mixed vowels *ʌ* and *ö* not occurring frequently.[1]

The consonantal system of these refrain vocables is strikingly restricted as compared with the spoken language. It is limited largely, though not entirely, to the breathing *h*, the labial spirants *f* and *v* (written *bh*), and the three varieties of the *l*, *n*, and *r* sounds. Complete absence of the preaspirated voiceless occlusives, *c*, *p*, *t*, is particularly noticeable. Also absent are palatal *g* and *d*; non-palatal *d* is very rare, apparently occurring only after *n*, when it is voiced.[2] *B*[3] and *m* are not very frequent; the sibilant *s* seems only to occur as representing *is*, 'and'; its palatal form is absent. The spirants represented in Gaelic by *ch* and *dh*, broad and slender, and in phonetic script by *x*, *ç*, *γ*, and *j*, are all uncommon. The guttural nasal *ŋ* does not occur, nor do nasalized vowels.

These are the consonant sounds that can be used initially, usually in open syllables. But except in the case of *h* there is by no means complete freedom to use any of these consonants with any vowel; *f* and *n* seem only to combine with *a*;[4] and such combinations as *bhu*, *bhao*, *bhe*; *lu*; *rao*, *re*; seem to be entirely avoided. No such syllable can begin with a combination of consonants except in the case of *'s* before *na*, which is permissible. In the case of closed syllables the choice of final consonants is even more limited, only *g*, *m*, *n*, and *l* being used, and possibly *v* and *r*.[5]

---

[1] Short *ö* is very rare. It is also not popular for rhyming purposes in verse, and sections such as the first in No. xv here where such rhyme occurs are unusual. *ʌ* is represented in Gaelic spelling by *ao*: unfortunately this spelling is sometimes used to represent *ö* as well.

[2] e.g. *héman du* (cf. K. C. Craig, p. 13).

[3] *B* is more frequent in lullabies.

[4] *F* occurs combined with *i* in the meaningless *Fire, fàire* in a few refrains.

[5] Depending on how the syllables are divided. This has not been standardized by editors.

Meaningless disyllables found in these refrains conform to these rules. Of these the most frequent is *hoireann, oireann*, which, however, is sometimes written *o rinn*. The *o* can occur lengthened. Others are *hillinn* and *hurabh*, which, however, could be written *hill inn* and *hu ra bh-*. Exceptional disyllables like *challa, laoithill* (*th* represents hiatus), *leathag*, etc., prevent the system from becoming monotonous and help to fix the refrain in the memory. *Éileadh* which occurs fairly frequently is often written *eile* 'another' in transcriptions, but the stressed *e* seems to be always long here.

An important aspect of these meaningless refrains is that by no means all the possible sequences of monosyllables seem to be acceptable. Thus, the syllable *fa* has only been found followed by syllables beginning with *r* or *l*. No phrase has been found beginning with *v* (*bh*). And while it is easy enough to find sequences like *hao ri, hi ri, hu ra, hu ru*, and *hó hò*,[1] these have not been found occurring in the opposite order. The syllable *gu*, too, only seems to occur after *ho* or *hu*.

The fact that only certain syllables are used and that certain sequences of them are not acceptable rules strongly against any possibility of the refrain syllables' being used to express pitch; for while it is quite easy to imagine a system in which such syllables were used to express the scale that is within the compass of the traditional singer's voice—and the syllables exist in considerably greater number than would be needed to do this—use of the syllables in this way as a kind of Gaelic tonic solfa would in practice produce disagreeable sequences such as *fa gu, ro hao*, and so on. In any case, considering the way in which the melodies vary from singer to singer, the meaningless refrains could not express the music exactly. All that can be said is that through the alternation of long and short vowels[2] they represent the rhythm roughly and that some of them suggest pitch vaguely, e.g. *hao* or *haodh* (*hɑː:, hɑː: γ*) may be associated with a high note,[3] and *fail iù* with a rising sequence.[4] Long vowels are usually not associated with a note shorter than a dotted quaver in 2/4 time or a crotchet in 6/8 time: but, as the timbre of the short vowels in these refrains is that of their long forms, it is sometimes very difficult to decide whether

---

[1] i.e. long close *o* followed by long open *o*.
[2] e.g. in the refrains to Nos. XVII and XL here.
[3] e.g. in the refrain to No. XVII bar 11.
[4] e.g. in the refrains to Nos. XIII *c, d, e*, and XXXI.

the vowel corresponding to a quaver in a song in 2/4 time sung in slower tempo should or should not carry the accent that marks length in conventional writing. A long vowel can also cover two associated notes that together take up the time indicated above; for example, with the liberty that is allowed to folk-singers, a figure like *hù rù* can represent in 2/4 time ♩ ♩ or ♩ ♪ ♪ or ♪ ♪ ♩. The maximum value represented by a long vowel in these waulking songs is a full beat in 2/4 or 6/8 time.

The time-length represented by a short vowel can vary from a demisemiquaver to a quaver in 2/4 time. Generally speaking it may be said that when a short vowel follows a long one in combinations like *Hì ri, É ho, hò ro*, etc., within the same bar, the short vowel 'robs' the long one of a shorter portion of the full time-value of the beat or pulse. This occurs frequently, see, for examples, songs Nos. 1*d*, bar 8; vii*b*, bar 6; xiii, bar 6; xv*b*, bar 3; xxv*a*, bar 1.

Quite as frequently, indeed possibly more often (for this is a common rhythmic feature of Gaelic music), a short vowel comes before a long one. This can be seen, for example, in songs Nos. iii*a*, bars 8 and 9; iv*a*, bar 5. A long vowel, both preceded and followed by a short one within the same bar, occurs, for instance, in No. xxi*b*, bar 7. In this case the vocables could also be freely interpreted as:

Hi ùr - abh ó

Where two short vowels follow each other, they will frequently be found to divide the waulking pulse equally, see, for example, song No. v, bar 2. Similarly, three short vowels in succession will divide the beat into three, see *e.g.* vi*b*, bar 2.

In song No. v, bar 6, there is an interesting example of the beat divided by four short vowels, one of which is an epenthetic one:

fal-(a)bh orr-a seinn.

(the epenthetic vowel being one which has developed in Scottish Gaelic pronunciation, between two consonants in certain circumstances: it is not indicated in writing or counted metrically, but as it is sung it is always restored in brackets in the musical transcriptions in this book. MacCormick frequently wrote it in his manuscript, though not in this instance).

Note that MacCormick here wrote *sèinn*; but in this word it is actually the nasal *nn* that is long, not the vowel. It may be added that in the case of disyllables such as *hoireann, hillinn, chalainn, laithill*, when the second syllable of these represents a long note preceded by a short one, the length attaches to the nasal or liquid consonant rather than to the vowel. In the case of *leathag*, a refrain-word that occurs only once in this collection, the -*ag* presumably being the diminutive suffix, would have a clear *a* sound in any case. Disyllables with lengthened first vowels represent long notes followed by short ones, except in the case of *hillinn* in song No. II where both syllables here are long.

When the first syllable of a long-short figure is rendered by a very short note, we get the characteristic 'Scots snap', *e.g.* song No. IX, bar 6. Here there is nothing to indicate that the opening syllables *Hi rì* should be sung in this manner; in most cases they would represent an ordinary semiquaver followed by a dotted quaver, or even the short and long notes of a triplet figure, ♪♩. Nevertheless, there are some pairs of vocables that seem more often than not to be interpreted in this shortened way, e.g. *hoireann* in song No. IX, bar 4 (the bar following that referred to above), with the second syllable coming as a very short note on the second beat. Another figure usually rendered as a snap is *libh ó* or *lebh ó*, see *e.g.* song No. XIV, bar 5.

There are a number of other vocable groups which strongly suggest a particular rhythm, though these are capable of variation in every case. Examples are:

Hì ri rì $\frac{6}{8}$

Ho ro éil-eadh $\frac{6}{8}$

Gheall-adh e (also, *u o ho*, and, *chall-a bhi*)

Nàil-ibh i $\frac{2}{4}$

Hi liù hi leò $\frac{6}{8}$ or $\frac{6}{8}$

The foregoing shows that the refrain syllables do have a rhythmic value, indicating which notes are long and which short, of course within the limits of the rigid pulse of the waulking; and innumerable fine gradations of rhythm are possible and discernible in performance. Thus the long-short figure may be expressed as a true dotted quaver followed by a semiquaver of 2/4 time, e.g. $\frac{2}{4}$ ♩. ♪ ; or alternatively it may be expressed as the more flowing long-short figure of 6/8 time, e.g. $\frac{6}{8}$ ♩ ♪♩ ♪. It may also be sung, and frequently is sung, as something between the two, as a kind of *lazy* dotted note, in which the dotted quaver is a fraction shorter, and the semiquaver a fraction longer, than the strict value of standard musical notation.

Still more is this freedom of rhythmic values to be seen in the dotted triplet of 6/8 time:

The typical Scottish Highland way of singing or playing the figure is to lengthen quite considerably the first note of the triplet so that the actual effect is something like this:

It is an effect particularly often heard in pipe-tunes.

One would not, of course, expect to find such subtle variations indicated by the meaningless syllables of these waulking-song refrains.

One of the most remarkable, and indeed crucial features of the refrain syllables in general is that, while short conventional groups of up to three or even four syllables may occur in different songs, actual duplication of a whole musical phrase of these syllables is so rare as to be practically non-existent. It would seem that in the initial composition of these refrains, whoever may have made them, duplication between one song and another was rejected on principle, either by the persons who made the tunes, or by consensus of agreement amongst the singers themselves—amongst whom *some-one* would be sure to notice and object to the fact that a particular sequence of vocables making up a phrase had already been used for another song. This shows that the musical significance of these meaningless syllables must be considered within the context of the particular song in which they occur, and that the meaningless refrain as a whole is a mnemonic device for recalling the song as a whole to the traditional singers' memories.

The following table of vocable sequences beginning with the syllable close *o*, or *ho*; *ó* or *hó* (*o* and *ho*, etc., being to some extent interchangeable in these songs) will show how little duplication there is to be found in the present collection in phrase-sequences of vocables beginning with the same commonly used syllables.

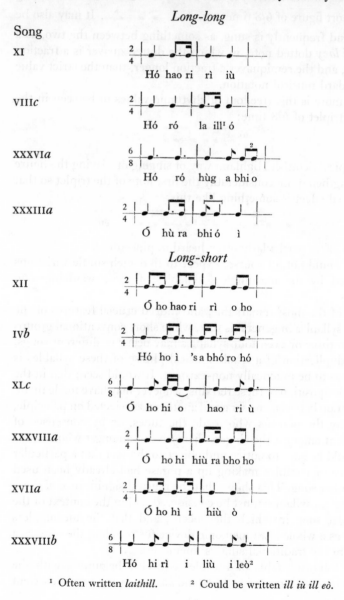

Long-long

Song

XI — Hó hao ri rì iù

VIIIc — Hó ró la ill[1] ó

XXXVIa — Hó ró hùg a bhi o

XXXIIIa — Ó hù ra bhi ó ì

Long-short

XII — Ó ho hao ri rì o ho

IVb — Hó ho ì 's a bhó ro hó

XLc — Ó ho hi o hao ri ù

XXXVIIIa — Ó ho hi hiù ra bho ho

XVIIa — Ó ho hì i hiù ò

XXXVIIIb — Hó hi rì i liù i leò[2]

[1] Often written *laithill*.   [2] Could be written *ill iù ill eò*.

Long-short (continued)

Song

XXIV*c*

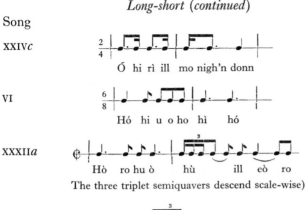

Ó hi rì ill mo nigh'n donn

VI

Hó hi u o ho hì   hó

XXXII*a*

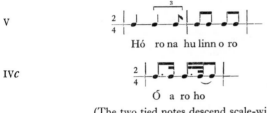

Hò   ro hu ò   hù   ill   eò   ro

The three triplet semiquavers descend scale-wise)

V

Hó   ro na hu linn o ro

IV*c*

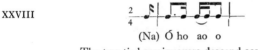

Ó   a   ro ho

(The two tied notes descend scale-wise)

XXVIII

(Na) Ó ho   ao   o

The two tied semiquavers descend scale-wise)

Short-long

III*b*

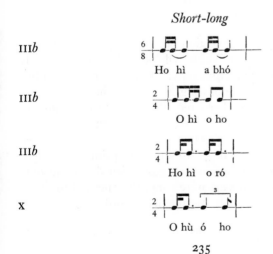

Ho hì   a bhó

III*b*

O hì   o ho

III*b*

Ho hì   o ró

X

O hù   ó   ho

235

Short-long (continued)

Song
IV*c*

O ró a bhì ó a ro ho

Short-short

VIII*b*

Ho i ó ho nàil-ibh ì

III*b*

Ho ro ghealladh i

XXIII*a*

Ho ro ho hao ri o hò

XXIX*b*

O ho hao rì nàil-ibh, ho ró ro hó hao rì

XIV*b*

O ho lebh ó ro hoireann ó

XXXIV

O ho hù ill eo ho, hao ri a ró

The extreme rarity of duplication of a whole phrase of refrain
syllables means that a line of these syllables will almost certainly
relate to one tune and to one tune only. The only exception to this
in our experience is the case of song No. XXXVIII here, where the
same refrain syllables have been recorded sung to two different
melodies;[1] we know of no other instance of this either within or
without the MacCormick Collection. This explains why, when
Scottish Gaelic poetry first began to appear in print in the eighteenth century, and the authors or collectors wished to indicate to
readers to what airs the poems were sung, they needed to do no
more than to give the (usually meaningless) words of the chorus

[1] See the tunes as transcribed on pp. 337 and 338.

as the 'tune'. Gaelic readers then were sufficiently acquainted with the corpus of Gaelic song to be able to recognize what air was meant immediately from this as a rule; whereas many modern readers would require that the tune be written in staff notation or in sol-fa. In earlier times readers who happened to be unacquainted with the airs could get a good idea of their rhythmic patterns from the meaningless refrains.[1] This is all the *notational* value such refrains could be said to possess; their real value was *mnemonic*, as the great majority of traditional singers, especially waulking women, could not read Gaelic in any case.

What distinguishes the refrains of Scottish Gaelic waulking songs sharply from those of most Western European folk-songs is their special phonetic structure, which makes their singing in a complete legato of uninterrupted tone easier than anything short of a solfeggio exercise; their numerous and intricate forms; and the very important part they play in carrying the main melodies of the songs. One can only speculate on what their history may be. If, as seems very likely, many of the tunes of these songs are much older than the words which are now sung to them, the meaningless syllables associated with their refrains may possess a very remarkable antiquity.

---

[1] Early books of Gaelic poetry would be read out loud by the few persons able to read Gaelic, to many who could not, and someone among the hearers would be likely to be able to identify the tunes from the refrain words in most cases.

IV

MUSICAL TRANSCRIPTIONS

FRANCIS COLLINSON

I

Ailein duinn, ó hì shiùbhlainn leat

(*a*) Mrs. Campbell (Bean Nill), Frobost, South Uist.

(*Sung without chorus*)

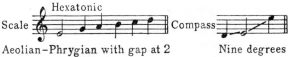

Scale · Hexatonic · Aeolian–Phrygian with gap at 2 · Compass · Nine degrees

Form: six phrases: A¹ A²‖B¹ C¹ C² B².

Form: six phrases: $A^1 A^2 \| B^1 C^1 C^2 B^2$.

Structure: a fourteen-bar melody: Verse 4, Refrain 10.

The singer commences the song with the refrain at ⊕ but with the opening bar changed as follows:

Refrain (*b*)

I

Ailein duinn, ó hì shiùbhlainn leat

(*b*) Sung by Mrs. Munro, South Uist

(Sung without chorus)

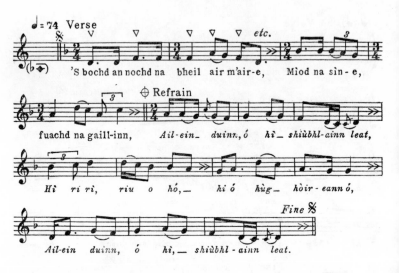

'S bochd an nochd na bheil air m'air-e, Mìod na sìn-e,

fuachd na gaill-inn, *Ail-ein_ duinn, ó hì_ shiùbhl-ainn leat,*

Hì rì rì, riu o hó,_ hi ó hùg_ hòir-eann ó,

Ail-ein duinn, ó hì,_ shiùbhl-ainn leat.

Scale — Hexatonic — Compass — Nine degrees

Phrygian–Aeolian with gap at 2

Form: six phrases: A B ‖ C¹ D E C². (Verse Refrain)

Structure: a fourteen-bar melody: Verse 4, Refrain 10.

The singer commenced the song with the refrain, at ⊕.

I

Ailein duinn, ó hì shiùbhlainn leat

(*c*) Sung by Mrs. Kate McCormick, Benbecula

(*Sung without chorus*)

Verse (8 syllables)

♩ = 84

Ail-ein duinn, a chiall 's a nàir - e!

(7 syllables)

Truagh nach robh mi ceart làmh riut, *Ail-ein duinn, ó hì,*

shiùbhl-ainn leat. Hao ri ri, ri ú hò, hi ò hùg

kòir eann ó, Ail-ein duinn, ó hì shiùbhl-ainn leat.

Variants

Ail-ein duinn, 'S truagh nach robh mi ceart làmh riut, Ge bè bodh'

no sgeir an tràgh thu, fàg an— làn thu Rìgh na Cath-rach

ùir no'n gain-eamh

Hexatonic

Scale   Compass

Aeolian-Phrygian with gap at 2   Nine degrees

Verse Refrain
Form: six phrases: A B ‖ C D¹ D² C.*
Structure: a fourteen-bar melody: Verse 4, Refrain 10.

 * *Note.* In the version which has a verse of seven syllables [shown as variant (*b*) above] the second phrase is roughly speaking a transposition of the first phrase, and the two phrases making up the verse should therefore here be considered as A¹, A².
 The refrain corresponds to Craig's version, and to M.S.C., p. 258.
 The singer commenced the song with the refrain at ⊕

I

Ailein duinn, ó hì shiùbhlainn leat

(*d*) Sung by Seonaid Shomhairle Bhig, Barra, and Mrs. Maclean, Barra

244

Form: six phrases: Verse‖Refrain
A B ‖C¹ D¹ D² C²
(with similarity of beginning in phrases A and B).
Structure: a fourteen-bar melody: Verse 4, Refrain 10.
The singer commenced the song at the verse 'Chuala mi' etc. as above.

II

'S mise bhean bhochd, chianail, thùrsach
(South Uist, centre)

Sung by Donald McIntyre, Paisley

(Without chorus)

Form: six phrases: Verse‖Refrain
A B¹‖C, B² D B³.
Structure: a twelve-bar melody: Verse 4, Refrain 8.
The verse lines are sung in the order 1, 2; 2, 3; 3, 4; etc.
The singer commenced the song with the refrain, at ⊕.

245

III

Nighean ud thall, bheil thu 't'fhaireachadh?
(South Uist, north end)

(*a*) Sung by Miss Kate MacDonald (Ceit Iseabail), Iochdar, and
chorus, at an actual waulking

Accentuation of preliminary waulking pulse before song begins:

In the recording, the pulse continues for one bar after the song has finished;

i.e. for two pulses, 1 strong and 1 weak. *e. g.*

As pentatonic 1st position   Five degrees
with fifth note missing or 'gapped'.

Form: four phrases: A¹ B A² B.

Structure: an eight-bar melody:

 Verse A, 1; Refrain A (solo) 1, (chorus) 2.
 Verse B, 1; Refrain (solo) 1, (chorus) 2.

III

Nighean ud thall (Benbecula)

(b) Sung by Miss Kate MacMillan, Torlum, Benbecula

(Sung without chorus)

Ionian–Mixolydian with gap at 7   Six degrees

Form: four phrases: A B¹ C B².

Structure: an eight-bar melody:

Verse A, 1; Refrain, (solo) 1, (chorus) 2.
Verse B, 1; Refrain (solo) 1, (chorus) 2.

The singer commenced the song with verse A as here, with, however, a repetition of bars 3 and 4.

Nighean ud thall (Barra, south end)

(*c*) Singer: Miss Mary Morrison, Earsary, Castlebay, Barra

(*With chorus*)

Introductory refrain; 1st time soloist, 2nd time chorus

Ho ro— gheall-adh a, o hì— o hó,

Verse of 4 syllables Refrain (solo) (*b*)(chorus)

Nigh-ean ud thall Hi ri— a bhó ho ro— gheall-adh a,

o hì— o hó.

another form of
(5 syllable verse)   5 syllable verse

Variants

Bheil thu 't'fhair-each-adh

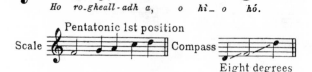

Ho ro gheall-adh a Ho ro gheall-adh a

(Atharraich) *Fine*

Ho ro—gheall-adh a, o hì— o hó.

Pentatonic 1st position
Scale Compass

Eight degrees

Note. B♮ occurs exceptionally in variant at *.

Form: Basically there are two phrases: A and B. The music of the verse, how-ever, only takes in half the verse line and therefore has to be repeated to complete the line. This has in a sense the effect of extending it to twice its length, in which case the form may be thought of as being in four phrases—A B A B.

Structure: a four-bar melody extended by repetition to eight bars: Verse 1. Refrain (solo) 1, chorus 2: all repeated to complete the verse line.

At the 'change of subject' or 'Atharraich' the two bars above are repeated first by the soloist then by the chorus. The next section of the text then continues to be sung to the tune from ✕ to ✕ as before.

The song ends with the same two additional bars as at the 'Atharraich', i.e. the chorus response, repeated, first by the soloist and then by the chorus.

III

Nighean ud thall (Barra, south end)

(*d*) Mrs. Mary Morrison (Bean Phluim), Barra, with Miss Annie Johnston singing the chorus

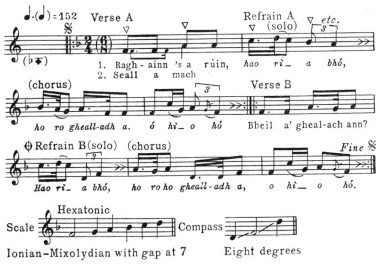

Form: four phrases: A¹ B¹ A² B².

Structure: an eight-bar melody:
  Verse A, 1; Refrain A (solo) 1, (chorus) 2.
  Verse B, 1; Refrain B (solo) 1, (chorus) 2.

The two sections alternate irregularly, too often for either to be classified simply as a variant. The song begins with the refrain at ⊕, the first bar being sung by the soloist and the remaining two bars by the chorus.

III

Nighean ud thall, bheil thu 't'fhaireachadh?
(Mingulay tradition)

(*e*) Sung by Mrs. Anna MacDougall (Anna Raghnaill Eachainn)
Castlebay

(*With chorus*)

Ionian–Mixolydian

Six degrees

Form: four phrases: A B: ‖ :C B.

Structure: an eight-bar melody:
  Verse A, 1; Refrain A (solo) 1, (chorus) 2.
  Verse B, 1; Refrain B (solo) 1, (chorus) 2.

The singer commenced the song with Verse A.

IV

Cairistiana
(South Uist, centre)

(*a*) Singer: Mrs. Campbell (Bean Nìll Mhóir), Frobost

(*Without chorus*)

Form: four phrases A¹ B A² B.

Structure; an eight-bar melody:
    Verse 2, Refrain (solo) 2, (chorus) 4.

The singer commenced the song with the refrain at ⊕.

IV

Cairistiana
(South Uist, north end)

(*b*) Sung by Mrs. Donald John MacLellan, Iochdar, South Uist
with chorus, at a genuine waulking

Nach fhreag-air thu, Chair-ist-ian - a, É— hó
hì rì, hó ho ì 's a bhó ro hó, é hó hì rì.

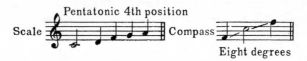

Scale — Pentatonic 4th position — Compass — Eight degrees

Form: four phrases: A B¹ C B².

Structure: an eight-bar melody: Verse 2, Refrain 6.

* The tempo varies during the performance. The mean tempo is as marked above.

The singer commenced the song at ⊕ with the form

Bhó ro ho,

the chorus chiming in at the 2nd beat of the second bar.

At 'Atharraich' the soloist repeats the last four bars of the time, which are further repeated by the chorus. The soloist then continues with the verse line from the beginning of the time, i.e. from the first 𝄋 .

IV

Cairistiana
(Barra, north end)

(c) Sung by Seonaid Shomhairle Bhig (Janet Mackinnon)
and chorus

Form: four phrases: A B C B.

Structure: an eight-bar melody, Verse 2, Refrain 6.

The singer commenced the song with the verse as above.

Cairistiana
(Barra, south end)

(*d*) Sung by Mrs. Mary Morrison (Bean Phluim), Barra

(*Without chorus*)

Form: four phrases: A B C B.

Structure: eight-bar melody:
  Verse 2, Refrain (solo) 2, (chorus) 4.

The singer commenced the song with the refrain at ⊕.

V

Cha n-eil mi gun nì air m'aire (South Uist, centre)

Sung by Mrs. Mary Steele, Bornish

(*Without chorus*)

Form: four phrases: A¹ B C A².

Structure: an eight-bar melody:
Verse A, 2; Refrain A, 2.
Verse B, 2; Refrain B, 2.

The singer, after the introductory refrain, sings the opening line to the concluding half of the tune, on which the song ultimately ends. This is therefore labelled Verse B.

Tha an latha an diu gu fliuch fuaraidh
(Barra, Mingulay tradition)

(*a*) Singer: Mrs. MacDougall (Anna Raghnaill Eachainn), with
Annie Johnston singing chorus

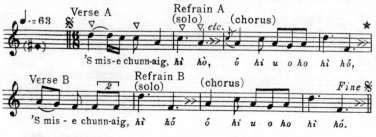

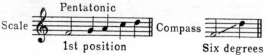

Form: four phrases: A B C B.

Structure: an eight-bar melody.
Verse A, 1; Refrain A (solo) 1, (chorus) 2.
Verse B, 1; Refrain B (solo) 1, (chorus) 2.

The singer commenced the song with verse A as above.

The song ended at ★. *Fine* indicates the more usual place of ending, the singer
repeating the last two bars (i.e. the chorus refrain), which is repeated by the
chorus in its turn.

Tha an latha an diu gu fliuch fuaraidh
(Barra, south end)

(*b*) Sung by Mrs. Mary MacNeil, and chorus

Form: four phrases: A B C B.

Structure: an eight-bar melody:
  Verse A, 1; Refrain A (solo) 1, (chorus) 2.
  Verse B, 1; Refrain B (solo) 1, (chorus) 2.

Each half-line of text is repeated. The first half-line ('S mise chunnaic) is irregularly repeated to the same melody, i.e. to the tune of Verse A. Thereafter the pattern is mainly to commence each new half-line to the tune of Verse B and repeat it to Verse A. The song ends with the repetition of the last two bars by the soloist, followed by a further repetition by the chorus

VI

Tha an latha an diu gu fliuch fuaraidh
(Barra, south end)

(*c*) Singer: Mrs. Mary Morrison ('Bean Phluim'), Earsary

(*With chorus*)

Form: four phrases: A B A B.

Structure: an eight-bar melody:
    Verse A, 1; Refrain A (solo) 1, (Chorus) 2.
    Verse B, 1; Refrain B (solo) 1, (Chorus) 2.

The singer commenced the song with Refrain B at ⊕ ; the song ended with a repetition of the last two bars by the soloist, followed by a further repetition by the chorus.

VII

Di-Sathuirne ghabh mi mulad
(South Uist, north end)

(*a*) Miss Penny Morrison, Iochdar, with chorus, at a real waulking

Scale: Pentatonic; 1st position

Compass: (Nine) Eight degrees

Form: five phrases: A B C D E.

Structure: an eleven-bar melody:
  Verse A (solo) 2; Refrain A (chorus) 5.
  Verse B (solo) 2; Refrain B (chorus) 2.

VII

Di-Sathuirne ghabh mi mulad
(Benbecula)

(*b*) Miss Kate MacCormick

(*Without chorus*)

Form: five phrases: A B C D E.

Structure: a ten-bar melody:
  Verse A, 2; Refrain A 4, Verse B, 2; Refrain B 2.

See note to VII (*c*) on reversal of accentuation of waulking pulse in each alternative cycle.

Di-Sathuirne ghabh mi mulad
(Barra, Mingulay tradition)

(c) Mrs. MacDougall ('Anna Raghnaill Eachainn'), Castlebay,
with Annie Johnston singing Chorus

Form: five phrases: A B C D E.

Structure: a ten-bar melody:
Verse A, 2; Refrain A, (chorus) 2; Verse B 2, Refrain (solo) 2, (Chorus) 2.

Notice the three-pulse bar at the end, reversing the accent in the next time round. The strong accent followed by the lesser accent, indicated by the signs below, is however conjectural in this performance, though the effect has been observed on other occasions.

▽ 1st time, 3rd time, etc.
△ 2nd time, 4th time, etc.

The singer commenced the song with verse A as here. The point of ending cannot be determined from the recording. Versions by other singers end at *, i.e. the end of the fourth bar, the shorter of the two refrains.

Di-Sathuirne ghabh mi mulad (Barra, south end)

(d) Sung by Miss Mary Gillies and Mrs. James MacNeil

Form: five phrases: A B C D E.

Structure: a ten-bar melody:
  Verse A 2, Refrain A 4; Verse B 2, Refrain B 2.

The singer commenced the song with Refrain B, at ⊕.

VIII

Rinn mi mocheirigh gu éirigh
(South Uist, north end)

(*a*) Singer: Miss Ceit Iseabail MacDonald, Iochdar, at a genuine
waulking

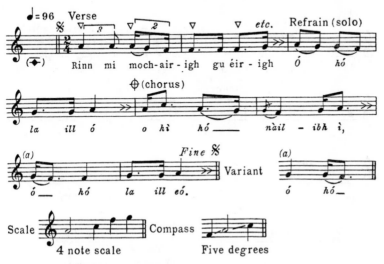

Scale: 4 note scale   Compass: Five degrees

Form: four phrases: Verse ‖ Refrain
                A   ‖ B¹ C B²

Structure: an eight-bar melody:
  Verse 2; Refrain (solo) 2, (chorus) 4.

The singer commenced with the chorus refrain at ⊕. The four introductory bars
from there to the end are sung first by the soloist and repeated by the chorus;
the song then proceeds from the ℅.

VIII

Rinn mi mocheirigh gu éirigh
(South Uist, centre)

(b) Singer: Mrs. Mary Steele, Bornish

(Sung without chorus)

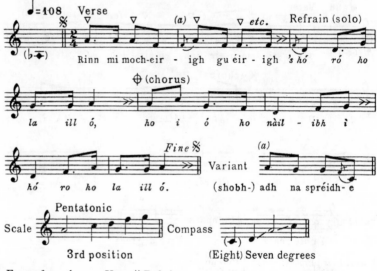

Form: four phrases: Verse ‖ Refrain
                A   ‖ B¹ C B²

Structure: an eight-bar melody:
  Verse 2; Refrain (solo) 2, (chorus) 4.

'Solo' and 'chorus' markings are conjectural in this performance, as in every
other case where the singers were recorded alone at the fireside. The singer
commenced the song with the chorus refrain, at ⊕.

264

VIII

Rinn mi mocheirigh gu éirigh
(South Uist, centre)

(*c*) Singer: Mrs. Campbell ('Bean Nill'), Frobost

(Sung without chorus)

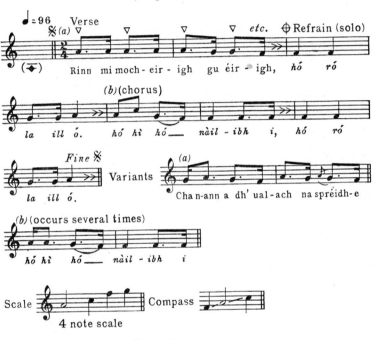

Scale 4 note scale

Compass

Form: four phrases: Verse ‖ Refrain
                A   ‖ B C B

Structure: an eight-bar melody:
  Verse 2, Refrain (solo) 2, (chorus) 4.

The singer commenced the song with the solo refrain, at ⊕.

VIII

Rinn mi mocheirigh gu éirigh
(Barra, Mingulay tradition)

(*d*) Sung by Mrs. MacDougall ('Anna Raghnaill'), Castlebay, with
Annie Johnston singing chorus

Chaidh na Dòmh-nall-aich dha'n linn-idh, *Ó hó la ill eó,*

o hi ó ho nàil - ibh na hó hó — la ill eó.

Scale — Pentatonic — 3rd position

Compass — Nine degrees

Form: four phrases: Verse ‖ Refrain
                A   ‖ B¹ C B²

Structure: an eight-bar melody:
  Verse 2, Refrain (solo) 2, (chorus) 4.

The singer commenced the song with the refrain at ⊕, the first two bars being
sung by the soloist and repeated by the chorus.

VIII

Rinn mi mocheirigh gu éirigh
(Barra, south end)

(*e*) Miss Mary Morrison, Earsary

Uisd - ein'ic 'ill' Easb-uig Cha-luim,'s ó hó— la ill eó,

o hì hó ho nàil - ibh, na hó ho ho la ill eó.

Variants

o hó ho ho o hì hó— ho

Uisd - ein 'ic 'ill' nàil - ibh na

Scale Hexatonic

Compass Nine degrees

Aeolian with gap at 5 (irregular.)

(The 5th (E) appears in variants.)

Form: four phrases: Verse ‖ Refrain
                     A¹ ‖ B C B

Structure: an eight-bar melody: Verse 2, Refrain 6.

The singer commenced with the refrain at ⊕; the first two bars were sung by the soloist, and the chorus joined in at the third bar. The song ended with the repetition by the soloist of the last four bars of the refrain, followed by a further repetition of the same four bars by the chorus.

IX

Dh'éirich mise moch Di-Dòmhnaich
(South Uist, north end)

Singer: Mrs. Archie Munro

(Sung without chorus)

End-of-phrase markings are here intentionally omitted as being doubtful and inconclusive.

In this unusual form of waulking melody, the musical phrase-rhythms seem to cut across the rhythm of the words. Considered from the musical point of view the phrasing of the melody would appear to be as follows:

Such musical scansion will not, however, fit the word rhythms of the poem. The verse part of the tune takes in lines one and two of the poem, and on the repetition of the melody the verse part of the tune commences with line two of the poem and takes in line three, and so on.

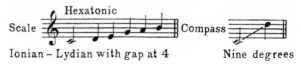

Scale — Hexatonic — Compass

Ionian – Lydian with gap at 4   Nine degrees

Form: Scanned as in the footnote, the form of the melody appears as A¹ B A² C.

Structure: In the form of the tune as governed by the words, the structure is that of a nine-bar melody:
  Verse 3; Refrain (solo) 2, (chorus) 4.

The singer commenced the song at the first 𝄋 as written.

X

'S fliuch an oidhche nochd 's gur fuar i
(Benbecula)

Sung by Mrs. Kate McCormick, Hacklett

(Without chorus)

Mixolydean, with gap at 6   Six degrees

Form: four phrases, A B C B.   * Conjectural.

Structure: an eight-bar melody:
  Verse A, 1; Refrain (solo) 1; (chorus) 2.
  Verse B, 2; Refrain (solo) 1; (chorus) 2.

269

XI

Thug mi gaol do'n nighinn duinn
(South Uist, centre)

Sung by Mrs. Campbell ('Bean Nill') with Mrs. Patrick MacPhee
singing the chorus

(With the B♮ of the variant the scale is Hexatonic, Phrygian-Locrian with gap
at 5.)

Form; four phrases: Verse ‖ Refrain
A ‖ B¹ C B²

Structure: an eight-bar melody:
Verse 2; Refrain (solo) 2, (chorus) 4.

The singer commenced the song with the solo refrain, at ⊕.

XII

Gura mise tha fo mhulad 's mi air tulaich na buaile
(South Uist, centre)

Sung by Mrs. Campbell ('Bean Nìll') and Mrs. Patrick MacPhee
at Frobost

Form: four phrases: A B¹ C B².

Structure: an eight-bar melody:
  Verse 2; Refrain (solo) 2, (chorus) 4.

The singer commenced with the solo refrain, at ⊕.

↑ indicates that the A♮ is sung slightly sharp throughout the song (bar 3).

The E♭ and A♮ in bar seven are constant and distinct resulting in the unusual vocal interval of an augmented fourth.

XIII

Gura mise tha làn airteil (South Uist, centre)

(*a*) Sung by Miss Kate MacDonald, Peninerine

(Sung without chorus)

* The singer ends the song here.
Φ Normal end of this type of song.

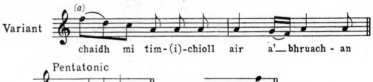

Variant

chaidh mi tim-(i)-chioll air a'—bhruach - an

Scale
5th position

Compass
Eleven degrees

Form: five-phrases: Verse ‖ Refrain
A B ‖ C D E

Structure: a ten-bar melody: Verse 4, Refrain 6.

The singer commenced the song with the verse as here.

The second line of each verse couplet becomes the first line of the succeeding couplet.

The singer ended the song with the solo refrain, but the song normally ends with the chorus refrain as with others of the same type.

272

XIII

Gura mise tha làn airteil (Benbecula)

(*b*) Sung by Mrs. Fanny MacIsaac, Torlum

(Sung without chorus)

Scale — Hexatonic

Phrygian—Aeolian with gap at 2

Compass — Eight (Ten) degrees

Form: five phrases: Verse ‖ Refrain
               A B ‖ C¹ D C²

Structure: a ten-bar melody: Verse 4, Refrain 6.
The singer commenced the song with the verse as written.

XIII

Gura mise tha làn airteil
(Eriskay)

(c) Singer: Mrs. Norman MacInnes

(*With chorus*)

Form: five phrases: Verse ‖ Refrain
A B ‖ C¹ D C²

Structure: a ten-bar melody: Verse 4, Refrain 6.

The singer commenced the song with the refrain, i.e. at ⊕. She ended the performance with the 'solo' refrain, at the point marked with an asterisk, but the song would normally probably end with the 'chorus' refrain. The 'solo' and 'chorus' refrain entries are conjectural, as all singers joined in on this occasion at the 'solo' part.

XIII

Gura mise tha làn airteil
(Barra, Eriskay tradition)

(*d*) Sung by Mrs. James McDougall ('Floraidh Alasdair') Leideag
and chorus

Hexatonic

Dorian with gap at 2

(The low B occurs only in a variant)

(Ten) Eight degrees

Form: five phrases: Verse ‖ Refrain
               A B ‖ C¹ D C²

* Conjectural.

Structure: ten-bar melody: Verse 4, Refrain 6.

The singer commenced the song with the verse as above written; it ended with a repetition of the last four bars by the soloist followed by a further repetition by the chorus. The soloist here made the following variant.

hi   rí   il   eó   fa   liù   il   eó   etc.

XIII

Gura mise tha làn airteil (Barra, north end)

(*e*) Singer: Ruairi Iain Bhàin (Roderick MacKinnon), Isle of Barra

(*Without chorus*)

Form: five phrases: Verse ‖ Refrain
              A B   ‖ C D C

Structure: a ten-bar melody:
Verse 4, Refrain (solo) 2; (chorus) 4.

Of the verse couplets, the second line of each couplet becomes the first line of the succeeding couplet and is therefore sung to the first part of the verse melody. The singer commenced the song with the verse as here written.

* Word not distinct on recording.

XIII

Gura mise tha làn airteil
(Barra, south end)

(*f*) Sung by Mrs. John Galbraith, Earsary, Barra, with chorus

The E is weak, only occurring once in the tune (semiquaver, 2nd bar after 𝄋).

Form: four phrases: Verse ‖ Refrain
               A   ‖ B¹ C B²

277

Structure: an eight-bar melody: Verse 2, Refrain (solo) 2; (chorus) 4.
Each line of the text is sung twice.

    * The singer here prefixed the verse line with an anacrusis note, enunciating
the unstressed word *Is* in full, which is not usually done.

XIII

Gura mise tha làn airteil
(Barra, north end)

(g) Sung by Miss Janet MacKinnon ('Seonaid Shomhairle Bhig')
and Mrs. MacLean, Northbay

Form: four phrases: Verse ‖ Refrain.
           A   ‖ B¹ C B²
Structure: an eight-bar melody: Verse 2; Refrain (solo) 2, (chorus) 4.
The song begins with the solo refrain, i.e. at ⊕.

XIV

Gura mise tha fo ghruaman
(South Uist, centre)

(*a*) Singer: Miss Anna MacDonald and chorus, Peninerine

Form: four phrases: A¹ B A² B.

Structure: an eight-bar melody: Verse 4, Refrain 4.

↓ ↓ = very much flatter than written. Such a note might be explained as an example of the curious intonation sometimes found in the performance of folk-singers, particularly in the Hebrides. It could be regarded as a quarter-tone. The singer commenced the song with the Refrain at ⊕. *♮ = up to pitch.

279

XIV

Gura mise tha fo ghruaman
(Eriskay)

(*b*) Sung by Mrs. Marion MacInnes ('Bean Dhòmhnaill Iain')

(*Sung without chorus*)

Scale: Hexatonic — Dorian, with gap at 2

Compass: Nine degrees

Form: four phrases: Verse ‖ Refrain—(with close similarity between the
A B ‖ C D   second bar of C and the first bar of D.)

Structure: an eight-bar melody: Verse 4, Refrain 4.

The singer commenced the song with the refrain, at ⊕. In an actual waulking
the four bars would be repeated by the chorus.

XV

'S e nochd a' chiad oidhche 'n fhoghair
(South Uist, north end)

(a) Sung by Miss Kate MacDonald, Iochdar, and chorus, at a genuine waulking at Gerinish

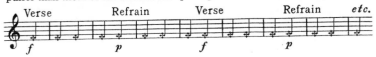

Form: Five phrases: A¹ A² B C D.

Structure: A nine-bar melody:
Verse A, 2; Refrain A 4; Verse B, 2; Refrain B, 1.
At * the chorus sing both versions, and it is not possible to determine which is the correct one.

In this actual waulking, the verse lines were accompanied by much louder pulses than those of the refrain. The pulse pattern is:

XV

'S e nochd a' chiad oidhche 'n fhoghair
(South Uist, centre)

(b) Sung by Miss Kate MacDonald (Peninerine), without chorus

Form: five phrases: A¹ A² B C D.

Structure: a nine-bar melody:
    Verse A, 2; Refrain A, 4.
    Verse B, 2; Refrain B, 1.

XV

'S e nochd a' chiad oidhche 'n fhoghair (Benbecula)

(c) Sung by Mrs. A. J. MacLellan, Hacklett

(With chorus)

283

(d) becomes regular (𝄋)Verse A

hao   ri   ó   Dol   seach-ad rubh - a   le gaill~inn, E hó

Pentatonic

Scale   Compass

3rd position   Eight degrees

Form: five phrases: A¹ A² B C D.

Structure: a ten-bar melody:
   Verse A, 2; Refrain A, 4.
   Verse B, 2; Refrain B, 2.

Notice that the waulking pulse (here conjectural) is thrown into cross accent by the first ¾ bar, but is restored to normal accentuation by the second ¾ bar.

The rhythmic caesura of one whole minim in the final bar is quite irregular. This changes during the course of the song to the more usual form of end-rhythm shown in the last variant, and was probably mis-remembered by the singer.

XVI

Bhean ud thall, gu dé th'air t'aire? (Barra, south end)

(a) Sung by Miss Mary Gillies, Mrs. James MacNeil, and Mrs. Mary Johnston, Barra

Introductory bars

♩ = 60

(b♭)
Ro   ho   lill eó,   ro   ho   lill eó,

𝄋 Verse A
(a)
Refrain A
(b)
'M fac- a   tu Ragh' - all_   no_ Ail - ein?   Laoi leó ho ró,

Verse B
(c)
trom orr - a chó,   fair à   lill   eó,_   'M fac - a   tu Ragh' -

Refrain B
Fine 𝄋
-all_ no Ail - ein?   Ro   ho lill eó,   ro ho lill eó.

Variants

Laoi leó ho ró

Scale Phrygian

Compass

Eight degrees

Form: four phrases: A B C D.

It is debatable, however, if Refrain A might not be reckoned as consisting of two phrases (2 bars and 1 bar) instead of one phrase as here construed, in which case the form will be A B C D E.

Structure: a nine-bar melody:
Verse A, 2; Refrain A, 3; Verse B, 2; Refrain B, 2.

The singer finished the song at the end of Refrain A. In an actual waulking, however, the song would almost certainly end with the shorter refrain (Refrain B) at 'Fine' as marked.

XVI

Bhean ud thall, gu dé th'air t'aire? (Barra, south end)

(b) Sung by Annie Johnston

(*Without chorus*)

Bhean ud thall, gu dé_ th'air t'air - e?

Ró_ hò *laill leó,* Ró_ hó *laill leó,* Mòr - an bròin gun

cheòl fo - near_ dhomh, *laoi leó hò ró,*

trom orr - a hó_____ *fair à* _____ *lill leó.*

Variant

Mòr - an bròin gun cheòl fo - near dhomh,

The song begins at the first ℅ as above.

The scale reckoned from the last note of the tune is:

Locrian

It is debatable, however, whether the tonal centre of the melody may not be felt to be C, rather than E; and constructed upon C the scale will appear as:

Mixolydian

Scale   Compass

Eight degrees

Form: five phrases: A B C D E.

Structure: a nine-bar melody:
  Verse A, 2; Refrain A, 3.
  Verse B, 2; Refrain B, 2.

The singer commenced the song at the beginning of the tune as here written. This is actually the second half of the tune, i.e. the verse which is followed by the shorter refrain, and is therefore labelled Verse and Refrain B.

Siuthadaibh, siuthadaibh, a mhnathan
(Benbecula)
(Le Màiri Nighean Alasdair Ruaidh, ma's fhìor)

(a) Sung by Mrs. A. J. McLellan and chorus

The feel of the tune is Dorian, with D as tonal centre, rather than Aeolian.

Form: from 𝄋 to 𝄋 A B A B, four phrases of two sections. (The end of the section at each half phrase is marked ⟩.)

The tune, however, is strongly felt by the transcriber to be ternary, with the opening four bars (here shown as 'introductory refrain') forming an integral part of the melody. If this be accepted then the last four bars of one round of the melody must be regarded as also the first four bars of the next round.

Structure (from 𝄋 to 𝄋): a sixteen-bar melody:
  Verse A, 2; Refrain A (solo) 2; (chorus) 4.
  Verse B, 2; Refrain B (solo) 2; (chorus) 4.

Verses 'A' and 'B' are here so nearly identical that the melody from 𝄋 to 𝄋 could have been written as eight bars repeated instead of sixteen as here. The metrical structure is, however, very unusual in that the verses of five syllables *alternate regularly* with longer verses of six or seven syllables, and it therefore seems appropriate to write these out below their proper rhythmic modifications of the verse melody. The words were probably originally sung to a different kind of tune, which was not a waulking melody originally.

XVII

Siuthadaibh, siuthadaibh, a mhnathan
(South Uist)

(*b*) Sung by Mrs. Alex Morrison, Milton, South Uist

(*Without chorus*)

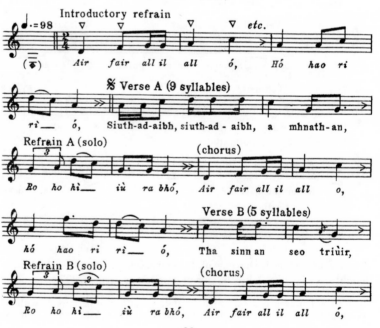

Scale · Hexatonic · Phrygian–Aeolian, gap at 2nd · Compass · Ten degrees

Form: four phrases (each composed of two sections): A B C D.

Structure (from 𝄋 to 𝄌): a sixteen-bar melody:
  Verse A, 2; Refrain A, (solo) 2, (chorus) 4.
  Verse B, 2; Refrain B (solo) 2, (chorus) 4.

See notes *re* form and structure in versions (*a*) and (*c*).

XVII

Siuthadaibh, siuthadaibh, a mhnathan
(South Uist, north end)

(*c*) Sung by Mrs. Nicholson, Iochdar, and chorus, at an actual
waulking

Form: from 𝄋 to 𝄋. there are eight phrases: A B, C D, E B, C D.

The divisions might, however, here be reckoned as sections rather than phrases, with two sections to a phrase, the form then being four phrases, A B C B, with similarity of ending between A and C. (The sections at each half phrase are marked with the symbol ⟩.)

Structure: a sixteen-bar melody:
    Verse A, 2; Refrain A (solo) 2, (chorus) 4.
    Verse B, 2; Refrain B (solo) 2, (chorus) 4. But see note *re* Form above.

As with the Mrs. Alex Morrison version, the feel of the tune is ternary, with the opening (introductory) four bars similar to the last four, and sounding therefore like an integral part of the melodic structure.

XVIII

Gura mis' tha fo éislein
(South Uist, south end)

(*a*) Norman MacMillan, Kilphedar

(*Sung without chorus*)

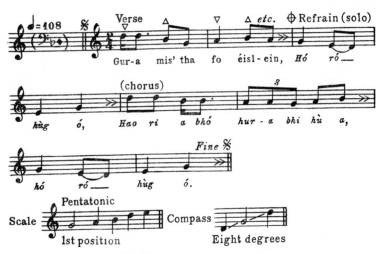

Scale — Pentatonic — 1st position

Compass — Eight degrees

Form: four phrases: A¹ B A² B.

Structure: an eight-bar melody:
  Verse 2; Refrain (solo) 2, (chorus) 4.

The singer commenced the song with the refrain, at ⊕.

Gura mis' tha fo éislein
(South Uist, north end)

(*b*) Sung by Ceit Iseabail MacDonald, Iochdar, and chorus, at a genuine waulking

Variants

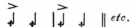

Scale: Pentatonic, 5th position — Compass: Eight degrees

Form: four phrases: Verse ‖ Refrain
                        A ‖ B C B

Structure: an eight-bar melody:
  Verse 2; Refrain (solo) 2, (chorus) 4.

The waulking pulse has the accentuation:

  ♩ ♩ ‖ ♩ ♩ ‖ *etc.*

The tempo quickens after a few cycles.

XVIII

Gura mis' tha fo éislein
(Benbecula)

(c) Sung by Mrs. A. J. MacLellan, Hacklett, and chorus

Scale and compass: similar to XVIII (b), i.e. pentatonic 5th position, compass eight degress.

Form: four phrases: Verse || Refrain
A¹ || B A² B

Structure: an eight-bar melody: Verse, 2; Refrain (solo) 2, (chorus) 4.

* This is the regular melody for the second part of the song, where the rhyming vowel is short *a* instead of long *é*.

The singer constantly adapts the melody to fit the stresses and vowel lengths of the verses.

Mi dualach, mi donn
(Benbecula)

Singer: Miss Kate MacMillan, Torlum

(Without chorus)

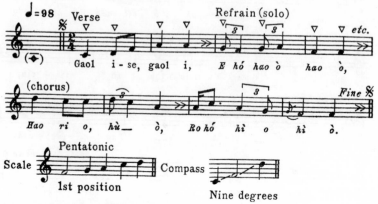

Form: four phrases: A B¹ C B².

Structure: An eight-bar melody:
Verse 2; Refrain (solo) 2, (chorus) 4.

The singer commenced the song with the verse, as here.

'S mise 's daor a cheannaich
(South Uist, centre)

Singer: Miss Kate MacDonald, Peninerine

(Without chorus)

Scale **Pentatonic** 4th position Compass **Six degrees**

Form: four phrases: A B C D.

Structure: an eight-bar melody:
Verse A, 2; Refrain A, 2; Verse B, 2; Refrain B, 2.

XXI

Dhòmhnaill òig mhic Dhòmhnaill 'ic Ruairi
(South Uist, north end)

(*a*) Sung by Miss Penny Morrison, Iochdar, at a genuine waulking
at Gerinish

Introductory refrain

Hoir-eann ó ho hì iù o, Hi ur-abh ó
ro hug éil-eadh, Hoir-eann ó, ho hì iù o.

Verse
A Dhòmhn-aill òig mhic Dhòmhn-aill 'ic Ruair-i

Chunn-a mi dol suas an dé thu, Hoir-eann ó
ho hì iù o, Hi ùr-abh ó ro hug éil-eadh,
Hoir-eann ó, ho hì iù o.

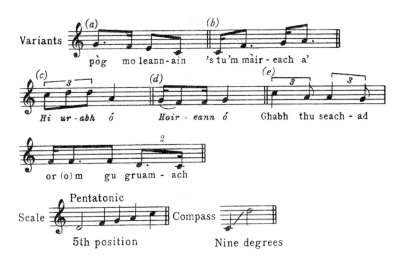

Variants

(a) pòg mo leann-ain (b) 's tu'm màir-each a'

(c) Hi ur-abh ó (d) Hoir-eann ó (e) Ghabh thu seach-ad

or (o)m gu gruam-ach

Scale — Pentatonic — 5th position   Compass — Nine degrees

Form: five phrases: Verse ‖ Refrain
                       A B ‖ C B C

Structure: a ten-bar melody: Verse 4, Refrain 6.

XXI

Dhòmhnaill òig mhic Dhòmhnaill 'ic Ruairi
(Benbecula)

(*b*) Sung by Mrs. Kate MacCormick, Hacklett

(*Without chorus*)

Tha mi sgìth a' siubh-al beinn-e, Ri lath-a soill-eir_

_ gun ghréin ann, *Hoir - eann ó*, *ho hì hiù o*,

Hi ùr - abh ó, *ro hug éil - eadh*, *hòir-eann ó ho hì hiù o.*

Variants

(*a*)

Cliù dha'n Tì_ aig a bheil m'fhort-an

(*b*)

Ged nach do chois - inn thu bréid dhomh

Scale — Pentatonic — 4th position — Compass — Nine degrees

Form: five phrases: Verse ‖ Refrain
               A B ‖ C D C

Structure: a ten-bar melody: Verse 4, Refrain 6.

The singer commenced the song with the refrain at ⊕.

Marbhaisg air a' mhulad, 's buan e
(South Uist, centre)

(a) Sung by Miss Kate and Miss Anna MacDonald, Peninerine

Form: six phrases: Verse || Refrain   Structure: a twelve-bar melody:
              A B || C D E C   Verse 4; Refrain (solo) 2, (chorus) 6.

The singer commenced the song with the chorus refrain, at ⊕.

XXII

Marbhaisg air a' mhulad, 's buan e
(South Uist, centre)

(*b*) Sung by Mrs. Campbell ('Bean Nìll'), Frobost

(Without chorus)

Scale: Pentatonic, 2nd position

Compass

Form: five phrases: Verse ‖ Refrain
                 A B ‖ C D C

(It would also be possible to consider the second phrase of the refrain as consisting of two phrases of two bars each. This would make six phrases, i.e. A B ‖ C D E C.) Phrase E is indicated by the sign >.

Structure: a twelve-bar melody:
    Verse 4, Refrain (solo) 2, (chorus) 6.

The singer commenced the song with the solo refrain, at ⊕.

XXIII

'S muladach mi is mi air m'aineoil
(South Uist, centre)

(*a*) Singer: Miss Kate MacDonald, Peninerine

(*Without chorus*)

Refrain B

Hi   rì   ri   ri   ri   a bhó

Scale — Pentatonic, 1st position — Compass — Nine degrees

Form: four phrases: A B C D.

Structure: an eight-bar melody:
  Verse A, 2; Refrain A($\frac{3}{4}$), 2.
  Verse B, 2; Refrain B($\frac{2}{4}$), 2.

The singer began the song as here. This corresponds with MacCormick. The singer, who only sang five lines of the song in all in the recording, commenced with the verse which was followed by the *shorter* refrain. This is contrary to the customary practice, and this verse and short refrain is therefore here labelled Verse B, and the following verse and longer refrain labelled Verse A. The song would normally end with Refrain B (the shorter refrain) and this is therefore conjecturally marked *Fine*. The accentuation of the waulking pulse is conjectural and is inserted throughout the melody to show the cross-accents which would occur at the $\frac{3}{4}$ bars.

XXIII

'S muladach mi is mi air m'aineoil
(South Uist, centre)

(*b*) Sung by Mrs. Campbell ('Bean Nill'), Frobost

(*Without chorus*)

Form: four phrases: A B C D.

Structure: an eight-bar melody:
Verse A, 2; Refrain A, 2.
Verse B, 2; Refrain B, 2.

'S muladach mi 's mi air m'aineoil
(Barrg, South end)

(*c*) Sung by Annie and Calum Johnston, Castlebay

Form: four phrases: A¹ B A² C.

Structure: A nine-bar melody:
Verse A, 2; Refrain A, 3.
Verse B, 2; Refrain B, 2.

Cha dìrich mi an t-uchd le fonn
(South Uist, north end)

(*a*) Sung by Miss Penny Morrison, Iochdar

(*Without chorus*)

Scale: Pentatonic 1st position

Compass: Eight degrees

Form: four phrases: Verse ‖ Refrain
A¹ ‖ B A² B

Structure: an eight-bar melody:
Verse 2; Refrain (solo) 2, (chorus) 4.

The 'solo' and 'chorus' markings are conjectural.

The singer sang only a few lines of the song in this recording.

XXIV

Cha dìrich mi an t-uchd le fonn
(Benbecula)

(b) Sung by Miss Effie Monk, Torlum

(Without chorus)

Lydian–Ionian with gap at 4   Nine degrees

The B♮ in the third variant makes the scale Ionian for that stanza.

Form: four phrases: Verse ‖ Refrain ⊕ Commencement of song.
                A   ‖ B C B

Structure: an eight-bar melody:
     Verse 2, Refrain 6.

The notes in bar 6 marked with the sign ↑ are uncertain in intonation and are often sung sharper than the written notes.

XXIV

Cha dìrich mi an t-uchd le fonn
(Benbecula)

(*c*) Sung by Mrs. Kate MacCormick, Hacklett

(*Without chorus*)

Cha dìr - ich mi 'n t-uchd le fonn

Refrain (solo)

Ó hi rì ill mo nigh'n donn, Hì rì ill

mo nigh'n donn, Ó hi rì ill mo nigh'n donn.

Verse of 8 syllables

Ban - (a) - chag a' chrodh - laoigh__ 's nan aigh-ean__

Verse of 8 syllables

Dian - adh na gamhn - a 'nan aigh-ean__

Verse of 7 syllables

'S e__ mo cheist a' fleasg-ach donn__ Seòl - adh o Eig -

9 syllables

- e gu Rùm Le òr dear-(a)g 'sle air - (i)-gead pronn

Scale — Hexatonic

Compass — Eight degrees

Ionian-Lydian, with gap at 4

307

Form: four phrases: Verse ‖ Refrain
A ‖ B C B

Structure: an eight-bar melody:
Verse 2; Refrain (solo) 2, (chorus) 4.

The markings 'solo' and 'chorus' are conjectural.

The singer commenced the song with the refrain at ⊕.

Note. The singer begins the verse on note A as often as on F, as in the last two variants.

XXV

Nighean chruinn donn, dut is éibhinn
(South Uist, centre)

(*a*) Sung by Mrs. Campbell ('Bean Nill'), Frobost

(*Without chorus*)

Variants

Na bric 'sna brad - ain___ a' leum_ dhut

(becomes regular)
(a)   (b)

òir-eann ò___ ro. Cha mhar - aich' ach mac duin' uas - ail.

Scale | Dorian | Compass

Seven degrees

Form: five phrases, A B C D E with similarity of ending of C and E.

Structure: a ten-bar melody:
  Verse A, 2; Refrain A, 4.
  Verse B, 2; Refrain B, 2.

Refrain B was sung twice at break in song (cp. text line 902/3).

The song finishes with the introductory refrain.

XXV

Nighean chruinn donn, dut is éibhinn
(Benbecula)

(b) Singer: Miss Effie Monk, Torlum

(*Without chorus*)

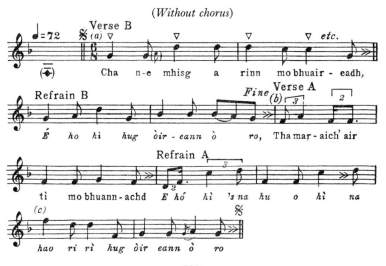

♩=72 % Verse B
        (a) ▽   ▽   ▽   ▽ etc.

Cha   n-e mhisg   a   rinn   mo bhuair - eadh,

Refrain B   *Fine* Verse A
                               (b)

É   ho   hì   hug   òir - eann   ò   ro,   Tha mar - aich' air

            Refrain A

tì   mo bhuann - achd   E hó   hì   's na   hu   o   hì   na

(c)   %

hao   rì   rì   hug   òir   eann   ò   ro

309

Variants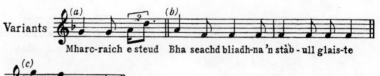

Mharc-raich e steud Bha seachd bliadh-na 'n stàb - ull glais-te

hao ri rì hug

Scale  Compass

Dorian–Aeolian, with gap at 6   Ten degrees

(*a*) Variant with long stressed vowel.

(*b*) This variant occurs in second part of song, where the rhyming vowel is short.

Form: five phrases A B C D E.

Structure: a ten-bar melody:
Verse A (here sung after Verse and refrain B) 2; Refrain A, 4.
Verse B (here sung first) 2, Refrain B, 2.

The singer commenced the song at the first 𝄋 as written.

Of this song, version (*a*) sung by Mrs. Campbell ('Bean Nìll') is the correct form, ending with the short refrain. Here, in version (*b*), the sequence is inverted to show the proper phrase-sequence of the melody. The verse and refrain first sung is here labelled B, and the second A.

Note constant adaptation of the melody to word stresses and vowel length here also.

XXVI

Gura mis' tha fo mhulad air an tulaich luim fhuair
(South Uist, centre)

(*a*) Singer: Mrs. Campbell ('Bean Nill'), Frobost

(*Sung without chorus*)

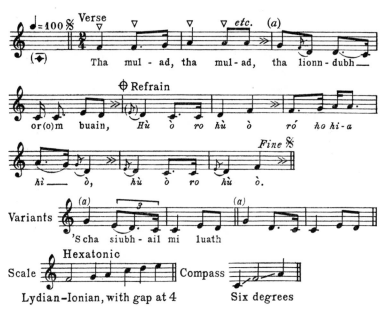

Tha mul - ad, tha mul - ad, tha lionn - dubh —

or(o)m buain, Hù o ro hù ò ró ho hi - a

hì — ò, hù ò ro hù ò.

Variants

'S cha siubh - ail mi luath

Scale — Hexatonic

Lydian–Ionian, with gap at 4

Compass — Six degrees

Form: five phrases: A B || C D C.

Structure: a ten-bar melody: Verse 4, Refrain 6.

The singer commenced the song with the refrain at ⊕.

Gura mis' tha fo mhulad air an tulaich luim fhuair
(Benbecula)

(*b*) Singer: Mrs. Kate MacCormick, Hacklett

(*With chorus*)

Lydian–Ionian, with gap at 4

Basic compass Six degrees
Compass in variants, Ten degrees

Form: five phrases: Verse ‖ Refrain
           A B ‖ C D C

Structure: a ten-bar tune:
  Verse 4; Refrain (solo) 2, (chorus) 4.

The singer commenced the song with the refrain (fifth bar) at ⊕.

XXVI

Gura mise tha fo mhulad air an tulaich luim fhuair
(Barra, south end)

(*c*) Sung by Miss Mary Gillies, Castlebay

(*With chorus*)

Gur - a mis' tha fo mhul - ad Air an tul - aich

luim fhuair, Hì hò ro hù o, Chall - a hì o —

hì hò hì — hò ro hù o.

Scale — Hexatonic

Compass — Eight degrees

Lydian–Ionian, with gap at 4

Form: five phrases: Verse || Refrain
                A, A transposed || B C B

Structure: a ten-bar melody:
  Verse 4, Refrain 6.

The singer commenced the song at the refrain, at ⊕, the first two bars being sung solo, and the chorus chiming in along with the soloist at the third bar.

Variants   (*a*) in opening   also (*a*)

The song ended similarly to the commencement, i.e. with repetition from ⊕ to the end, the soloist singing the first two bars and the chorus chiming in for the last four bars.

313

XXVII

Tune not recovered, see Notes, p. 183.

XXVIII

Chaidh mi do'n bheinn ghabhail fradhairc
(South Uist, centre)

Sung by Mrs. Duncan MacDonald, Peninerine

(Without chorus)

314

Variants

Struth a - gus gaoth 'N iar 'na h-agh - aidh

Scale — Four note   Compass

Five degrees

Form: four phrases: A B C D (C and D ending similarly).

Structure: an eight-bar melody:
    Verse A, 1; Refrain A, 1;
    Verse B, 1; Refrain B, 1;
    Verse C, 1; Refrain C, 1;
    Verse D, 1; Refrain D, 1.

The melody consists of four sections, A, B, C and D; each section providing the air for a *half verse* of the poem, followed by a refrain. The point in the melody at which the song ends shows that the singer commences the song with a variant of the second half of the tune, which is therefore here labelled Verse and Refrain C and D. The use of additional refrain syllables to the verse sections of the melody to indicate '*atharrachadh*' or change of subject is unusual, the normal practice being to sing the refrain three times at this point.

XXIX

Dh'éirich mi moch madainn àlainn
(South Uist, north end)

(*a*) Sung by Miss Penny Morrison, Iochdar

(*Without chorus*)

Dorian–Aeolian, with gap at 6   Eight degrees

The B♮ in variant (*b*) would make the scale Dorian, but this is exceptional to the rest of the recording.

The E in the scale is weak, occurring only once in the tune as a short note.

Form: six phrases: A B C A B C.

Structure: a six-bar melody:
Verse A, 1; Refrain 2;
Verse B, 1; Refrain 2.

See notes in version (*b*) sung by Mrs. MacDougall regarding the extension of the tune by repetition to complete the whole line of text.

The words used here by the singer are connected with a different song (No. XXVII), of which the tune was not recovered.

XXIX

Dh'éirich mi moch madainn àlainn
(Barra, Mingulay tradition)

(*b*) Sung by Mrs. MacDougall ('Anna Raghnaill Eachainn'),
Castlebay; with Annie Johnston singing the refrain

Scale — Hexatonic — Dorian, with gap at 2

Compass — Eight degrees

Form: six phrases: A B C :‖: A B C.

(The use of $\frac{3}{4}$ time is dictated by the solo and chorus divisions of the refrain into two equal lines, as set down in MacCormick's text. The resultant phrase division is musically clumsy, but unavoidable.)

Structure: a six-bar melody:
  Verse A, 1; Refrain A (solo) 1, (chorus) 1;
  Verse B, 1; Refrain B (solo) 1, (chorus) 1.

Each half of the melody is repeated to the same (half-line) text. The notes of Verse and Refrain A are the same as those of Verse and Refrain B, except for rhythmic modification of the end of the verse melody to suit short or long vowels. As the 'verse' melody only takes in a half-line of text the melody is extended from four to eight bars by repetition to complete the text line.

Note. Presumably at a waulking the Introductory refrain would be sung solo first time, and by chorus second time.

317

XXX

Cha labhair mi 'n t-òran
(South Uist, north end)

(*a*) Sung by Miss Penny Morrison, Iochdar

(*With chorus*)

Introductory refrain, 1st time solo, 2nd time chorus

Hì hoir-eann hì hiu o, hì— hoir-eann ò ro ho.

Verse — Refrain (solo)

Cha— labh-air mi 'n t-òr-an, Hì hoir eann ò ro ho,

(chorus) — Fine

Hì hoir-eann hì hiu o, hì— hoir-eann ò ro ho.

Scale — Pentatonic — 1st position — Compass — Six degrees

Form: four phrases: Verse ‖ Refrain
A ‖ B¹ C B²

Structure: an eight-bar melody:
Verse 2, Refrain (solo) 2, (chorus) 4.

XXX

Cha labhair mi 'n t-òran
(South Uist, north end)

(b) Sung by Miss Kate MacDonald ('Ceit Iseabail'), Iochdar at
a genuine waulking

Form: four phrases: Verse ‖ Refrain   Structure: an eight-bar melody:
                A ‖ B¹ C B²   Verse 2, Refrain (solo) 2, (chorus) 4.

Note. Several lines of text were sung by the singer before the first line of
verse transcribed here (which bears the title of the song) but these are hard
to make out in the recording and have not been transcribed.

Notice the difference between the dotted and undotted notes in the verse
melody and in the variants of it. This corresponds to the difference between
long and short vowels in the text; viz. the long *ò* of *òran* and the short *a* of *facal.*

The song ended with the soloist repeating the chorus refrain which was then
repeated by the chorus.

XXX

Cha labhair mi 'n t-òran
(South Uist, north end)

(*c*) Sung by Miss Catriona Caimbeul, Loch Carnan

(*With chorus*)

Form: four phrases: Verse ‖ Refrain
                     A   ‖ B C B

Structure: an eight-bar melody: Verse 2, Refrain (solo) 2, (chorus) 4.

The singer ended the song by repeating the refrain, which was repeated in its turn by the full chorus.

The chorus sang the refrain in the key a fifth above that of the soloist throughout. This is shown clearly in the pitch of the introductory bars. From 𝄋 to 𝄋 the large notes show the notes actually sung by the chorus; the small notes indicate these reduced to the same key as that of the soloist, which are at the correct pitch. The soloist frequently chimes in at the last note of the chorus refrain—a fifth below the chorus—before singing the verse line from the 𝄋.

XXX

Cha labhair mi 'n t-òran (South Uist, centre)

(*d*) Sung by Miss Kate MacDonald, Peninerine

(*With chorus*)

Form: four phrases: Verse ‖ Refrain
A ‖ B¹ C B²
Structure: an eight-bar melody:
Verse 2, Refrain (solo) 2, (chorus) 4.

XXXI

Is moch an diu a rinn mi éirigh
(Barra, south end)

(*a*) Sung by Mrs. James MacNeil, Leideag

(*With chorus*)

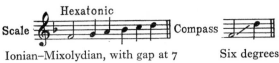

Scale Hexatonic

Compass Six degrees

Ionian–Mixolydian, with gap at 7

Form: four phrases: Verse ‖ Refrain
                        A   ‖ B¹ C B²

Structure: an eight-bar melody:
  Verse 2, Refrain (solo) 2, (refrain) 4.

Variant (*b*) corresponds to a displacement of the long stressed rhyming vowel *é*
by the short vowel *a*.

XXXI

Is moch an diu a rinn mi éirigh
(Barra, south end)

(*b*) Singer: Mrs. John Galbraith, Castlebay

(*With chorus*)

Is moch an diu a__ rinn mi__ éir - igh,

Fail ill ò ro,_ fail iù ill ó, Fail iù ill ó

ho - ro éil - eadh, Fail_ ill ó ro,_ fail iù ill ó.

Variants

Dhìr-ich mi suas gual, an t-sléibh-e,

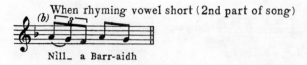

When rhyming vowel short (2nd part of song)

(b)

Nìll_ a Barr-aidh

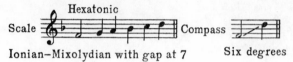

Scale   Hexatonic   Compass   Six degrees

Ionian–Mixolydian with gap at 7

Form: four phrases: Verse ‖ Refrain
        A   ‖ B¹ C B²

Structure: eight-bar melody:
    Verse 2; Refrain (solo) 2, (chorus) 4.

The performance commences with the solo refrain at ⊕ sung by the soloist. The chorus chimed in at the third bar of the refrain.

There is the suggestion of a waulking pulse to be heard in the background throughout the song, consisting of two evenly accented beats in the bar, *e.g.*

This cannot of course be accepted as definitive as no cloth

was actually being waulked during this performance. The song ends with the last 4 bars sung three times:
    1st; by the chorus.
    2nd; by the soloist, indicating ending.
    3rd; by the chorus.

* The tempo accelerated as the song proceeded.

Siùbhlaidh mi 's fàgaidh mi 'm fearann
('An fhìdeag airgid')
(Barra, Mingulay tradition)

(*a*) Sung by Mrs. MacDougall, Castlebay, with Annie Johnston
singing the chorus

Có sheinn-eadh an __ fhid - eag air - (i)-gid,

Hì rì ill iù ill eò ro, Có feir - eadh nach

seinn-inn_fhìn i, Hò ro hù ò, hù ___ ill eò __ ro.

Variants

Cha bhuill ghaois-ne, cha bhuill chain-(i)-be Ul - ag - an òir

air gach ceann dhiu, Clog-ad - a cruadh-ach mu d' ghruaig cham-(a)-laich

Clog-ad - a cruadh-ach mu d' ghruaig cham-(a)-laich

Scale Hexatonic **Compass**

Dorian–Mixolydian, with gap at 3rd · Eight degrees

Form: four phrases: A B C D.

Structure: an eight-bar melody:
Verse A, 2; Refrain A, 2; Verse B, 2; Refrain B, 2.

* 9-syllable line and svarabhakti (epenthetic) vowel, see p. 231.

Siùbhlaidh mi 's fàgaidh mi 'm fearann
('An fhìdeag airgid')
(Barra, east side)

(b) Sung by John MacKinnon, Craigston

(*Without chorus*)

The singer ended the song with Verse B, at *, no refrain following. The normal point of ending would be at the second 𝄎. He began the song also with Verse B.

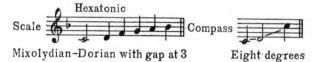

Mixolydian–Dorian with gap at 3   Eight degrees

Form: four phrases: A B C D.

Structure: an eight-bar melody:
   Verse A, 2; Refrain A, 2;
   Verse B, 2; Refrain B, 2.

XXXIII

Cha déid mise, cha déid mi (South Uist, centre)

Sung by Miss Kate MacDonald, Peninerine

(*Without chorus*)

327

Form: four phrases: Verse ‖ Refrain
A¹　　‖ B A² B

Structure: an eight-bar melody: Verse 2, Refrain (solo) 2, (chorus) 4.

The singer commenced the song with the chorus refrain; at ⊕. Nearly all through the song the singer omitted the chorus refrain, singing only the solo refrain. Singers often do this when singing the song alone, without a chorus taking part in the performance. She actually ended the song at the end of the solo refrain, but this is irregular in the tradition, and the song should undoubtedly end with the chorus refrain.

XXXIV

Cha n-eil falt orm air fuireach (Benbecula)

Miss Effie Monk, Torlum

(*Sung without chorus*)

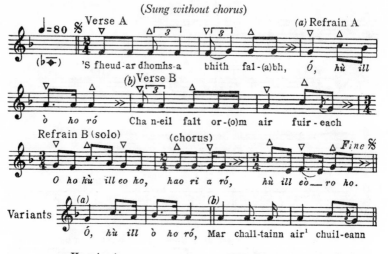

Variants

Ó, hù ill ò ho ró, Mar chall-tainn air¹ chuil-eann

Scale — Hexatonic　　Compass —

Ionian with gap at 6　　　　　Six degrees

Form: five phrases: A B C D E.　　¹ *Sic.*

Structure: a nine-bar melody:
　Verse A, 2; Refrain A, 2; Verse B, 2; Refrain B (solo) 1; (chorus) 2.

The first of the ¾ bars would throw a waulking pulse of strong accent followed by subsidiary accent into cross rhythm; the regular rhythm is restored by the second three-four bar. The accentuation is however conjectural as the song was performed without any chorus singers. The singer, who was old, only sang a few lines, and only sang each line once. She commenced the song with Verse A as written.

XXXV

Chraobh nan Ubhal (Barra, South end)

(*a*) Sung by Calum Johnston ('Calum Aonghais Chaluim')
Castlebay

(*Without chorus*)

Scale

Ionian

Compass

Nine degrees

Form: four phrases: A B C D.

Structure: an eight-bar melody:
  Verse A, 2; Refrain A, 2;
  Verse B, 2; Refrain B, 2.

The grace-notes marked with an asterisk, all unusually wide in interval from their principal note, are characteristic of Calum Johnston's singing style. It is possible that they owe their origin to the technique of the bagpipes, of which he is a skilled player.

XXXV

Craobh nan Ubhal
(Barra, north end)

(b) Sung by Roderick MacKinnon ('Ruairi Iain Bhàin') Northbay

(*Without chorus*)

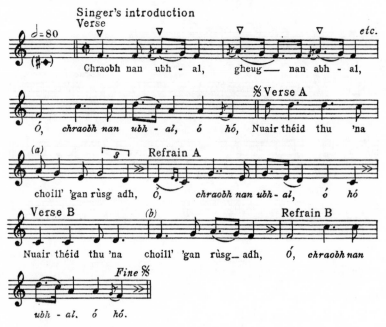

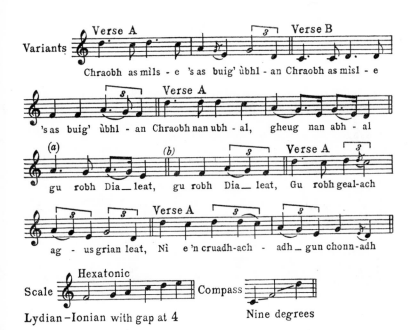

Variants

Verse A ... **Verse B**

Chraobh as mìls - e 's as buig' ùbhl - an Chraobh as mìsl - e

Verse A

's as buig' ùbhl - an Chraobh nan ubh - al, gheug nan abh - al

(a) (b) **Verse A**

gu robh Dia — leat, gu robh Dia — leat, Gu robh geal-ach

Verse A

ag - us grian leat, Ni e 'n cruadh-ach - adh — gun chonn-adh

Scale **Hexatonic** Compass

Lydian – Ionian with gap at 4   Nine degrees

Form: four phrases: A B C D.

Structure: an eight-bar melody:
  Verse A, 2; Refrain A, 2;
  Verse B, 2; Refrain B, 2.

XXXV

Craobh nan Ubhal (Barra, north end)

(*c*) Sung by Janet MacKinnon, Northbay (words imperfectly remembered), with Mrs. MacLean joining in the chorus

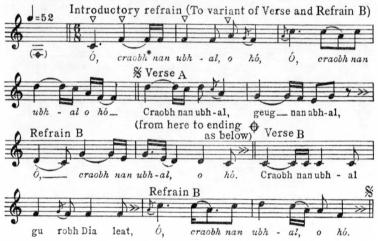

The song ends with the following variant of the introductory refrain, following Refrain A:

Form: four phrases: A B C D.

Structure: an eight-bar melody:
    Verse A, 2: Refrain A, 2;
    Verse B, 2: Refrain B, 2.

* *Sic* throughout the refrain, *craobh*, not *chraobh*.

The singer sang lines 1 and 2 each once, line 3 twice, and line 4 once.

XXXVI

Ailein, Ailein 's fhad an cadal
(South Uist, centre)

(*a*) Sung by Duncan MacDonald, Peninerine, South Uist

(*Sung without chorus*)

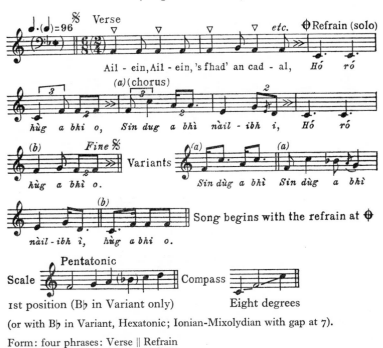

Scale Pentatonic

1st position (B♮ in Variant only)   **Compass**   Eight degrees

(or with B♮ in Variant, Hexatonic; Ionian-Mixolydian with gap at 7).

Form: four phrases: Verse ‖ Refrain
                A   ‖ B C A

Structure: an eight-bar melody:
   Verse 2; Refrain (solo) 2, (chorus) 4.

XXXVI

Ailein, Ailein, 's fad' an cadal (Barra)

(b) Sung by Nan MacKinnon, Isle of Vatersay, without chorus

(Recorded in Edinburgh by F. C. 17/11/64)

Form: four phrases: Verse ‖ Refrain
    A   ‖ B C B

Structure: an eight-bar melody:
    Verse 2, Refrain 6.

Note. This singer possesses the idiosyncrasy of singing all her songs (except *puirt-a-bial*) at a very slow tempo. The tempo here marked does not therefore necessarily bear any relation to the tempo at which the song would be sung at an actual waulking.

XXXVII

Latha dhomh 's mi 'm Beinn a' Cheathaich
(Barra, South end)

(*a*) Sung by Mrs. Mary Morrison ('Bean Phluim'), Earsary

(*With chorus*)

accelerating considerably towards the end

(*a*) Verse (1st section, 8 syllables to the line) ⊕ Refrain (solo)

𝅘𝅥𝅭 = 66

Lath - a   dhomh   's mi 'm Beinn   a' Cheath-aich, *Air*

(*b*) (chorus)

fair al ill ó,   *Ro ho bha hó,*   *Hoir - eann is   hó,   ho*

(*c*)   *Fine*

ró   hi ó, ___   *Hi   rì   ho ro__ bha,   hó   hug ò   ro*

Variants   (*a*)   (*b*)

Cha   b'e caig - eann   *Hoir - eann is   hó,   ho*

(*b*)   (*c*)

Hoir-eann is   hó,   ho   ró   hi ó, ___   *Hi*

2nd section, 12 syllables to the line, extending to 13 and 14 syllables:

Air

Nam   bith - inn 'nam nigh - inn fo   ligh - e   mo   ghruaig - e

Air

also   *etc.*

The singer commenced the song with the refrain, i.e. at ⊕.

Pentatonic

Scale   Compass

1st position   Nine degrees

335

Form: four phrases: Verse ‖ Refrain
             A   ‖ B C D

Structure: an eight-bar melody:
  Verse 2; Refrain (solo) 2, (chorus) 4.

At (*b*) one group of the chorus voices sang the upper notes throughout the song, resulting in a rudimentary but certainly unintentional two-part harmony.

XXXVII

Latha dhomh 's mi 'm Beinn a' Cheathaich
(Barra, north end)

(*b*) Sung by Janet MacKinnon, Northbay, without chorus

336

Form: four phrases: Verse ‖ Refrain
                    A   ‖ B A² C
Structure: an eight-bar melody:
    Verse 2; Refrain (solo) 2, (chorus) 4.
The singer commenced the song with the Verse as written.

XXXVIII

'S fhada bhuam a chì mi 'n ceò
(Eriskay)

(*a*) Sung by Mrs. Duncan MacInnes

(*Sung without chorus*)

Dorian–Aeolian, with gap at 6   Ten degrees

Form: three phrases: Verse ‖ Refrain (but see below)
                     A   ‖ B C
Structure: a six-bar melody:
    Verse 2, Refrain 4.
The singer is apparently omitting the solo refrain which, in all likelihood,
would correspond to the last phrase (i.e. two bars) of the chorus refrain, as in
the other version here given. This would give the full refrain the usual ternary
form, i.e. (here) Verse ‖ Refrain
              A   ‖ [C] B C
The singer commenced the song with the refrain, at ⊕.

'S fhada bhuam a chì mi 'n ceò
(Barra, Mingulay tradition)

(b) Singer: Mrs. Alex Johnston, Castlebay

(Without chorus)

'N cual-a sibh mar dh'éir - ich dhòmhs'?—

Hó   hi   rì   hi   liù   i   leò,   hó   hó   hi

iù   ra   bhó,   hó   i   rì   i   liù   i   leò.

Variants

Hó hi rì hi, Hó i ri i_ liù i leò,_ Hó_ i ri ri

Scale — Hexatonic — Compass

Mixolydian, with gap at 6   Six degrees

Form: four phrases: Verse ‖ Refrain
              A   ‖ B C B

Structure: an eight-bar melody: Verse 2, Refrain 6.

The singer commenced the song with the refrain, at ⊕. The chorus joined in along with the soloist after 4 bars.

338

XXXIX

Tha an oidhche nochd fuar
(South Uist, centre)

(*a*) Sung by Mrs. Campbell ('Bean Nill')

(*Without chorus*)

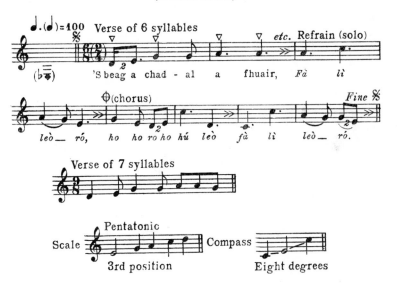

Form: four phrases: Verse ‖ Refrain
                A   ‖ B¹ C B²

Structure: an eight-bar melody:
   Verse 2, Refrain (solo) 2, (chorus) 4.

The singer commenced the song with the chorus refrain, at ⊕. At 'Atharraich'
the singer repeats the chorus refrain.

XXXIX

Tha an oidhche nochd fuar
(Eriskay)

(*b*) Sung by Mrs. John MacInnes

(*With 'impromptu' chorus*)

Tha 'n oidhch-e nochd fuar, *Air fà li*

leò— hó, Ó ho ro 's na hù ill eo, air

fà li leò— hó.

Variant — (*a*) Verse of 7 syllables

Bidh sinn pòsd' le min-ist-eir, *Air*

Scale — Hexatonic

Aeolian–Phrygian with gap at 2

Compass — Seven degrees

Form: four phrases: Verse ‖ Refrain
A ‖ B C B

Structure: an eight-bar melody:
Verse 2; Refrain (solo) 2, (chorus) 4.

The singer commenced the song with the solo refrain at ⊕.

The song ends with a repetition of the full refrain (solo and chorus).

XL

'S mise chunnaic an t-iaonadh
(South Uist, north end)

(*a*) Sung by Miss Penny Morrison, Iochdar, South Uist

(*With impromptu (male) chorus*)

Mi - se chunn - aic an t-iaon - adh

Mad - ainn mhoch 's mi 'g iarr - aidh chaor - ach, *Ó ho hi ò—*

(chorus) *hao ri ù, Ó hi hi ò— hi ri iù,*

Ó ho hi ò, hao ri iù.

Variant Nigh-ean donn a' *etc.*

Scale — Hexatonic
Ionian –Myxolydian, with gap at 7

Compass — Nine degrees

Form: five phrases: Verse ‖ Refrain
A ‖ BC D C

Structure: a ten-bar melody:
Verse 4, Refrain (solo) 2, (chorus) 4.

The singer commenced the song with the refrain at ⊕.

'S mise chunnaic an t-iaonadh
(South Uist, centre)

(*b*) Sung by Mrs. Campbell ('Bean Nìll'), Frobost
(Without chorus)

'S e mo bhas - an dhaibh bu chuach - an

Tarr-aing uisg' a lod - ain fhuar - a, Ó___ ho hì ò

hao ri iù, Ó ho hi ò, hi rì ri ù,

ó___ ho hi ó, hao ri iù.

Variants

Thill air mo cheum, chaoch-ail m'ast - ar

Bha mi 'nam ruith Hi rì ri iù.

This variant becomes regular towards the end.

Scale 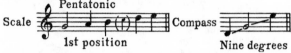 **Compass**

Pentatonic

1st position   Nine degrees

* The (gapped) C appears in two variants, the last becoming regular. This changes the scale to Hexatonic; Mixolydian-Ionian, with gap at 7.

Form: five phrases: Verse ‖ Refrain
              A B ‖ C D C

Structure: a ten-bar melody:
  Verse 4; Refrain (solo) 2, (chorus) 4.

The singer commenced the song with the chorus refrain at ⊕.

XL

'S mise chunnaic an t-iaonadh
(Benbecula)

(c) Sung by Mrs. Angus John MacLellan, Hacklett

(*Without chorus*)

Introductory refrain (variant of melody of refrain in song)

(♥) Ó ho hi ò,— hao ri ù, Ó ho hi ò,—

hao ri ù, Ó ho hi ò— hao ri ù.

Verse

Nach mi - se chunn - aic an t-iaon - adh, Mad-ainn mhoch 's mi

Refrain (solo)

'g iarr - aidh chaor - ach, Ó ho hi ò, hao ri ù,

(chorus)

Ó ho hi ò, hao ri ù, Ó ho hi ò hao ri ù.

Verse

Variants

Mad-ainn mhoch 's mi 'g iarr-aidh chaor-ach, Nigh-ean donn a'

Verse

chuail-ein chraobh-aich, Nigh-ean donn a' chuail-ean chraobh-aich 'S i 'na suidh' air.

(a) Verse

lic na faoil - inn Craic - eann cúl a cinn m'a h-aod - ann.

343

Craic-eann a lamh - an m'a sgaoir-dein 'S theann mi null an

còmh - rag ciùin rith', 'S dh'fharr-aid mi dhi gu dé h-adh - bhar,

No dé id - ir bha____ i caoin-eadh? Chì mi bà - ta

staigh a' mhaoil - e, ceath-rar air ràmh 's fear 'ga stiùr - adh,

Bean 'na deir-eadh 's i sior-chaoin - eadh 'S chì mi bà - ta

staigh a'___ bhuail - e, Ó ho hi ò hao ri ù.

'S ann a bh'unn - ta bal-aich shuar - ach, Ghabh iad gu dor -

us bial uamh-a,___ 'S e mo bhas - an dhomh bu chuach - an.

Scale   Ionian   Compass

Nine degrees

Form: five phrases: Verse ‖ Refrain
A B ‖ C D C

Structure: a ten-bar melody:
Verse 4; Refrain (solo) 2, (chorus) 4.

BIBLIOGRAPHY

DESCRIPTIONS OF WAULKING

BOSWELL, *Journal of a Tour to the Hebrides with Samuel Johnson, 1773*, Yale University, 1963. (P. 152.)

BURT, Edward, *Letters from a Gentleman in the North of Scotland*, London, 1822. (Vol. ii, p. 48. Written around 1730.)

CAMPBELL, Donald, *A Treatise on the Language, Poetry, and Music of the Highland Clans*, Edinburgh, 1862. (Pp. 175–6).

CARMICHAEL, Alexander, *Carmina Gadelica*, Edinburgh, 1928, 1941. (Vol. i, p. 306; vol. iv, pp. 88–89.)

GARNETT, T., *Observations on a Tour through the Highlands and part of the Western Isles of Scotland*, London, 1800. (Vol. i, p. 158.)

GEIKIE, Sir Archibald, *Scottish Reminiscences*, Glasgow, 1904. (Pp. 264–5).

GOODRICH FREER, Ada, *The Outer Isles*, London, 1902. (Pp. 254–62; quoted here.)

GORDON-CUMMING, C. F., *In the Hebrides*, London, 1883. (P. 273.)

JOHNSTON, Annie, in *Gaelic Folksongs from the Isle of Barra*, London, 1950. (Pp. 8–9; in translation; quoted here.)

LOCKHART, J. G., *Life of Sir Walter Scott*, Edinburgh, 1838. (Vol. 3, p. 230; quoted here.)

MACCULLOCH, John, *The Highlands and Western Isles of Scotland*, London, 1824. (Vol. ii, p. 398, followed by a discussion of the scales used in Highland folk-music.)

MACDONALD, Patrick, *A Collection of Highland Vocal Airs never hitherto published*, Edinburgh, n.d. (*c.* 1780). (P. 10.)

MACDONALD, Rachel, 'When I think of Scarp', *Scots Magazine*, lxxxiii. 35–36.

MACFADYEN, John, *Sgeulaiche nan Caol*, Glasgow, 1902. (P. 43.)

MACKELLAR, Mary, 'The Waulking Day'. Paper read to the Gaelic Society of Inverness on 9 March 1887. *Transactions of the Gaelic Society of Inverness*, xiii. 201. (Quoted here.)

MACLEAN, Calum I., *The Highlands*, London, 1959. (Pp. 74–75.)

MACLEOD, Kenneth, in *Songs of the Hebrides*, London, 1909. (Vol. i, p. 22.)

BIBLIOGRAPHY

MARTIN, Martin, *A Description of the Western Islands of Scotland*, London, 1716. (Second edition, p. 57; quoted here.)

NECKER DE SAUSSURE, L. A., *Voyage en Écosse et aux Îles Hébrides*, Geneva, 1821. (Vol. ii, pp. 272 and 348; quoted here.)

PENNANT, Thomas, *A Tour in Scotland* (in 1769), fifth edition, London, 1790. (Vol. ii, pp. 328–9; quoted here.)

REA, Frederick, *A School in South Uist*, edited by J. L. Campbell, London, 1964. (Pp. 31–33. Rea's description of Donald MacCormick, pp. 27–28, is quoted here.)

SHAW, Margaret Fay, in *Folksongs and Folklore of South Uist*, London, 1955. (Pp. 72–73.)

SHAW, William, *An Analysis of the Galic Language*, second edition, Edinburgh, 1778. (Pp. 136–7; quoted here.)

TOLMIE, Frances, *Journal of the Folksong Society*, London, 1911. (Vol. iv, pp. 147–9.)

GENERAL

COLLINSON, F., *The Traditional and National Music of Scotland*, London, 1966.

KENNEDY FRASER, Marjory, *A Life of Song*, London, 1929.

MURRAY, Amy, *Fr. Allan's Island*, New York, 1920. (Contains valuable comments on the nature of Gaelic folk-tunes with twenty-six examples, taken down on Eriskay in 1905.)

MUSICAL TRANSCRIPTIONS

(a) OBJECTIVE

CREIGHTON, Helen, and MACLEOD, Calum, *Gaelic Songs in Nova Scotia*, National Museum of Canada, Bulletin no. 198, 1964.

McDONALD, The Revd. Fr. Allan, *Bàrdachd Mhgr. Ailein, the Gaelic poems of Fr. Allan McDonald of Eriskay*, edited by J. L. Campbell, Edinburgh, 1965. (Contains three Christmas hymns in the style of waulking songs, to traditional airs, pp. 98, 100, 102.)

MACDONALD, Keith Norman, *The Gesto Collection of Highland Music*, Leipzig, 1895. (Some of the transcriptions were done by Frances Tolmie.)

—— *Puirt-a-Beul or Mouth Tunes*, Glasgow, 1901 and 1931. (Contains some waulking songs.)

MURRAY, Amy, 'An Fhideag Airgid (with music)', *Celtic Review*, ii. 201.

—— 'Child Songs in the Island of Youth', *Celtic Review*, ii. 314. See also *Fr. Allan's Island*, in which these tunes were reprinted.

SHAW, Margaret Fay, *Folksongs and Folklore from South Uist*, London, 1955. (Includes thirty-two waulking songs.)

—— 'Six Hebridean Folksongs', *Journal of the English Folk Dance and Song Society*, 1943; 'Seven Hebridean Folk Songs', ibid., 1944. (Vol. iv.)

BIBLIOGRAPHY

SHAW, Margaret Fay, 'Gaelic Folksongs from South Uist', *Studia Memoriae Belae Bartók Sacra*, Budapest, 1957. (Pp. 417–33.)

TOLMIE, Frances, 'One Hundred and Five Songs of Occupation from the Western Isles of Scotland', *Journal of the Folk Song Society*, London, 1911.

(b) ART VERSIONS

DUN, Finlay, *Orain na'h-Albain*, Edinburgh, n.d. (c. 1860).

KENNEDY-FRASER, Marjory, and MACLEOD, Kenneth, *Songs of the Hebrides*. Vol. i, London, 1909; vol. ii, London, 1917; vol. iii, London, 1921.

—— —— *From the Hebrides*, Glasgow, 1925.

—— —— *More Songs of the Hebrides*, London, 1929.

MACMILLAN, Fr. John, McGLYNN, Patrick, and LEWIS, F. W., *Gaelic Songs of the Isles of the West*, London, 1930. (Two volumes.)

RECORDINGS

CAMPBELL, J. L., JOHNSTON, Annie, and MACLEAN, John, M.A., *Gaelic Folk Songs from the Isle of Barra*, set of five twelve-inch discs with book of words and translations, London, 1950. (Contains seven waulking songs.)

SCHOOL OF SCOTTISH STUDIES, *Gaelic and Scots Folk Tales, Gaelic and Scots Folk Songs, Scottish Instrumental Music*, with three long-playing discs, Edinburgh, 1960. (The Gaelic folksongs are transcribed and translated by James Ross, with musical notes by Francis Collinson.)

ARTICLES IN PERIODICALS

ANDERSSON, Professor Otto, 'On Gaelic Folk Music from the Isle of Lewis', The *Budkavlen*, Åbo, Finland, 1952.

BASSIN, Miss Ethel, 'The Debt of Marjory Kennedy Fraser to Frances Tolmie'. Paper read to the Gaelic Society of Inverness on 28 March 1958. *Transactions*, xxxix–xl. 334.

CAMPBELL, J. L., 'Songs of the Hebrides', *Scots Magazine*, January 1958.

—— 'Some Notes on Scottish Gaelic Waulking Songs', *Éigse*, viii. 87.

—— 'More Notes on Scottish Gaelic Waulking Songs', *Éigse*, ix. 129.

COLLINSON, F., 'Songs of the Hebrides', *Scotsman*, 6, 7, and 8 January 1958.

ROSS, James, 'The Sub-Literary Tradition in Scottish Gaelic Song-poetry', *Éigse*, viii. 1.

—— 'Further Remarks on Gaelic Song Metres', *Éigse*, viii. 350.

—— 'A Classification of Gaelic Folk Songs', *Scottish Studies*, i. 95.

347

BIBLIOGRAPHY

PERIODICALS

An Gàidheal, Glasgow, 1873–7 (six volumes). (A number of traditional Gaelic tunes are printed in this magazine.)

Celtic Review, Edinburgh, 1904–16. (*C.R.*)

Éigse, A Journal of Irish Studies, Dublin, 1939–.

Gairm (Scottish Gaelic quarterly), Glasgow, 1952–.

Journal of the Folk Song Society, London, 1898–1931.

Journal of the English Folk Dance and Song Society, London, 1932–.

Scottish Gaelic Studies, Oxford, 1926–.

Scottish Studies, Edinburgh, 1957–. (Journal of the School of Scottish Studies, Edinburgh University.)

Transactions of the Gaelic Society of Inverness, Inverness, 1870–. (*T.G.S.I.*)

PRINTED TEXTS

CAMPBELL, J. F., *Leabhar na Féinne*, London, 1872.

CRAIG, K. C., *Orain Luaidh Mairi nighean Alasdair*, Glasgow, 1949. (K. C. C.)

CARMICHAEL, Alexander, *Carmina Gadelica*. Vol. iv, Edinburgh, 1941 (pp. 88–99); vol. v, Edinburgh, 1954 (pp. 2–83). (*C.G.*)

GILLIES, John, *Sean Dain agus Orain Ghaidhealach*, Perth, 1786.

HENDERSON, The Revd. Dr. George, *Làmh-Sgrìobhainnean Mhic-Neacail*. Paper read to the Gaelic Society of Inverness on 14 December 1911. *Transactions*, xxvii. 340.

—— 'Arthurian Motifs in Gadhelic Literature', *Miscellany presented to Kuno Meyer*, Halle, 1912.

MACDONALD, Alexander, *Aiseiridh na Sean Chánoin Albanaich*, Edinburgh, 1751.

MACDONALD, The Revd. A., and MACDONALD, The Revd. A., *The MacDonald Collection of Gaelic Poetry*, Inverness, 1911. (McD.)

MACDONALD, Ranald, *Comh-Chruinneachadh Orannaigh Gaidhealach*, Edinburgh, 1776.

MACLEAN, Calum I., 'Traditional Songs from Raasay and their Value as Folk-Literature'. Paper read to the Gaelic Society of Inverness on 25 February 1949. *Transactions*, xxxix–xl. 176.

MACPHERSON, D. C., *An Duanaire*, Edinburgh, 1868.

O'RAHILLY, Cecile, *Five Seventeenth-Century Political Poems*, Dublin, 1952.

DICTIONARY

McDONALD, Fr. Allan, *Gaelic Words from South Uist and Eriskay*, edited by J. L. Campbell, Dublin, 1958. (Explains a number of words that occur in old waulking songs.)

BIBLIOGRAPHY

MS. TEXTS

CAMPBELL, J. L., transcriptions of ediphone, disc, wire, and tape recordings made in South Uist, Barra, and Nova Scotia.

CARMICHAEL, Alexander, papers in Edinburgh University Library.

HENDERSON, The Revd. Dr. George, papers in Glasgow University Library.

JOHNSTON, Annie, manuscript collection of traditional Gaelic folksongs, many taken down from her mother and from the late 'Ealasaid Eachainn', kindly put at my disposal for copying in 1937.

MCDONALD, The Revd. Fr. Allan, manuscript collection of waulking songs, and song texts in folklore notebooks.

MACDONALD, The Revd. Angus, the Killearnan collection of Gaelic songs. (Mostly made in Uist between 1874 and 1895. Most of these songs were printed in the *MacDonald Collection of Gaelic Poetry*, but the manuscript, which is beautifully written, gives more information about the reciters than the book does.) (K.)

MACINTYRE, Donald (the Paisley Bard), manuscript collection of waulking songs taken down by himself, kindly put at my disposal.

MACLACHLAN, Donald, of Connel, manuscript collection of traditional Gaelic songs and stories, including some from Uist, kindly put at my disposal by The Rt. Revd. the Bishop of Argyll and the Isles with the consent of Miss Margaret Maclachlan. (O.)

MACLEAN, The Very Revd. Canon Duncan, manuscript collection of waulking songs made when parish priest of Bornish, South Uist, kindly put at my disposal.

MACKINNON, late Capt. Donald J., manuscript collection of texts of traditional Gaelic songs, mostly from Barra, kindly put at my disposal by Mrs. MacKinnon.

GLOSSARIAL INDEX

A

à (= e, *pronoun*), *he*, 663.
abhal, *apple*; geug nan a., 1246.
acaire, *anchor*, 1310.
acarsaid, *anchorage*, 196.
achadh, *field, plain*; cha choisich mi 'n t-a., 926; *g.* air feadh an achaidh, 920; Achadh Luachrach, *a place name*, 811.
ad, *hat*; *g.* làn na h-aide, 918.
adag, *sheaf*, 1290.
adhart, *forward*; air a., 603.
adhbhar, *cause*, 170, 1381.
agh, *pl.* aighean, *hinds*, 399; *heifers*, 883, 886; aighean dàra, 1233.
aghaidh, *face*; h-a. air cuan, *her prow towards the sea*, 88; air a. nam mórbheann, *on the face of the moor*, 327; 'na h-a., *against her*, 987.
aiceid, *affliction, illness*; a. chuim, *consumption*, 662.
aigeanntach, *valiant, spirited*, 1239.
aighear, *joy*, 397, 702; *g.* aighir, 1303.
aighearach, *joyful*, 754.
aigne, *mind*, 1368.
ailis, *reproach*; a chuir orm an a., 101; thog iad ormsa mar a., 1195.
aindeoin, '*unwill*'; dha m' a., *whether I like it or not*, 481; dha'n a., *in spite of themselves*, 4.
aineachd, ? ainbhfiach, *debt*, 836. *Or* ain-iochd?
aineoil, '*unacquaintance*'; air a h-a., 194; air m'a., 828, 856.
ainneamh, *seldom*, 766.
ainneamhachd, *infrequency, seldomness*, 109.
airce, *necessity, want*, 1291.
aire, *attention*; air m'a., 1, 143, 507, 933; air t'a., 568.
àireamh (*vb.*), *count, number*, 64.
airgiod, *silver*; a. pronn, 875; *g.* fìdeag airgid, 1152; trì chrainn

airgid, 1156; crios nam ball airgid, 1245; *d.* strian de'n a. gheal, 910.
àirigh, *shieling*; air à., 682, 1075; air à. na buaile, 1078.
airteal, *misery, sadness*; *g.* làn airteil, 443.
aiseag, *ferry*; bàta g'an a., 258; *g.* bàta 'n aisig, 268.
àite, *place*, 1230; à. falaich, 33; à. daingeann, 34.
aithne, *knowledge*; *in phrase* 's aithne *or* b'aithne dhomh, 147, 157, 219, 310, 315, 1136, 1174, 1179, 1312.
aithneadair, *connoisseur*, 728.
aithnich, *recognize*, 295, 1253; *cond.* dh'aithnghinn, 350; aithnichinn, 705.
aitreabh, *habitation*, 917.
àlainn, *beautiful*, 1020, 1325.
almte, ? *treated with alum*, 997.
altrum, *nursing, rearing*, 238.
amharc, *looking at*, 406; *past* dh'amhairc, 1023.
anabharrach, *exceeding*, 1231.
anail, *breath*, 489.
anam, *soul*, 21, 104, 562.
anart, *linen*, 737, 740; air an a. chaol bhàn, 676; léine chaol dha'n a. Ghailmhinn, 1243; pìosan caola geal' an a., 23; *associated with* sìoda, *silk*, 120, 559; *shroud*, 513; an léine chaoil an a. ascaoin, 273; Gus an déid mi 'san làr Anns an a. chaol bhàn, 388; *g.* anairt, 120.
aobrann, *ankle*, 1392.
aodach, *clothing*, 496, 720; *sails*, 692, 1377.
aodann, *face*, 1391; *g.* fhir an aodainn shoilleir, 725; a. nach greannach, 834.
Aoine, *Friday*, 64. *See note.*
aonar, *alone*; 'nam a., 210.
aonaran, *alone*; 'm a., 966.
aotrom, *light*, 381.
àrach, *rearing*, 1048.

bearradh, *crest of a ridge*; na féidh air bh., 8.

beathaich, *feed*, 637.

beinn, *hill, hill-grazing, moorland*, 1360; a' bh. àrd, 489; Beinn a' Cheòthain, 966; 'sa bh., 590; théid 'na bh., *on to the hill*, 542; rachadh 'na bh., 1005; o'n gharbh-bh., 304; *g.* dìreadh na beinne, 80; mullach beinne, 322; ri siubhal beinne, 771.

beith, *birch*, 576.

beòir, *beer*, 240, 1050.

beud, *misfortune, pity*; b'e 'm b. e, 552; nach éireadh b. dhi, 1099.

beul, bial, *mouth*, 227, 380, 663; beul na comhairl', 128; bial dearg tana, 835; *entrance*, am bial gach niosgaid, 69; am bial Chaol Ìle, 133; gu dorus bial uamha, 1397; gu bial fainge, 322; *edge*, beul na stuaidhe, 475; bho bheul na tuinne, 1009; *part of a gun*, gunna bheòil bhòidhich, 492; gunna a' bheòil laghaich, 544.

Beurla, *English (language)*; sgoil na B., 19; luchd B., 638.

beus, *custom*, 848; b. do thalla, 147, 157; b. do thùrlaich, 1136; *pl.* beusan, 1110.

biadh, *food*, 1291.

bian, *skin (of a person)*, 250.

biaoirlinn, *galley*, 132, 607, 609, 612, 691, 1309; air a bh. chaoildhuibh dharaich, 192. (*Pronunciation and rhyme require this spelling.*)

biast mhaol, *otter*; an riochd na béiste maoile, 207.

binn, *sweet-voiced*, 652, 1109, 1110, 1276; *comp.* binne, 784, 1007.

biorshuileach, *sharp-eyed*, 652.

bìth, *pitch*, 564.

blàr, *battle*; chuirinn am b. le Cloinn Dòmhnaill, 215, 316.

blàthach, *buttermilk*; *g.* na blàthcha, 1077.

bleideil (*adj.*), *blethering*, 979.

bliadhna, *year*, 118; seachd b., 906; bòid am b., 1000.

bó, *cow*, 149; bhó dhubh, 901; bhó mhór, 884; bhó ruadh, 901; *nom. pl.* bà dàra, 743; *g. pl.* buaile bhó, 189.

bochd, *poor, poorly*, 1208.

bog, *soft*; *comp.* buige, 1254.

bogha, *bow*, 315, 972; b. an iubhair, 591.

bòid, *voyage*, 4.

bòid, *vow*, 999, 1000, 1099; b. is gealladh, 1014.

boineid, *bonnet*; dianadh an ùmhlachd le'm b., 825; boineidean gorma 'gan lùbadh, 1275; b. chùil-bhig, 469; b. dhubhghorm, 1321; luadhadh nam boineidean, 1346.

bonn, *coin*, 588, 876.

bonn, *sole of the foot*; fo bhonn, 865; *d. pl.* air am bonnaibh, 824.

bòrd, *table*; bualadh b., 1042; luadhadh nam boineidean mu'n bh., 1346; *d. pl.* daoin' uaisle mu bhòrdaibh dùmhail, 287; daoin' uaisle mu bhòrdaibh, 362; *a board (in a coffin)*, ciste nam b., 141 (*equivalent to* clàr); (*in a boat*) air bh. a fuaraidh, 366; falbhaidh mi air bhòrdaibh daraich, 1129.

botal, *a bottle*, 787.

bòtann, *boot*, 865.

bothag, *bothy*; b. an t-sùgraidh, 1080; *d.* am bothaig bhig an iomall tuatha, 376.

bothan, *bothy*; b. gun tughadh, 624; am b. beag an iomall mòintich, 354; am b. beag cumhag air àirigh, 681.

bradan, *salmon*; *pl.* bradain, 889.

bràiste, *brooch*, 683.

bràthair, *brother*, 31, 263, 561, 1231; *pl.* bràithrean, 61, 589, 897, 1030, 1065, 1398.

breac, *trout*; *pl.* bric, 889.

breacan, *plaid*; cirb dhe do bh. craobhach, 1391; *g.* fear bhreacain, 1004; an lùib mo bhreacain, 248, 1097.

bréid, *kertch (formerly worn by married women in the Highlands)*; nach dug b. dhomh, 348; nach do choisinn thu b. dhomh, 760.

breug, *lie*; *g.* gealladh bréige, *a false promise*, 756; òl a' bhuideil bhréige, 551; *pl.* breugan, 1197; thog iad oirnn na breugan, *they told lies of us*, 1236.

brìodal, *flirtatious talking*, 504, 528, 769.

g. pl. ruagadh nan caorach, 1296; 'g iarraidh chaorach, 1374.

capull, *a horse*, 246.

car, *a trip*, 185; *a trick*, 193.

cara, *a relation*; car', 1203, 1205; *d. pl.* charaibh, 1205.

carach, *tricky*, 755.

carachadh, *moving*, 86.

càradh, *see* càirich.

caraid, *friend, relation*; *pl.* càirdean, 269, 749, 1101.

càrnach, *mound*; *d.* air a' chàrnaich, 1022.

carra-cheann, *tufted head*; *g.* lacha bheag a' charra-chinn, 474.

carraig, *fishing-rock*, 3.

cas, *foot*, 400, 1342; *a haft*, 996; *g.* ceum mo choise, 858; *d.* do dhà chois, 1392; *also in expression* an cois, *beside*, 1189; *pl.* casan, 199, 245, 259, 909. *See also* gearrachas.

cathan, *wild goose*; sealgair a' chathain, 417.

ceangal, *restraint*, 59; *act of tying or binding*, 169, 515, 738, 884. (*Pronounced* ceamhal *in Uist and so written by MacCormick in lines* 515, 738, *and* 884.)

ceann, *head*, 319, 450, 1003; c. na céille, 128; *figuratively*, an c. do mhórshluaigh, 849; *end*, c. a' bhàigh, 534; c. an rathaid, 92, 1298; bho cheann a' chlachain, 1317; *prow of a boat*, 1301; *g.* cùl do chinn, 39, 804, 1391; falt a cinn, 555; lacha bheag a' charra-chinn, 474; stìom mo chinn, 336; *d. pl.* air an ceannaibh, *on their ends*, 99; *d. s.* cionn, *in phrase* os cionn, *above*, 566, 1266; os a cionn, 617; os mo chionn, 625; a chionn, *because*, 689.

ceannach (*n.*), *buying*; gun ch., *for nothing*, 22, 1077.

ceannachadair, *purchaser*, 727.

ceannaich (*vb.*), *to buy*, 677, 745.

ceannard, *chief*, 96.

ceap, *stocks*, 168.

cearbach, *defective*, 995.

ceàrr, *wrong*; neo-cheàrr, 1025.

cearrag, *left hand*; *g.* fear cearraig, 369.

ceathrar, *four persons*, 599.

ceil, *conceal*; nach c. mi air càch, 386; 1177, 1358.

céile, *a mate*, 628, 758, 1212; c. leapadh, *a bedfellow*, 266; *a husband*, 1318; *in phrase* a chéile, *each other*, 20, 283, 294, 629, 770, 788, 790, 1101.

ceirb, cirb, *a corner of a garment*; ceirb dha m' thrusgan, 1018; cirb dhe do bhreacan, 1393.

ceist, *a term of endearment*; c. nam ban, 701, 975; troma-cheist nam ban, 703; mo cheist, 399, 465, 520, 522, 524, 765, 866; mo cheist air, 484.

Céitein, *May*, 11; an fhochainn Ch., 276.

ceò, *mist*, 326, 1278, 1331.

ceòl, *music*, 569, 1040; *g.* seinn a ciùil, 1091.

ceòl-gàire, *sound of laughter*, 989, 1036.

ceud, *a hundred*; *pl.* ceudan, 637.

ceudfath, *faculty*, 59.

ceudghaol, *first love*, 279; *g.* c. falaich, 1013.

ceum, *step*, 109; c. astair, 622; fois orra ch., 339; c. mo choise, 858; c. stòlda, 930.

ceutach, *graceful*, 636, 944, 1219.

ciad, *a hundred*, 1070.

ciall, *sense*; *as asseveration*, a ch., 236; *g.* air bheagan céille, 554; ceann na céille, 128; fàgail na céilleadh, 60; a laoigh mo chéilleadh, 17.

cian, *far-off*, 111.

cinneadh, *clan, relations*, 1057; cinne, 415 (*in identical contexts*).

cìoch, *breast*; bainne-c., 241, *etc.*; *pl.* cìochan, 103, 351, 482; c. geala, 529.

cion, *a term of endearment*; tha mo ch. air, 557.

cir (*n.*), *comb*, 346.

cìr (*vb.*), *to comb*, 450.

cirb, *see* ceirb.

circeag, *female grouse*; *g.* na circeige duinne, 421, 1329.

ciste, *chest*; tha do phreasain am ch., 954; am chistidh, 671; *coffin*, 74; ciste nam bòrd, 141; ciste chaol, 272, 514; ciste chumhag nan clàr, 389, 1370. (*The dative case is usually* cistidh *in speech*.)

355

ciùin, *calm*, 115, 148, 414, 1216; *g. fem.*
ciùine, 558.
clach, *stone*; *g.* am prìosan cloiche, 594; *d.* chaidh i ri cloich, 845.
clachan, *village*; baile bòidheach a' chlachain, 237; bho cheann a' chlachain, 1317.
cladach, *shore*; *g.* cladaich, 1266.
claidheamh, *sword*, 972; *pl.* claidhmhnean, 257.
claistinn, *hearing*, 1276.
clàr, *a board*, ciste chumhag nan c., 389, 1370; c. fhuine, *a baking board*, 1002.
clàran, *dim. of* clàr; c. cumain, 183.
clàrsach, *harp*, 82; seinnear c. nan teud druidte, 584; c. ghrinn, 1139; *d.* le clársaich, 1040.
cleachd (*vb.*), *use*, 355.
chleachdach (*adj.*), *waving, flowing* (of hair), 249.
cléithe, *see* cliath.
cliabh, *breast*; c. na h-eala, 250.
cliar, *clergy*; *g.* cléire, 762, 1100.
cliath, *waulking table*; *g.* fuaim na cléithe, 1107; air chùl cléithe, 1111.
clisgeadh, *frightening*, 668.
clò, *cloth*, 1341.
clogad, *helmet*; c. cruadhach, 1244.
clòimh, *wool*, 1219.
cluain, *a plain*, 925; *metaphorical*, 1400; an fhairge ghlas 'na cluainean, 809; c. rainich, 829.
cluas, *the forepart of a lugsail or a jib*; *d.* cluais, 941.
cluasag, *pillow*, 946, 1401; *d.* air cluasaig, 813.
cnàimh, *bone*; bhristinn c., 71.
cnàmh (*vb.*), *decay*, 1187.
cnoc, *mound*; caisteal air gach c., 1105, 1225; air chnoc àrd, 1241; *d. pl.* le cnocaibh, 1061.
cnocan, *little mound*; *g.* air taobh cnocain, 330.
coileach, *blackcock*; mharbhte . . . . . c. dubh air bàrr géige, 1084; *g.* sealgair a' choilich, 1328; sealgair coilich thu, 1363; sealgair . . . . . choilich dhuibh, 402.
coille, *wood*, 808; shiùbhlainn beinn is c. leat, 1360; chunnaic mi do choill' 'ga rùsgadh, 49; *d.* mar chuthaig an coill', 382 *and* 654; do'n choill'

iùbhraich, 1140, 1252; do'n choill' fhiosraich, 1146, 1259. (*The dative is coillidh in Uist dialect.*)
coimhead, *watching*; c. uam, 830.
coimhideachd, *keeping watch over*, 800.
coinneamh, *meeting*; cumail c. ri, 277; mu'n c., 827.
còir (*adj.*), *kindly*, 1343; *pl.* còire, 498.
còir (*n.*), *right*; chumadh c. ruinn, 187; bu chòir dhomh, 298; nach b'i chòir i, 337; bu ch. dha, 348; bu ch. dhut, 357; an c. no 'n eugcoir, 550.
coireach, *responsible*, 1174.
coisich, *to walk*, 926, 928.
coisiche, *walker*, 1228.
coisinn, *earn*, 760, 761, 763.
coite, *a boat* (*derogatory term*), 614.
colbh, c. chuilce, ?, 579. *See note.*
coluinn, *body*, 1341.
com, *body, thorax*; *g.* fuil do chuim, 44; aiceid chuim, 662.
comas, *power*, 816.
comhairle, *counsel*, 128, 1114.
còmhdach, *clothing*, 324.
còmhdhail, *meeting*; am. ch., 329.
còmhlan, *a band*, 1269, 1405.
còmhnard (*adj.*), *level*, 361, 844.
còmhnard (*n.*), *level ground*, 929.
còmhradh, *conversation*, 509.
comunn, *a company*, 820.
copa, *a cup*; *pl.* copanan dearg, 1221; *see* cupa.
cor, *condition*, 167.
corca, *oats*, 1062 (*Uist for* coirce).
còrdadh, *agreement, promise to marry*, 358, 359, 690.
còrn, *a roll of cloth*; c. an t-sròil uaine, 436.
corrach, *rough*, 321.
corran, *sickle*; *g.* air chùl corrain, 1111.
còta, *coat*, 335, 708; bann mo chòta, 859; fear chòta ghuirm, 1029.
còtan, *a little coat*; *g.* chòtain eangaich, 1226.
cothlamadh, deise chothlamaidh, *clothing of wool of mixed colours*, 1242.
cra-bhata, *a cravat*, 647.
cràdh, *pain*; *pl.* cràidh, 661.
craiceann, *skin*, 1391, 1392; *g.* gilead do chraicinn, 648.
crann, *mast*; *pl.* siùil bhàna ri crainn gheala, 517; buill chaola ri crainn gheala, 565, 578; trì chrainn airgid,

eireachdail, *handsome*, 1359.

éirich (*vb.*), *rise*, 659, 1020; *happen*, 631, 1099.

éirigh, *arising*, 274, 282, 478, 481, 627, 631, 778, 794, 1092; fhuair mi ghruagach dhonn gun é., 1096.

eirthir, *shore*, 1176.

éisdeachd, *listening to*, 1237.

éislein, *misery, unhappiness*, 626.

éisleineach, *miserable, unhappy*, 829.

eislig, islig, *bier*, 73.

eòlach, *knowledgeable*, 213, 314, 414, 495, 696, 1056.

eòlas, *acquaintance*, 340.

eòrna, *barley*, 341, 1062, 1288.

eud, *jealousy*; na bi 'n e. rium, 278.

eudail, *cattle, wealth*; *in expression* m'eudail, *my darling*, 95, 145, 155, 277, 853.

eugcoir (*n.*), *wrong*, 550, 1098.

F

facal, *a word*, 254, 1053.

fad, *length*, 640, 1023.

fadhail, *sea ford*, 534, 985.

faghaid, *a hunting, hue and cry*, 533, 542.

fàilte, *welcome*, 1070.

fàin, gu f., *gently*, 1011 (= gu faoin).

fàinne, *a ring*, 347; f. òir, 1104.

fàinneach, *ringleted*, 40, 63.

faire, *watching*, 437.

faireachadh, *watching*, 84.

fàireadh, *skyline*, 1023.

fairge, *ocean*, 1151; f. ghlas, 809.

fairlich, dh'fhairlich orm a chur air fuadach, *I failed to expel it*, 461, 797.

falach, *secret*; sùil mo cheudghaol falaich, 1013.

fàlaire, *a palfrey*; f. chrùidheach, 51.

falamh, *empty, poor*, 1016; f. dheth, 1120.

fallaid, *leavings of meal*, 840.

fallain, *healthy* (*often equivalent to 'alive'*), 29, 571, 844.

falt, *hair* (*of a human*), 1186, 1217; f. mo chinn, 451; f. a cinn, 555; g. an fhuilt chleachdaich, 249.

fang, *fank*; g. bial fainge, 322.

faobhar, *a cutting edge*; f. ghleòis, 846.

faoileag, *seagull*; g. na faoileige glaise, 642.

faoilinn, *stony beach*, 1390.

Faoillich, na F., *the equinoxes*, 616.

farasda, *easy*, 1011.

fàrdrach, *galley*, 816.

farsuinneachd, *breadth*, 1118.

fàs (*vb.*), *grow*, 1143, 1162, 1256.

fàsach, *desert*; d. 'san fhàsaich, 987.

fastadh, *engaging*, 1312.

feabhas, air f., *however well*, 480.

feadan, *usually the chanter, here rather the drones of a bagpipe*; f. àrd, 83, 1041; f. dùmhail, 289; f. siùbhlach, 290; f. toll, 869.

feamain, *seaweed*; do chluasag an fh., 946; anns an fh., 943; 'san fh., 837, 1340 (*all in connexion with drowning*).

feannadh, *flaying*, 149.

fear, *a man*; *voc.* fhir, 338; *g. s. and n. pl.* fir; *g. pl.* fhear, 537; *d. pl.* fearaibh, 255, 817; *one person or thing of masculine gender*, 212, 687, 1376, 1377, 1406; f. a b'fheàrr dhiu, 1028; f. a' chùil dualaich, 452; f. an leadain bhòidhich, 765; f. aodainn shoilleir, 725; f. bhreacain urad, 1004; f. cearraig, 369; f. chòta ghuirm, 1029; f. crìon, 1178; f. fallain, 571; f. fionn, 1027; f. foinnidh, 817; f. gasda, 1354; f. geal, 890, 1324; f. làimhe deise, 370; f. mhealladh na h-òinsich, 350; f. òg, 154, 355, 537; f. tapaidh, 915.

fearachas, *manliness*, 96.

fearail, *manly*, 217, 308, 782, 833, 1056.

fearann, *land*, 88, 146, 854, 1128; g. fearainn, 1118, 1119.

feasgar, *evening*, 148, 982.

féile, *hospitality*; g. Iain Mùideartach na f., 53, 77.

féill, *a holy day, festival*; g. air là féille, 764.

féith, *sinew*; *pl.* féithean, 57.

féith, *bog*; g. féithe, 1224.

feitheamh, *waiting*, 840.

feòil, *flesh*, 58, 245, 246.

feucannt, *peacock-like*; òganach . . . f., 782; cùirteir f., 1235.

feudar (*vb.*), nam b'fh., *if need be*, 1222.

GLOSSARIAL INDEX

G

gabhail (*vbl. n.*), *taking*; g. fuachda, 199; gh. fradhairc, 984; ghabh i 'n t-òigeir, 540; gun gabhadh tu banntrach mar chéile, 758; ghabh mi mulad, *I became sorrowful*, 223; *sing a song*, beul a gh. an fhuinn, 380; gabhamaid òran, 789; *with* mu, *dress, prepare, put in order*; g. umad, 226; g. mu'n bheul, 227; g. mu'n t-sùil, 228.

gadhar, *dog*; g. gadhair, 535, 545.

gailleann, *gale*, 5; g. gaillinn, 2; d. gaillinn, 563, 573.

gaineamh, *sand*, 32, 487.

gainne, *scarcity*, 1132.

gainntir, *see note to line* 321.

gàirich, *to laugh*, 941.

gairm, *to call*, 1277.

gaisgeach, *hero*, 1313.

galan, *gallon*, 98.

galar, *disease*; g. fios mo ghalair-sa, 105; *pl.* galair, 661.

Gallach (*adj.*), *foreign*, 997.

gallan, *a lad*; g. gallain, 535.

gamhain, *stirk*, 885; *pl.* na gamhna, 886; g. *pl.* nan gamhna breaca, 445; nan gamhna caola, 1382.

gaol, *love*, 379, 673, 674, 970, 974, 1235, 1338; g. miad mo ghaoil ort, 894.

gaoir, *cry*; g. nan creach, 294.

gaoth, *wind*; g. làidir, 1064; g. an ear, 1250; g. an iar, 86, 986, 1250; d. le gaoith a tuath, 198.

gàrradh, *stone wall*, 1234.

geal, *white, fair*, 327, 890, 1323, 1324; *comp.* gile, 250; pl. geala, 529.

gealach, *moon*, 85, 1249.

geala-ghruagach, *a fair young girl*, 375.

geall, *a wager*, 318, 1033, 1034.

geall (*vb.*), *to promise*, 433.

gealladh, *a promise*, 90, 714, 1014; g. bréige, 756.

gearain, *complaining*, 144, 695.

geàrr (*vb.*), *to cut*; gearradh shìoda, 120; g. leum, 124.

gearrachas, *short foot*; earbag bheag nan g. cuimir, 1008; earba bheag nan g. caol, 1170.

gearrachù, ? *terrier*; *pl.* gearrachoin, 545.

gearran, *pony, garron*; *nom. pl.* gearrain, 899; *g. pl.* ghearran, 1124.

geata, *a gate*; g. nan seachd glasan, 913.

geug, *branch*; g. nan abhal, 1246; g. air bàrr géige, 1084.

geugaire, *hero*; g. fionn, 832.

geumraich, *bellowing*, 293.

geur, *sharp*; *pl.* geura, 257.

giadh, *goose*; g. glas, 473; g. a' gheòidh, 641, 1293; geòidh, 1363.

giamanach, *hunter*, 490, 492, 1168.

gibht (*vb.*), *give away*, 432, 433.

gilead, *whiteness*, 648, 707.

gille, *lad*, 543; *pl.* gillean, 423, 783, 880, 1353.

gin, *anyone*, 902, 1165.

giollan, *lad*, 301; *also* glas-ghiollan, *q.v.*

giorag, *panic*; nach leubh an g., 305.

giùlain (*vb.*), *to carry*, 1341, 1342.

giùlan, *a bier*.

giuthas, *a pine*, 566, 577.

giùthsach, *a pine wood*, 1206.

glac (*n.*), 'nur glacaibh, *in your grasp*, 1320.

glaine, *a glass*, 1345.

glaisean, *sparrow, small bird*; g. an riochd a' ghlaisein, 1292.

glaiste, *locked*, 906.

glan, *clean, bright*; *pl.* glana, 165, 561.

glaodhaich, *to cry*, 1378.

glas, *a lock*; *pl.* glasan, 913.

glas-ghiollan, *a callow youth*, 345.

glasadh, *becoming grey*; an là a' g., 1277.

gleann, *glen*; *pl.* gleannan, 497.

gleannan, *little glen*, 1082; *pl.* gleannain, 1017.

gleidheadh (*vb. n.*), *keeping, preserving*, 276.

gleus, *lock of a gun*, 184; bha g. ort, *you were ready for action*, 55; g. tha faobhar ghleòis oirr', *it has a sharpened edge*, 846.

gluais, *move*, 815.

glùn, *knee*, 67, 103, 619; d. glùin, 177; *pl.* glùinean, 1274.

gnothach, *errand*, 126, 810; g. gnothaich, 131.

gobhar, *goat*; g. chròcach, 172.

goid, *to steal*, 171, 172, 174.

goirid, *short*, 1178.

goirteas, *pain*, 661.

gòrach, *foolish*, 345, 508, 1175.
gòraiche, *foolishness*, 331.
gorm, *blue*, 834; *comp.* guirme, 252.
gradan, *meal from grain from which the chaff has been burnt*; g. min ghradain, 1284.
gràdh, *loved one*, 268, 394.
graigh, *herd, flock*; *g.* air thùs na graighe, 546.
gràinne, *nap on cloth*; cur g. air léintean, 121; chuireadh g. grinn air bhannan, 560.
gràisg, *rabble*; *g.* na gràisge, 992.
greannach, *sullen*, 834.
greannmhor, *lively, active*, 1154.
Gréigis, *the Greek language*, 639.
greis, *a short spell of time*, 988, 989.
grian, *sun*, 1249; g. gheal, 327; *g.* Rìgh na gréine, 549; *d.* fo'n ghréin, 68; gun ghréin oirr', 772.
gruag, *head of hair, locks*, 450, 685; g. fhàinneach, 63; *g.* gruaige, 726, 738; (fleasgach) na gruaige duibhe, 138; lighe mo ghruaige, 1322; *d.* air deagh-ghruaig, 469.
gruagach, *maiden*, 432; g. laghach, 882; g. dhonn, 248, 1096; *d.* do gheala-ghruagaich, 375; *pl.* gruagaichean, 153, 561, 827.
gruaidh, *cheek*, 951; 's deirge a g., 251; g. thana, 521; g. mhìn-dearg, 531; *pl.* gruaidhean, 428; gruaidhean dearg daithte, 1073.
gruaim, *gloom*; an g. rium, 744; fo ghruaim, 390, 801; thug e'n latha an diu fo gh. dhiom, 463; fear . . . nach biodh g. air, 1324; fear . . . gun gh., 1354.
gruamach, *gloomy*, 751.
gruaman, *gloom*; fo gh., 476.
guala, *shoulder (of a hill)*, 1021, 1095; (*of a person*) g. bac mo ghuaille, 814; far mo ghuaille, 454; *d.* orra ghualainn, 470; ri (a) ghualainn, 1326; *pl.* guaillean, 800.
guanach, *light, neat and pretty*, 474.
gucagach, *foaming*, 778.
guileag, *cry (of swan)*, 179.
guirmead, *blueness*, 709.
gunna, *gun*, 176, 182, 1026, 1320; a gh. ri ghualainn, 1326; do ghunnasnaip orra ghualainn, 470; g. nach diùltadh, 490; g. bheòil bhòidhich,

492; g. caol a' bheòil laghaich, 544; giamanach a' gh. chaoil, 1168.
gur, *brood*; bheireadh g. as an fhuarniod, 422, 1329.
guth, *voice*, 535, 536, 1110; g. cinn, 1109.

I

ialadh, *creeping*, 177.
iall, *thong*; nan i. almte, 997.
ian, *bird*, 1088, 1189; *pl.* na h-eòin, 493; *metaphorically, a chief*, 302.
ianadair, *fowler*, 1192.
iaonadh, *wonder*, 1211.
iaonadh, *dexterity, prowess, exploit*; 's mise chunnaic 'n diu an t-i., 203; 's mise chunnaic an t-i., 1373. *See* Éigse, viii. 249 (eangnamh).
iar, *west*, 86, 986, 1250.
iarann, *iron*; *g.* iarainn fhuair, 57.
iarann-muilinn, *a mill-pin*, 184.
iarla, *earl*; *pl.* iarlachan, 851.
iarrtas, *petition, prayer*; M'i. air Rìgh na Cathrach, 31; m'i. air Rìgh na gréine, 549.
iasg, *fish*, 1160.
ìm, *butter*, 1076.
impis, *an i., on the point of*, 555.
iomairt, *attempt*, 426; i. air an tàileasg, *playing at backgammon*, 1037.
iomradh, *mention*; gun i. air, 992.
ionann, *like*; cha n-i. 's mar dh'éirich dhomh, *not as it happened to me*, 631; 's i. sin 's mar atà, 665.
ionndrainn, *missing*, 1055.
ionnraic, *upright, honourable*, 247.
ìseal, *low*, 136, 847.
islig, *see* eislig.
iteach, *feathers*, 1148.
iubhar, *yew*; g. bogha an iubhair, 591.
iùbhrach, *of yew*; *d.* do'n choill' iùbhraich, 1140.

L

là, *day*, 391, 772, 1277, 1295; 's fhad' o'n là sin, 81.
labhair, *speak*, 1052.
là bràch, *day of judgement*, 30.
lacha, *wild duck*; lacha bheag, *mallard*; l. bheag a' charra-chinn ghuanaich, 474; l. bheag a' mhuineil chaoil, 1171; *g.* an riochd na lachann, 641; an riochd na l., 1293.

lag, *dell*; l. an fhraoich uaine, 449; l. am bi luachair, 1327.

lagan, *little dell*; l. lasrach, 903, 916 (*probably a place name*).

laghach, *well-shaped, nice, pretty*, 544, 882.

laghadh, *shaping*, 1371.

Laideann, *the Latin language*, 638.

làidir, *strong*, 28, 213, 217, 308, 314, 372.

laise, *flush*; l. 'nan gruaidhean, 428.

làmh, *g.* làimhe, *d.* làimh, *hand, arm*, 1002; *often in connexion with steering boats*, l. air an stiùir nuair bu chruaidhe, 368; l. stiùradh nan stuagh, 395, 1355; l. a reubadh a' chuain ghlais, 1204; *g.* fear làimhe deis', 370; bac mo làimhe, 39; *d.* guma slàn do'n làimh a dh'fhuaigh i, 371; (an stiùir) an làimh mo leannain, 574, 781; an làimh nan gillean, 783; an làimh an Leòdaich, 785; an làimh riut, *beside thee*, 36; *of valorous deeds*, b'e 'n l. ri tapadh e, 1316; cha deach an l. dheas gu feum dhut, 78; bogha 'na làimh lùthmhor, 591; as do làimh gun earbainn m'anam, 562; 's e mo l. -sa fhuair a shaothair, 1394; *in love songs*, l. air a ciochan, 351; mo l. air do chiochan, 529; *asseveration*, air mo làimh, 70.

lamhanan, *gloves*; l. sìoda, 958.

làn (*adj.*), *full*; l. airteil, 443; *pregnant*, 664.

làn (*n.*), *full tide*, 38; l. an dùirn, *handful*, 301; l. na h-aide, *hatful*, 918.

langan, *bellowing (of deer)*, 1087.

laogh, *calf*; do'n l. bheag, 885; *pl.* laoigh, 292, 1161; *fawn*, l. breac, 1083; l. breac ballach, 9; *as term of endearment*, a laoigh mo chéilleadh, 17.

làr, 'san l., *into the ground*, 387.

lasgaire, *a youth*; leis an l. dhonn, 657, 862.

latha, *day*, 54, 267, 463, 801; fo. l., 779; ro'n l., 1085, 1089; gu latha, 1305.

leaba, *bed*, 947, 962, 1264, 1400; *g.* gun chéile leapadh, 266; *d.* an l. bhig luachrach, 718; air an leabaidh, 412; 's mi 'n leabaidh, 1054; do'n leabaidh, 1209.

leac, *flagstone, tombstone*; *g.* bruach do lice, 72; *d.* air lic, 206; *pl.* leaca troma na dileann, 137; *see* fuarleac.

leacach, *slope*; *g.* leacaich, 444; *d.*, 1278.

leacan, *cheeks*, 649.

leacainn, *hillside*, 1405.

leadan, *head of hair, locks*; *g.* fear an leadain bhòidhich, 765; *g. pl.* luchd nan l., 822.

leag, *kill, shoot*, 493, 1169.

leaghadh, *melting*, 548.

leanabh, *baby*, 102, 114.

leann, *beer*; l. daithte, 240; l. làidir, 1050; *g.* leanna, 1125, 1306. (*Pronounced* liùnn.)

leannan, *sweetheart, lover*, 26, 140, 329, 366, 713, 831, 994, 1028, 1167, 1196, 1199; *g.* leannain, 413, 574, 793, 934, 1012, 1055.

leas (*idiom of*), cha ligeadh e l. siod, *he need not (do) that*, 243.

leathad, *slope*, 321, 401; *d. pl.* leòdaibh, 1061.

leathar, *leather*; crios do l., 998.

léigh, *doctor*, 68.

léine, *the old Highland shirt*, 13, 334; *g.* fear léine bàine, 1029; *d.* an léine chaoil, 273; *pl.* léintean, 707, 768, 780; léintean rìomhach, 121.

léireadh, *paining*, 10.

leobhar (*dial. for* leabhar), *book*, 129.

Leòdach, *a MacLeod*, 785.

leòis, *see* leus.

leòmhainn, ?; Sìol Ailein nan long l., 216; Sìol Ailein nan long leòmhann, 317.

leòn, *a wound*, 1339.

leubh (*dial. for* leugh), *read*, 129, 305.

leubhadair, *reader*, 728.

leum (*n.*), *a leap*, 124.

leum (*vb.*), *to leap*, 125, 889, 913.

leumnaich, *leaping*, 292.

leus, *blister*; *pl.* leòis, 427, 1042.

liadan, *strips* (*literally* 'breadths'), 335.

lig, *to broach*; ligeil fìona, 982; *to lay*, l. mi m'uileann, 1022.

lighe, ? *flood*; l. mo ghruaige, 1322.

lìon (*n.*), *flax*, 1222.

lìon (*vb.*), *to fill*; l. an stòp, 1345.

lìonmhor, *numerous*, 1026.

litir, *letter*, 672.

liùgadh, *bending down*, 1145.

loch, *a loch or lake*, 804.

GLOSSARIAL INDEX

stocainn, *stocking*; *g.* stocainn bhàinghil, 488; *pl.* stocainnean, 325.

stoirm, *noise*; s. nan each, 1268. *See note.*

stòl, *stool of repentance*, 761.

stòlda, *sober, respectable*, 930.

stòp, *a can or stoup*, 1345; *pl.* stòip, 98.

stràid, *? a street*; s. na meala, 1116.

streap (*vb.*), *to climb*, 644.

streup (*n.*), le s., *after a struggle*, 766.

strian, *bridle*; s. sleamhuin, 52; s. de'n airgiod gheal, 910.

stròicean, *tatters*, 686.

struth, *a stream*, 986.

stuadh, *a gable*; *g.* tùr na stuaidhe, 156; *? pinnacle*, Giùbhsaich na stuaidhe, 1206.

stuadh, *a wave*, 395; *g.* o bheul na stuaidhe, 475; *g. pl.* nan stuadh, 1355; *d.* 'san stuaidh, 945.

suaicheantas, *badge*; s. dearg, 1244.

suain, *sleep*, 1398.

suairce, *handsome*, 1216.

suarach, *indifferent, not caring for*, 510; bha mi s. mu d' dhéidhinn, 752; air am bu sh. òl sinéabhar, 786; an loch mu'n robh mi s., 804; *superlative*, de'n anart bu shuaraiche, *of the most contemptible rag*, 740.

suas, 'ga cur suas, *setting her to windward*, 394.

suathadh, *rubbing*, 1285.

subh, *a berry*; s. craobh, *raspberry or dewberry*, 1162 (*not 'woodbine' as translated by Fr. Allan McDonald for the sake of rhyme*).

sùgradh, *flirting, love-making*; bothag an t-sùgraidh, 1080.

suigeanta, *merry*, 1240.

sùil, *eye*; s. a bha cuimir, 228; s. ghorm, 834; 's guirme a s., 252; chaogadh tu 'n t-s., 491; ùir air s., 1012, 1013; *g.* miann mo shùl, 406.

suirghe, *wooing*, 1103.

T

tacan, *short space of time*, 358.

tadhail (*vb.*), *visit*; *fut.* tadhlaidh, 94, 95; tadhlamaid, *let us visit*, 1344. (*Preposition air with persons, an with places.*)

tadhal, *act of visiting*, 130, 604.

taghadh, *choosing, choice*, 538, 547; fo th. na gruaige, 726.

tagsa, *support*, 623.

taigh, *house*, 1265; t. glaiste, 723, 733; t. bàn, 1266; t. mór, 92, 158, 201, 202, 361.

taigh-òsda, *inn*, 349, 1344.

tàileasg, *backgammon*, 1037.

tainead, *scarcity*; t. mo bhuaile spréidhe, 12; t. mo chruidh-laoigh air buailidh, 900; chuir e mo chuailein an t., 110.

talamh, *earth*, 106; t. ìseal, 136; t. toll, 33.

talla, *hall*, 147; t. nan ròiseal, 416, 1058.

tàmh (*n.*), *rest*; chaidh orra, 'n tàmh 1369.

tàmh (*vb.*), *to rest*, 1035.

tana, *thin*, 521, 835.

taobh, *side*, 808, 974, 1169; a t. leòinte, 67; o th. na tuinne, 180; gacha t. dhi, 209; gacha t. dhiom, 212; gacha t. na Beinn' Cheathaich, 405; air t. cnocain, 330; nach sìninn mo th. ri balach, 1015; cha sìninn mo th. geal ri taobh balaich, 1323. *See also* tùbh.

taod, *halter*, 169.

taomadh, *baling*, 1376.

tapadh, *an able feat*, 1316.

tapaidh, *able*, 255, 915, 1215.

tathaich, *to visit*, 93.

té, *one female person, a woman*, 455; mise . . . mar thé dhiù, *I like one of them*, 556.

teanal, *pl.* teanail, *goods*, 501.

teanga, *a tongue*, 844.

teann, *tight*, 1357; *comp.* teinne, 859.

teann (*vb.*), *begin*; t. ri, 331; *to tighten*, 479; *to draw near to*, 1380.

teannagheall, *hard and fast wager*, 318.

teàrnadh, *descending*, 80, 444; *driving downwards*, 401.

teàrr, *tar*, 1372.

teileach, *? blubbery*; ròn teileach, 419. (*Recte* beileach, *thick-lipped.*)

teine, *fire*; t. mór air bheagan luatha, 159.

teisteil, *of good reputation, chaste*, 980.

teud, *string of a musical instrument*; seinnear clàrsach nan t. druidte, 584.

INDEX OF PERSONS AND PLACES

PRINTED IN GREAT BRITAIN
AT THE UNIVERSITY PRESS, OXFORD
BY VIVIAN RIDLER
PRINTER TO THE UNIVERSITY